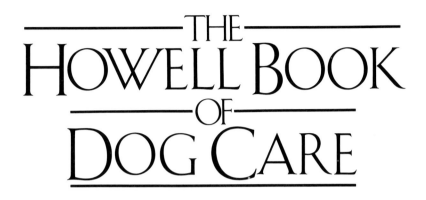

THE HOWELL BOOK OF DOG CARE

THE HOWELL BOOK OF DOG CARE

TIM HAWCROFT, B.V.Sc. (Hons) M.A.C.V.Sc.

HOWELL BOOK HOUSE
NEW YORK

MAXWELL MACMILLAN CANADA
TORONTO

MAXWELL MACMILLAN INTERNATIONAL
NEW YORK OXFORD SINGAPORE SYDNEY

I dedicate this book to my father, Eric Hawcroft

Howell Book House
Macmillan Publishing Company
866 Third Avenue
New York, NY 10022

Maxwell Macmillan Canada, Inc.
1200 Eglinton Avenue East
Suite 200
Don Mills, Ontario M3C 3N1

Macmillan Publishing Company is part of the Maxwell
Communication Group of Companies.

Library of Congress Cataloging-in-Publication Data

Hawcroft, Tim. 1946–
The Howell book of dog care / Tim Hawcroft.
p. cm.
Includes index.
ISBN 0-87605-573-0
1. Dogs. 2. Dogs—Health. I. Title.
SF427.H326   1992   91-29383   CIP

Macmillan books are available at special discounts for bulk
purchases for sales promotions, premiums, fund-raising, or
educational use. For details, contact:

Special Sales Director
Macmillan Publishing Company
866 Third Avenue
New York, NY 10022

10 9 8 7 6 5 4 3 2 1

Printed in Hong Kong

Originated by Weldon Publishing
a division of Kevin Weldon & Associates Pty Limited
Sydney, Australia

CONTENTS

ACKNOWLEDGEMENTS

It was only through the encouragement and patient understanding of my wife, Jan, and children, Melanie, Samantha, Damien and Edwina, and the assistance of my father, Eric, in planning, researching and proofreading, that I was motivated to complete this book.

My sister, Judy Shields, had the daunting task of typing, retyping and deciphering my notes. She accomplished it in a spirit of cheerful co-operation and with much admired accuracy.

I would like to thank my partner, Dr David Loneragan, and all the staff at Gordon Veterinary Hospital: Dr Andrew Morgan, Dr Sue McMillan, and the nurses, Jennifer Reber, Kim Tupper and Diane Spalding, for their kindly advice and generous co-operation.

My special thanks are extended to the following for promptly and generously meeting my requests for information: the American Kennel Club (US) for supplying statistics and literature; the Australian National Kennel Council for kindly giving permission to publish extracts from breed standards; the Kennel Club (England) for supplying statistics and other information; and the New South Wales Canine Council and its manager, Patricia Cooper, for providing breed standards and liaising with the Australian National Kennel Council.

I am also extremely grateful to: Jenny Daniels, a kindly and constructive critic of the obedience training section of the manuscript; Lyn Gibson and her handsome dog Deefa, for being most co-operative models for the visuals in the obedience training section; Ruth Winn, who was so generous of her time in providing information and photographs of the Cocker Spaniel, assisted by Julie Lawson and Frank Werner; the Metropolitan Mid Week Dog Training Club, Primula Park, Lindfield, Sydney, which gave me unqualified co-operation as a photographer at its meetings; Dr Paul Macqueen (Pfizer Agricare Pty Ltd) for his personal involvement in providing slides and diagrams; and Professor Andrew Wood (Department of Veterinary Radiology, University of Sydney), who provided facilities for making the x-ray slides.

My sincere thanks go out to those individuals, companies, and dog clubs and societies and their secretaries who responded generously to my request for information and visuals:

Dog clubs and societies, NSW:
Australian Silky Terrier Club
Border Collie Club
Boxer Club
Cavalier King Charles Spaniel Club
Cocker Spaniel Society
Dachshund Club
Dobermann Club
Rhodesian Ridgeback Club

Diagrams were supplied by:
Dr Paul Macqueen (Pfizer Agricare Pty Ltd)
Dr Jeffrey Smith
Josephine Wing

Photographs were supplied by:
Lyn Britza
Gladys Cowie
Sonya Gatfield
Eric Hawcroft
Tim Hawcroft
Dr Paul Macqueen
Marendale Boarding Kennels
Lyall Menz
Sue Parker
Lauren Somers
Robyn Tresseder
Ruth Winn
Mrs Wisdom

INTRODUCTION

A dog is man's best friend. This old saying still rings true. The relationship owners have with their dogs offers an opportunity for developing a unique form of companionship, characterised by loyalty, caring, trust, enjoyable relaxation, and a feeling of security. A dog owner is seldom lonely; the companionship can be a source of therapy for the aged and lonely and for those who are ill, and a dog is always good company for the health walker and jogger.

Your relationship with your dog is more likely to be mutually satisfying if you remember that your dog is as much of an individual as you are, and has more or less the same needs. Its basic need is good health. You can ensure this by attending to such matters as veterinary care, nutrition, grooming, housing, recreation, communication, education and companionship.

Satisfying the needs of the dog involves the owner in daily activities as well as occasional visits to the veterinary surgery and perhaps to the grooming salon. In caring for your dog's physical and psychological needs, you will have to play an active role, which requires a certain know-how, patience and time. This book provides the know-how not only for pet owners and their families, but also for breeders, trainers, those attending dog-care courses, veterinary nurses and students.

The first four chapters, 'Breeds', 'Choosing your puppy or dog', 'Training' and 'Behaviour problems and correction', give you the necessary information to help you choose a dog, raise it and train it, and to deal with the common behaviour problems that surface occasionally.

The next six chapters are all directly concerned with the dog's health, and include guidance on when to call the veterinarian, first aid and how to administer medication; the A–Z section on diseases and health problems provides practical advice on the recognition, treatment and prevention of the many illnesses that dogs suffer and which an owner may be faced with from time to time; and the final chapter is a comprehensive one on breeding, a topic of interest to every dog owner.

You will find answers to most of your questions about caring for your dog in this book. For any other problems that might arise, seek advice from your veterinarian.

Opposite: These healthy, happy dogs would be loyal and affectionate pets.

BREEDS

Kennel club statistics—Registration—Breed standards
Varieties within breeds—Grouping of breeds
Most popular breeds—Crossbreeds and Mongrels

The evolution of the true dog, *Canis familiaris*, has taken place over millions of years. Some say the true dog first appeared in the evolutionary chain about fifteen thousand years ago, in Eurasia. Since that time, the number of different breeds, by the processes of genetic mutation and selective breeding, has increased, particularly in the last four or five hundred years. Today there are about four hundred different pure breeds, i.e. pedigreed dogs, although not all are registered.

Apart from the pure breeds (pedigreed dogs), there are the crossbreeds and the mongrels which comprise by far the greater proportion of the world's dog population.

Kennel clubs and other such bodies have been established at a national level in various countries as authorities to control the registration of pedigreed dogs, to maintain and develop breed standards and to promote the pedigreed dog. Note the statistics in Tables I, II, and III supplied by the Kennel Club (KC) (England), founded in 1873; the Australian National Kennel Council (ANKC) (Aust.), founded in 1958; and the American Kennel Club (AKC)(US), founded in 1884.

TABLE I	
AUTHORITY	NUMBER OF REGISTERED BREEDS
Kennel Club (Eng.)	201
Australian National Kennel Council (Aust.)	156
American Kennel Club (US)	133

There are about 400 different pure breeds of dog in the world today.

Opposite: The German Shepherd is a highly intelligent breed.

REGISTRATION OF A NEW BREED

A new breed to be approved, accepted and registered by a national authority (see Table I) must undergo rigorous testing formulae. Only when the new breed is registered by a national authority will it accept individual dogs of that breed for registration, provided of course, both of its parents are registered. The advantage of registering your pedigreed dog is that you can enter it in any dog show, obedience trial, tracking test, etc., organised under the aegis of the national authority.

BREED STANDARDS

The national authority also approves and issues a written standard for each registered breed. In the US, a national organisation for each breed initially formulates and approves the Standard for its breed. The Standard is a description of what a particular breed would look like if it were perfect, and it sets a goal for breeders as well as providing a measuring stick for judges. These standards can be obtained from a national authority or local club.

VARIETIES WITHIN BREEDS

Some breeds are divided into varieties, generally based on size, coat type or colour. For example, the Dachshund is classified into three varieties according to coat—Longhaired, Wirehaired or Smooth; the Poodle is classified according to size—Toy, Miniature or Standard; and the Bull Terrier is classified as white or coloured.

GROUPING OF BREEDS

When a breed is registered, it is classified in one of six or seven groups according to what use the breed was originally intended. Note the different groupings and order of groupings for the UK, Australia and the US. For a full list of breeds under each grouping, see p. 204.

Kennel Club (KC) (England)

Hounds
Gun dogs
Terriers
Utility
Working
Toys

Australian National kennel Council (ANKC)

Toys
Terriers
Gun dogs
Hounds
Working
Utility
Non Sporting

American Kennel Club (AKC) (US)

Sporting
Hound
Working
Terrier
Toy
Non Sporting
Herding

TABLE II	
AUTHORITY	TOTAL NUMBER OF PEDIGREED DOGS REGISTERED
Kennel Club (Eng.)	270,769
Australian National Kennel Council (Aust.)	84,738
American Kennel Club (US)	1,253,214

GROUPING OF BREEDS

Gun dogs: These are the companions and assistants of the open space sportsman and hunter. They locate, flush out and/or retrieve game. Usually they are very intelligent and good obedience training subjects.

Some of the well-known gun dogs are the Cocker Spaniel, Golden Retriever, Labrador Retriever, English Setter, Chesapeake Bay Retriever, the English Springer Spaniel and the Irish Setter.

The Irish Setter is a member of the Gun dog group, called Sporting dogs in the US.

TABLE III					
THE TEN MOST POPULAR BREEDS IN 1990 (BASED ON REGISTRATION STATISTICS)					
K.C. (ENG.)		A.N.K.C. (AUST.)		A.K.C. (US)	
BREED	REGISTRATIONS	BREED	REGISTRATIONS	BREED	REGISTRATIONS
Yorkshire Terrier	25,665	German Shepherd	8,621	Cocker Spaniel	105,642
Labrador Retriever	25,456	Rottweiler	6,928	Labrador Retriever	95,768
German Shepherd	18,908	Australian Cattle Dog	3,462	Poodle (all varieties)	71,757
West Highland White Terrier	18,688	Labrador Retriever	3,203	Golden Retriever	64,848
Cavalier King Charles Spaniel	16,823	Boxer	2,954	Rottweiler	60,471
Golden Retriever	15,983	Dobermann	2,820	German Shepherd	59,556
Cocker Spaniel	12,866	Staffordshire Bull Terrier	2,774	Chow Chow	45,271
English Springer Spaniel	11,349	Golden Retriever	2,710	Dachshund (all varieties)	44,470
Staffordshire Bull Terrier	7,609	Border Collie	2,701	Beagle	42,499
Boxer	6,949	Cavalier King Charles Spaniel	2,128	Miniature Schnauzer	39,910
TOTAL	160,296	TOTAL	38,301	TOTAL	630,192

Note: The Labrador Retriever, Golden Retriever and German Shepherd are the only dogs appearing in the first ten of each authority's list.

• England: If the Poodle varieties (Giant, Standard and Miniature) were included as one, the combined registrations would total 7,224 which is above the cut off point of 6,949 registrations for the Boxer.

• Australia: The same applies to the Poodle and also to the Chihuahua in Australia, each with combined registrations of 2,511 and 3,051 respectively which are above the cut off point of 2,128 for the Cavalier King Charles Spaniel. The Cocker Spaniel (2,043 registrations) and the Bull Terrier (2,000 registrations) are just below the cut off point.

• United States: The Shetland Sheepdog (39,870 registrations) and Shih Tzu (39,503 registrations) are just below the cut off point of 39,910 for the Miniature Schnauzer.

Hounds: The role of the Hound is to run down its quarry. The long-legged hounds such as the Greyhound depend on their sight and speed, whilst the shorter legged hounds such as the Dachshund and Bloodhound depend on their scent and endurance to hunt their quarry in a pack.

Examples of the Hound group are the Beagle, Dachshund, Saluki, Whippet, Bloodhound and Afghan Hound.

Terriers: Terriers in earlier times were bred to hunt, dig out and destroy vermin. Some, such as the Bull Terrier, were bred to fight one another in the pits and later to attack and destroy rats in the pits. Now, the Terrier is regarded as a versatile dog, suitable as a watch dog, and as a pet that is frisky, loves to play and enjoys human companionship.

Well-known terriers are the Bull, Staffordshire Bull,

Fox, West Highland White, and Airedale.

Toys: These dogs have been bred as lap dogs and companions for indoor living. They have been selectively bred to be small in size.

Some well-known Toys are the Australian Silky Terrier, Chihuahua, Pekingese, Yorkshire Terrier and Maltese.

Utility dogs: These dogs are not so specialised as the Working dog group. They undertake work roles usually of a more generalised kind. Many of the dogs listed by the Australian National Kennel Council in the Utility group are placed in the Working dog group by the Kennel Club (Eng.) and the American Kennel Club (US), e.g. Boxer, Dobermann, Mastiff, Rottweiler, St Bernard and Samoyed.

Working dogs: These are active dogs which need to exercise and to perform the specific task that has been bred into them.

The Australian Cattle Dog, German Shepherd, Old English Sheepdog and the Collie are good examples of this group.

Non Sporting: All dogs in the Australian National Kennel Council's Non Sporting group except the Great Dane appear in Kennel Club's (Eng.) Utility group, e.g. the Boston Terrier, Chow Chow, Dalmatian, Keeshond, and Poodle (Standard, Miniature). All dogs in the American Kennel Club's Non Sporting group, except the Bichon Frise (Toy—KC) and Finnish Spitz (Hound—KC), appear in the Kennel Club (England)'s Utility group.

Herding: This group, unique to the American Kennel Club, appears to be for those dogs that specialise in the herding of such stock as cattle and sheep. Most of the breeds included in this group are to be found in the Working dog group of the Kennel Club (Eng) and the Australian National Kennel Council, e.g. Australian Cattle Dog, Collie, German Shepherd, Old English Sheepdog and Shetland Sheepdog.

Sporting: This group is also unique to the American Kennel Club and mostly includes the Retrievers, the Spaniels and Pointers, such as the Golden Retriever, Labrador Retriever, Cocker Spaniel, English Springer Spaniel, German Shorthaired Pointer and Weimaraner. Most of these are found in the Gun Dog group of the Kennel Club (Eng.) and the Australian National Kennel Council.

A Chihuahua

Hounds ready for the hunt.

A Bull Terrier

A Dobermann

A Kelpie at work

An Old English Sheepdog

A Rough Collie

A Dalmatian

A pair of Golden Retrievers

MOST POPULAR REGISTERED BREEDS

The selection of the most popular breeds is based on registration statistics published in1990 by the Kennel Club (England), American Kennel Club (US) and the Australian National Kennel Council.(See Table III.)

AUSTRALIAN CATTLE DOG

The Australian Cattle Dog evolved in the 1840s from a cross between a smooth-haired Blue Merle Collie imported from Scotland and a native Australian dingo. It is said that in the 1870s the Bull Terrier, Dalmatian and the Black and Tan Bull Terrier were crossed with the evolving Australian Cattle Dog, in attempts to refine and fix the breed. About the turn of the century there was a variety of cattle dogs in Australia. The first standard for the breed was compiled in 1897 and subsequently revised in 1965.

The Australian Cattle Dog is intelligent, reliable and hard working.

The Australian Cattle Dog's head is broad and strong, with a powerful lower jaw.

The Australian Cattle Dog is a strong, compact, symmetrically built working dog. Its combination of substance, power, balance and hard muscular condition conveys the impression of great agility, strength and endurance. The height of the dog is 46–51 cm (18–20 in) and the bitch is 43–48 cm (17–19 in).

The head is strong, the skull is broad, the cheeks are muscular, and the muzzle is of medium length, deep and powerful.

The body is slightly longer than it is high, the topline is level, the chest is deep and the dog is strongly coupled.

The set of the tail is moderately low and at rest it should hang in a slight curve. It should carry a good brush.

The coat is smooth. It is a double coat with a short, dense undercoat. The outer coat is close, each hair straight, hard and lying flat, so that it is rain resisting. Under the body, to behind the legs, the coat is longer and forms near the thigh a mild form of breeching. On the head (including inside of ears) and to the front of the legs and feet, the hair is short. Along the neck it is longer and thicker.

The colour is either blue or red speckle. The blue should be blue, blue mottled or blue speckled with or without markings. The markings are black, blue or tan in specified areas. The red speckle colour should be of good even speckle all over including the undercoat, with or without darker red markings. Red markings are permissible on the body, but not desirable.

The dog should present an alert, watchful and intelligent appearance. It is suspicious and aloof, nevertheless loyal, trustworthy and protective of its owner. Noted for its ability and efficiency in working cattle, it is also recognised as a faithful and ever alert security dog.

BEAGLE

The Beagle, which is noted for its ability to scent, is a popular hound, especially in the field, where the hare is its quarry. Its name first appears in the literature of the time of King Henry VIII. Over the centuries it has varied in type. There has been the smooth and the rough, the tall, medium and dwarf size. A beagle club and association were formed in Great Britain in 1890–91 and since that time the breed has been stabilised and improved.

In general appearance, the Beagle is a sturdy, compactly built hound, conveying the impression of quality without coarseness. It is a merry hound whose essential function is to hunt, primarily hare, by following a scent. It shows great activity, stamina and is of even temperament; it is not aggressive nor timid. Its desirable height is 33–40 cm (13–16 in). In the US, two varieties are recognised: not exceeding13 in, and over13 in, but not exceeding 15 in.

Its coat is short, dense and weatherproof; its colour is any recognised hound colour other than liver.

The Beagle makes an affectionate, even-tempered pet.

The Beagle's facial characteristics include large brown eyes, broad nostrils and an alert expression.

The tip of the tail is white. The tail is sturdy, moderately long, set on high and carried gaily but not curled over the back.

As well as being popular in the hunt and show ring, it is growing in popularity as a family pet. It is clean, affectionate and ready to make friends.

BORDER COLLIE

The Border Collie instinctively wants to work sheep and herd cattle. It has the inherent attributes to do this and every owner should keep this in mind. It is said that its origins are in the Collies of the border regions of England and Scotland, hence the name, Border Collie.

Its general appearance is that of a well proportioned dog, the smooth outline showing quality, gracefulness and perfect balance, with sufficient substance to ensure that it is capable of long periods of work as required of a sheep dog. The height of the dog is 48–53 cm (19–21 in) and the bitch is 46–51 cm (18–20 in).

The Border Collie is double coated, with a moderately long, dense, medium textured top coat while the undercoat is short, soft and dense, making a weather resistant protection, with abundant coat to form mane, breeching and brush.

Its colour is black and white, blue and white, chocolate and white, red and white and the tricolour black, tan and white. In each, the basic body colour (first mentioned

Border Collies are intelligent, faithful, and responsive to training.

The Boxer is very patient with children, making it an ideal family pet.

in the various colours) must predominate and be the background colour of the dog.

The Border Collie is a highly intelligent dog, responsive to training, keen and faithful, with an inborn desire to work. It is a prolific winner in sheep dog trials and obedience competitions.

It is also a much loved family pet, loyal, trustworthy and good with children.

BOXER

The history of the Boxer's ancestry in Germany indicates that it has served as a hunting dog, general utility dog, circus dog, and guard dog. In the 1880s the Boxer was mated to a taller English import, often white in colour, and so the modern Boxer breed line was begun. The Boxer was imported into US after the First World War and its popularity was established in the 1930s.

The Boxer is of medium size: dogs 57–63 cm (22.5–25 in) and bitches 53–59 cm (21–23 in). In body weight the dog is approximately 30–32 kg(66–70 lb) and the bitch is 25–27 kg (55–60 lb). It presents a spirited noble bearing, clean muscled body, square build and a mobile expressive face.

Its coat is short, glossy, smooth and tight to the body. The colours are fawn or brindle. White markings are acceptable if not exceeding one third of ground colour.

The Border Collie has a well-proportioned, graceful appearance.

Fawn is in various shades from dark deer red to light fawn. Brindle is black stripes on previously described shades of fawn, running parallel to ribs all over the body. Stripes contrast distinctly with the ground colour, neither too close nor too thinly dispersed. Ground colour is clear, not intermingling with stripes.

The tail is set on high, customarily docked and carried forward. The American Boxer has cropped ears whereas the Australian standard states that they should be of moderate size, thin, set wide apart on highest part of skull, lying flat and close to cheek in repose but falling forward with a definite crease when alert.

The Boxer's loyalty, intelligence, affection, playfulness and patience with children, courage, and distrustfulness of strangers makes the Boxer an ideal family pet, show dog and guard dog.

The Boxer's coat is short, glossy and smooth.

Boxers have a spirited, noble bearing and a mobile, expressive face.

CAVALIER KING CHARLES SPANIEL

Tapestries and paintings dating back to the 15th century depict spaniels similar to the present day Cavalier King Charles Spaniel in their small size, tapered muzzle, feathered coat, colour markings and flatness of the top of the head. In England, King Charles I and II were responsible for the spaniels rapid growth in popularity and the given name, King Charles Spaniel. The first Duke of Wellington was responsible for one particular variety being known as the Blenheim.

By the 19th century, especially in the latter half, breeders had changed the original King Charles to a dog with a domed skull, a short-nosed, puglike face and a distinct stop. An American, Roswell Eldridge, visited England in 1926 and sought to revive interest in what he considered was the original breed type, i.e. one with a long face, no stop and a flat skull. He offered an annual prize through Crufts. and as a consequence of the developing interest that followed, the Cavalier King Charles Spaniel Club, so named to distinguish it from the contemporary King Charles Spaniel, was formed in 1928. It continued to flourish and in 1945 the Kennel Club recognised the Cavalier as a separate breed from the King Charles Spaniel and accepted it as a registered breed in its own right. The first Cavalier King Charles Spaniel championship was held in 1946. In that year, 60 dogs were shown as registered in the Kennel Club's records. In 1990, approximately 17,000 were registered. In the US, the Cavalier is registered in a more general group known as the Miscellaneous Class.

The Cavalier King Charles Spaniel is a small dog, active, graceful and well balanced, with a gentle expression. Its weight range is 5.4–8.1 kg (12–18 lb).

Its skull is almost flat between the ears. The stop is shallow. Length from base of stop to tip of nose about 3.75 cm (1.5 in). Nostrils are black and well developed without flesh marks. The muzzle is well tapered. Eyes are large, dark, round but not prominent, and spaced well apart. Length of tail is in balance with the body, well set on, carried happily, but never much above the level of the back. Docking optional; if docked no more than one third to be removed.

The coat is long, silky, free from curl. Slight wave is permissible. Plenty of feathering. Totally free from trimming.

The recognised colours are:

Black and Tan: Raven black with tan markings above the eyes, on cheeks, inside ears, on chest and legs and underside of tail. Tan should be bright. White marks are undesirable.

Ruby: Whole coloured rich red. White markings are undesirable.

Blenheim: Rich chestnut markings well broken up, on

The Cavalier King Charles is a small, graceful dog.

Characteristic of the Cavalier King Charles Spaniel are its large, dark eyes and gentle expression.

pearly white background. Markings evenly divided on head, leaving room between ears for much valued lozenge mark or spot (a unique characteristic of the breed).

Tri colour: Black and white well spaced, broken up with tan markings over eyes, cheeks, inside ears, inside legs, and on underside of tail. Any other colour or combination of colours most undesirable.

The Cavalier is an alert, friendly companion, suited to home and children. It requires grooming.

CHOW CHOW

The unique features of the Chow Chow in the dog world is its blue-black tongue and stilted gait. The common belief, though there are differences of opinion, is that it originated over 2000 years ago in China where it served as a Sporting, Working, Herding and sacred dog. From China it was accepted into England and the US in the late 1800s.

In appearance the Chow Chow is active, compact, short coupled, well balanced and leonine, proud and dignified in bearing. The height of the dog is 48–56 cm

The unique feature of the Chow Chow is its blue-black tongue.

The Chow Chow is proud and leonine in bearing.

Quiet and loyal, the Chow Chow responds well to training.

(19–22 in) , and the bitch is 46–51 cm (18–20 in).

The skull is flat, broad and the stop is not well pronounced. Well filled under the eyes. The muzzle is moderate in length and broad from eyes to end.

The ears are small, thick, slightly rounded at the tip, carried stiffly and wide apart but tilting well forward over eyes and slightly towards each other, giving the scowling expression of the breed.

The coat is either rough or smooth. The rough coat is profuse, abundant, dense, straight and stand-off. Outer coat is coarse in texture with soft woolly undercoat. The coat is especially thick around the neck forming a mane or ruff. The smooth coat is short, abundant, dense, straight, upstanding, not flat, and plush-like in texture.

The Chow Chow is whole coloured black, red, blue, fawn, cream or white, frequently shaded but not in patches or parti-coloured.

The Chow Chow is active, intelligent and quiet and responds well to training. It is loyal, an excellent watch dog and suitable for the home.

COCKER SPANIEL
(ENGLISH AND AMERICAN)

The Spaniel breed is believed to have originated in Spain in the 14th century. By the 17th century several types of spaniels had been imported into England where they were collectively referred to as Spaniels. The story goes that one type of spaniel was so good at flushing out the woodcock that it was subsequently referred to as the Cocker Spaniel. Hence its name.

In 1882 it was imported into the United States where breeders developed some of its characteristics along different lines from the original English Cocker import. Indeed, over the centuries that the Cocker had been in England, changes in it had also taken place, but towards the close of the 19th century its breed line had been established to the point where it was accepted for registration by the Kennel Club in 1892.

The English Cocker Spaniel makes a devoted and playful pet.

An English Cocker Spaniel. Note the square jaw.

An American Cocker Spaniel. Note the upturned nose.

However, the American Cocker and the English Cocker were still classified as one for competition purposes. In 1936 in the US and in 1970 in England they were recognised as separate breeds by the respective kennel clubs.

Both the American Cocker and the English Cocker in general appearance are described as merry, sturdy, sporting and well balanced. In temperament they are much the same, the English being gentle and affectionate yet full of life and exuberance and the American being equable with no suggestion of timidity. However, when seen together, they look different. Some of the details that help to make up their different looks are :

Size

The English Cocker is slightly taller.

English: Dog 39.5–41 cm (15.5–16 in)
                Bitch 38–39.5 cm (15–15.5 in)

American: Dog 36.25–38.7 cm (14.5–15.5 in)
                Bitch 33.75 –36.25 cm (13.5–14.5 in)

Eyes

English: Full but not prominent ,always dark brown or brown. In certain coat colours,dark hazel to harmonise with coat.

American: Eyeballs round, full and looking directly forward. According to coat colour eyes vary from dark brown to black; dark hazel; not lighter than hazel.

Muzzle

English: Square muzzle; straight; skull well arched from end of muzzle.

American: Gives appearance of nose being slightly upturned with slight dish effect on muzzle; short; skull slopes back slightly.

Coat

English: Flat, fine and silky. Should never be wavy or curly. Front legs defined with feathering at back of leg. Never profuse.

American: Profuse, quite heavy. Legs with quite heavy feathering. Not as silky as the English,may be slightly wavy.

The Cocker Spaniel is an affectionate and devoted pet. It is admired for its elegance and attractive head framed by long ears, its bustling movement and merry wagging tail. The Cocker is a versatile gun dog and an intelligent family pet, suitable for the large or small home where it can be exercised and groomed.

DACHSHUND

The Dachshund is classified in the Hound group and is referred to as a persevering hunter and tracker. In the past it was well known for hunting the badger. These days it is more commonly accepted as a family pet and is easily recognised as the dog with the long body, long neck, long head and short legs.

According to their coat, there are three types—Smooth-haired, Longhaired and Wirehaired. Each type is classified as Standard, 9–12 kg (20–26 lb) or Miniature, 4.5 kg (10 lb). Judges are requested not to award a prize to any miniature over 5.0 kg (11 lb).

Smooth-haired: Dense, short and smooth.

Longhaired: Soft and straight or only slightly waved.

Longest under neck; under body and be hind legs where it forms abundant feather ing on tail where it forms a flag.

Wirehaired: With exception of jaw, eyebrows, chin and ears the whole body covered with a short, straight, harsh coat with dense undercoat. Beard on chin, bushy eyebrows, hair on ears almost smooth. Legs and feet well but neatly furnished with harsh coat.

All colours are allowed (except in Dapples, which should be evenly marked all over) but no white is permissible save for a small patch on chest which is permitted but not desirable. The Dachshund is an active, intelligent, fearless, even-tempered and faithful dog that can be accommodated in a small area.

Smooth-haired Dachshunds

Longhaired Dachshunds

Wirehaired Dachshunds

DOBERMANN

Louis Dobermann, a German tax collector of the mid 19th century, is said to have bred the dog that carries his name. He was also known to be the keeper of the local animal shelter and as he kept no records, it is thought that he set out to breed a guard and companion dog. Experts suggest that in order to achieve his goal he may have used the Pinscher, Rottweiler, Manchester Terrier, Beauceron and Greyhound in his breeding experiments. The Dobermann was given official recognition in Germany in 1900. The first Dobermanns arrived in Australia in the 1950s .

Dobermanns are of medium size, muscular and elegant, with a well set body. Of proud carriage, they are compact and taut and capable of great speed. The ideal height for dog s is 69 cm (27 in) and for bitches it is 65 cm (25.5 in).

The body is square, the height from ground to highest point of wither is the same as length from forechest to rear projection of upper thigh. The forechest is well developed. The back is short and firm with strong, straight topline, sloping slightly from withers to croup.

The tail is customarily docked at the first or second joint.

The coat is smooth, hard, short, thick and close lying. An imperceptible undercoat on the neck is permissible. Hair forming a ridge on back of neck and/or along spine is highly undesirable.

The Dobermann is muscular and elegant, and capable of great speed.

An excellent guard dog, the Dobermann is protective, loyal and obedient.

The colour is definite black, brown, blue or fawn (Isabella) only, with rust red markings. Markings to be sharply defined, appearing above eye, on muzzle, throat and forechest, on all legs and feet and below tail. White markings of any kind are highly undesirable.

The Dobermann likes to be a part of the family; it is protective, loyal and obedient. Wary of strangers, even children, the Dobermann serves as a deterrent, and is recognised as an excellent guard dog. It is extremely intelligent and can accept training at four months of age. The dog thrives on attention, but needs a firm owner.

ENGLISH SPRINGER SPANIEL

The Spaniel breed goes back to at least the 14th century but it is not until the late 18th century that there is any written record of the usage of the Springer name. It is understood that it was given because of the dog's capability in 'springing game' for net, falcon or greyhound. The English Springer Spaniel breed was recognised by the Kennel Club in 1902 and later by the American Kennel Club.

The English Springer Spaniel is a strong, robust, Sporting dog of medium size that works well in water and on land. It resembles the Cocker Spaniel though larger, being highest in leg and raciest in build of all the British land spaniels. Its approximate height is 51 cm (20 ins).

In body it is strong, neither too long nor too short. Chest is deep with well sprung ribs. Loin is muscular, strong with slight arch and well coupled.

The tail is set low, never carried above level of back and well feathered with lively action. Customarily docked.

The coat is close, straight and weather resisting, never

coarse. Moderate feathering on ears, forelegs, body and hindquarters.

The colour is liver and white, black and white, or either of these colours with tan markings.

The English Springer Spaniel is an intelligent dog, obedient, friendly, with a happy disposition. It enjoys family life including children. Reserved with strangers, it has proved to be a good watch dog.

The English Springer Spaniel is a robust dog of medium size.

With its happy disposition, the English Springer Spaniel enjoys family life.

GERMAN SHEPHERD

The German Shepherd was first bred from the working sheepdog in Bavaria just over a hundred years ago. In the short time since then, it has become most popular and is used by the Armed Forces, Police Drug Squads, persons with impaired vision, and security officers. Families keep them as pets and guard dogs.

The German Shepherd is a powerful, well muscled, versatile working dog. It is attentive, alert and tireless, with keen scenting ability. The ideal height for dogs is

The German Shepherd is a powerful, well-muscled dog.

Intelligent and responsive to training, the German Shepherd makes a loyal and courageous companion.

62.5 cm (25 in) and for bitches it is 57.5 cm (23 in); 2.5 cm (1 in) above or below the ideal is permissible.

The German Shepherd has a weather resistant coat; an outer one of straight, hard, close lying hair as dense as possible and a thick undercoat, usually grey or fawn except in all black dogs.

Its colour is sable or black or black saddle with tan, or gold to light grey markings. All black, all grey or grey with lighter or brown markings throughout are referred to as Sables. Blues, livers, albinos, whites (i.e. almost pure white dogs with black noses) and near whites are highly undesirable.

The German Shepherd is highly intelligent, and responds to obedience training and affection. As a family pet it needs to be groomed regularly and to be given the opportunity to exercise in space. The kennel yard should allow it a reasonable amount of freedom. It is not nervous or overly aggressive or shy, and it is extremely loyal and courageous.

GOLDEN RETRIEVER

It is said that a Flat Coated Retriever was mated to a Tweedside Spaniel bitch and some of the progeny were mated to an Irish Setter, the final result being the Golden Retriever. It was continually refined and in 1913 the Kennel Club recognised it as a true British breed.

The Golden Retriever is symmetrical, well balanced, active, powerful and a level mover. The height of the dog is 56–61 cm (22–24 in) and the height of the bitch is 51–56 cm (20–22 in).

Black German Shepherds are referred to as Sables.

Golden Retrievers are intelligent dogs that respond well to training.

The Golden Retriever is always ready for a swim.

It is a gentle and even tempered dog, with a kindly expression.

Its body is balanced and short coupled with a level topline.

Its coat is wavy or flat with good feathering and it has a dense water resisting undercoat.

Its colour is any shade of gold or cream but neither red nor mahogany. A few white hairs on the chest only is permissible. The nose is black.

The Golden Retriever is an intelligent dog, easy to train, popular as a family pet, show dog, obedience trial dog and gun dog. It is friendly, quiet, with a kindly expression and even temperament.

LABRADOR RETRIEVER

The origins of the Labradors are said to be in Newfoundland where they were known as the fisherman's assistant; they used to tow the nets and small boats to shore and retrieve fish.

They were imported into England in the early 19th century and were well established by the end of the century. They were appreciated as an excellent sporting dog in water and on land, and later on as a competitive show dog.

The Labrador is a short coupled, strongly built, very active dog with a keen love of water. The height of the dog is 56–57 cm (22–22.5 in) and the bitch is 54–56 cm (21.5–22 in).

The coat is short, dense, without wave or feathering, firm to the touch. and with a weather resistant undercoat The colour is wholly black, yellow or liver/chocolate. Yellows range from light cream to red fox. A small white spot on the chest is permissible.

A distinctive feature of the breed is the tail which is very thick towards the base, gradually tapering towards the tip, medium length, free from feathering, but clothed thickly all around with a dense, thick, short coat thus giving it a rounded appearance, described as the 'otter' tail. The tail may be carried gaily, but should not curl over the back.

The Labrador is popular as a household pet, gun dog, and guide dog for the blind. It is even tempered, keen and biddable, with a strong will to please. It has a kindly nature, with no trace of aggression and is a devoted companion.

MINIATURE SCHNAUZER

The Schnauzer, of German origin, was first used as a cattle dog and ratter. In more recent times it has become very popular as a family pet and reliable watch dog. There are three types of Schnauzer—Giant, Standard and Miniature. All three are distinctly different breeds.

The Miniature Schnauzer appeared around the turn of the century and its breed standards were first set in the early 1920s.

A Yellow Labrador

A Black Labrador

Labradors make excellent 'seeing eye'/guide dogs.

The Miniature Schnauzer has a coarse wiry coat, 'pepper and salt' in colour.

An affectionate family companion, the Miniature Schnauzer is suited to indoor and outdoor living.

In general appearance, the Miniature is similar to the Standard Schnauzer. It is sturdily built, robust, sinewy, nearly square (length of body equal to height at shoulders), and its rectangular head is accentuated by trimming. The Miniature bitch is 33 cm (13 in) in height and the dog is 35.5 cm (14 in).

The tail, which is set on and carried high, is customarily docked to three joints.

The coat is harsh, wiry and short enough for smartness, with dense undercoat. Clean on neck and shoulders, ears and skull. Harsh hair on legs. Furnishings fairly thick but not silky.

The colours are all pepper and salt with even proportions, or pure black, or black and silver, i.e. solid black with silver markings on eyebrows, muzzle, chest and brisket, forelegs below the point of the elbow, inside of hind legs below the stifle joint, on vent and under the tail.

The Miniature Schnauzer is an affectionate, family companion dog. It is alert, reliable, intelligent, suited to indoor or outdoor living, fond of children, reserved, and a good watchdog. Useful in controlling rodents.

POODLE

Poodles are classified as Standard over 38 cm (15 in) in height, Miniature under 38 cm (15 in) and over 28 cm (11 in) and Toy under 28 cm (11 in). The breed is said to have originated in Germany and from there it was brought to France which is often thought to be its homeland. Many onlookers are intrigued by its unique grooming. Despite the variety of clips that are to be seen, it is strongly recommended that the traditional lion clip be adhered to.

In appearance it is well balanced and elegant, with a very proud carriage. The coat is very profuse, dense and of good harsh texture. All short hair is close, thick and curly.

All solid colours are acceptable. White and creams to have black nose, lips and eyerims; black toenails desirable. Browns to have dark amber eyes and black points or deep amber eyes with liver points.

Blacks, silvers and blues to have black nose, lips, eyerims and toenails. Creams, apricots, browns, silvers and blues may show varying shades of the same colour up to 18 months. Clear colours preferred.

A Standard Poodle

This black Standard Poodle has a black nose, lips and eyerims.

A Toy Poodle

The Poodle originally was used as a Sporting dog, but is now more commonly known as a family pet, entertainer and a competitor in obedience trials. The Poodle is highly intelligent, gay spirited and good tempered; it likes to please and entertain.

ROTTWEILER

The Rottweiler was named after the town of Rottweil, Germany, where it was bred. As the story goes, it was used as a butcher's dog to guard large sums of money carried in a wallet tied around its neck when the butcher went on cattle buying trips in the country.

The Rottweiler is above average in size, compact and powerful, permitting great strength, manoeuvrability and endurance. The height for dogs is 63–69 cm (25–27 in) and for bitches it is 58–63.5 cm (23–25 in).

The coat is double, with a top coat of medium length, and is coarse and flat. The undercoat—essential on the neck and thighs—does not show through the top coat. Hair may be a little longer on back of forelegs and breechings. Long or excessively wavy coat is highly undesirable.

Its colour is black, with clearly defined rich tan to mahogany markings, not exceeding 10 per cent of the body colour. Areas with markings are the throat; cheeks; forelegs from carpus downward to toes; inside of rear legs from hock to toes, but not completely eliminating black from back of legs, and under tail. Markings also consist of a spot over each eye; a strip around each side of muzzle

The Rottweiler is above average in size, compact and powerful.

A natural guard dog, the Rottweiler can be a loyal pet, if obedience trained.

but not on bridge of nose; and two clear triangles on either side of the breastbone. White markings highly undesirable. Undercoat is grey, fawn or black.

The Rottweiler is loyal, good natured, self assured, fearless, biddable, with natural guarding instincts.

STAFFORDSHIRE BULL TERRIER

When bull baiting was banned by the British government in 1835, its followers turned to dog fighting which had a strong following in Staffordshire. Interested breeders tried to develop a breed for the pits (dog fighting arena) that had the fighting tenacity and strength of the Bulldog and the agility of the Terrier. Herein lies the origins of the Staffordshire Bull Terrier, recognised by the Kennel Club in 1935. In the US, a similar but larger dog was developed from British imports in 1870, and in 1935 the breed was recognised by the American Kennel Club as the American Staffordshire Terrier.

The Staffordshire Bull Terrier is agile, active and muscular. It is smooth coated, well balanced and has great strength for its size.

The standard weight for the dog is 13–17 kg (28–58 lb) and for bitches it is 11–15.5 kg (24–34 lb). Desirable height at wither is 35.5–40.5 cm (14–16 in), these heights being related to the weights.

Its body is close coupled, with level topline, wide front, deep brisket, well sprung ribs, muscular and well defined.

Its coat is smooth, short and close. The colour may be red, fawn, white, black or blue or any one of these colours with white. The colour may also be any shade of brindle, or any shade of brindle with white. Black and tan or liver colour is highly undesirable.

A highly intelligent, multi-purpose dog. Though courageous and a fighter, the Staffordshire Bull Terrier is peaceful unless aroused, and fits into the domestic or guard dog categories according to how it is trained.

WEST HIGHLAND WHITE TERRIER

The West Highland White is a native breed of Scotland and like other Terrier breeds was used as a vermin catcher in earlier days. In 1909 it was accepted for registration in the Kennel Club's Stud Book. Its popularity spread to the US where it was also registered by the American Kennel Club.

The West Highland is strongly built. It exhibits in a marked degree a great combination of strength and activity. The height is approximately 28 cm (11 in).

The skull is slightly domed and the head is thickly coated with hair. The jaws are strong and level, the nose is black and fairly large, forming a smooth contour with rest of muzzle.

The tail is 13–15 cm (5–6 in) long, covered with harsh hair, no feathering, as straight as possible, carried jauntily, not gay or carried over back. On no account should tail be docked.

The Staffordshire Bull Terrier was bred to fight, but is a peaceful, reliable dog unless aroused.

The West Highland White is a small dog, suitable as a house companion.

The West Highland is double coated. Outer coat consists of harsh hair, about 5 cm (2 in) long, free from any curl. The undercoat, which resembles fur, is short, soft and close. The colour is white.

The West Highland White Terrier is a small dog requiring just a short time of daily grooming. It is active, game, hardy, with high self esteem. This alert, gay, self reliant and friendly dog is a suitable house companion.

YORKSHIRE TERRIER

The breed is thought to stem from the many types of terriers that were to be found in Yorkshire in the 1800s, i.e. the Clydesdale or Paisley, Skye, and Black and Tan (Manchester) Terriers.

It was registered in the first volume of the Kennel Club's records as a Broken-Haired Scotch Terrier or Yorkshire Terrier. Later, it was registered solely as the Yorkshire Terrier in recognition of the county where its breeding from mixed origins was refined and stabilised.

The Yorkshire Terrier is very compact and neat, with an upright carriage conveying an air of importance. Its weight is up to 3.1 kg (7 lb).

Its body is compact with moderate spring of rib, good loin and level back. The general outline conveys an impression of a vigorous and well proportioned body. The hair on body is moderately long, perfectly straight (not wavy), glossy, of fine silky texture. Fall on head long, rich golden tan, deeper in colour at sides of head, about ear roots and on muzzle where it should be very long. Tan on head not to extend onto neck nor must any sooty or dark hair intermingle with any of the tan. The coat hangs down evenly on each side, a parting in the middle extending from nose to tail end.

The coat colour is dark steel blue (not silver blue) extending from occiput to root of tail, never mingled with fawn, bronze or dark hairs. Hair on the chest is rich, bright tan. All tan hair is darker at the roots than in the middle, shading to still lighter at the tips.

The eyes are dark, sparkling with a sharp intelligent expression. The ears are small, v-shaped, covered with very short hair coloured very deep rich tan.

The Yorkshire Terrier, a Toy dog, is alert, intelligent, hardy and spirited with an even disposition. The Yorkie as it is affectionately known is recommended as a house pet. It is small, loyal, friendly, clean, and a playful companion.

CROSSBREEDS AND MONGRELS

A mongrel is a dog of no definable breed. Whilst you might recognise a trace of different breeds in these dogs, no one breed is strongly dominant. Sometimes the term mongrel is used in an offensive, derogatory fashion but that is not the sense in which it is used here.

By contrast, the term crossbreed strictly interpreted applies to a dog which is a product of the mating of two different breeds. In general practice, if a dog shows the physical characteristics of a definite breed as well as the more subtle characteristics of another breed, it is referred to as a crossbreed, e.g. a dog that has the strong appearance of a German Shepherd, but also has the genes of some other dog in its make, is known as a German Shepherd cross.

Sometimes the crossbreed and mongrel are unfavourably contrasted with the pedigreed dog. It is well to remember that all dogs belong to the species *Canis familiaris*, and have similar endearing qualities. Furthermore, most pedigreed dogs of today come from a breed line that had its genesis in the crossbreed.

The crossbreed and mongrel are survivors and often intelligent. Usually they are affectionate, loyal and make good family pets.

The size of the crossbreed and mongrel population (an estimate of over a million in Australia, several million

The Yorkshire Terrier is an alert and playful companion.

A German Shepherd Cross

A Cattle Dog Cross

in the UK and many millions in the US) magnifies a common problem associated with the dog population of any country.

Some irresponsible, non-caring owners unthinkingly accept or buy a dog, find they cannot cope with it, and abrogate their responsibility by abandoning the dog or allowing it to stray, or by surrendering it to a dog caring body, such as the RSPCA or the ASPCA.

Some permanent method, such as the Trovan System, for identifying dog ownership is necessary in any programme devised to control the stray, abandoned, neglected dog population (see Identification, p. 44).

Allowing the dog to breed indiscriminately also contributes to the problem of a burgeoning dog population. The simple remedy is to have the dog neutered or spayed (see Birth control, p.199). It is a remedy which is also a safeguard for the dog's health.

A mongrel is a mixture of breeds.

CHOOSING YOUR PUPPY OR DOG

Why do you want a dog?—Responsibilities of a dog owner—Which breed to choose?
Puppy or adult dog?—Male dog or female (bitch)?—What to look for
Hereditable diseases and defects—Where to buy—Boarding kennels—Identification

D o not choose a dog on impulse because it is cuddly, or fashionable, or because you feel sorry for it. Keep these reasons well in the background of your decision-making.

WHY DO YOU WANT A DOG?

Is it to be a companion for yourself, the children or the family? Do you want a guard dog, a house dog, a yard dog, a show dog or a dog for breeding? Having decided why you want a dog, consider the responsibilities of a dog owner.

RESPONSIBILITIES OF A DOG OWNER

When buying a puppy, six to eight weeks of age, you are taking on a commitment for a period of approximately eight to 16 years. During that time you are committed to the following responsibilities:

Feeding: Your dog needs to be fed at least once a day.

Grooming: This task will vary according to the length of the dog's hair. Shorthaired breeds, such as the German Shorthaired Pointer, require little time compared with longhaired breeds, such as the Old English Sheepdog, which require daily grooming. Some breeds, such as the Poodle, need to have their hair cut a number of times a year which is usually done by a professional dog groomer. If you have limited time to devote to grooming, a shorthaired dog is a sensible choice. Hot wet climates are more suited to shorthaired dogs.

Housing: Small dogs are better suited to living indoors. Even though they are in the house, you need to provide a basket or dog bed where they can rest or sleep. Dogs living outside need shelter from the wind, rain, sun and snow, and a fenced off area to stop them from roaming and to allow adequate exercise.

Health care: You have to organise a regular worming programme, annual booster vaccinations and a check up by your veterinarian.

Which one to choose?

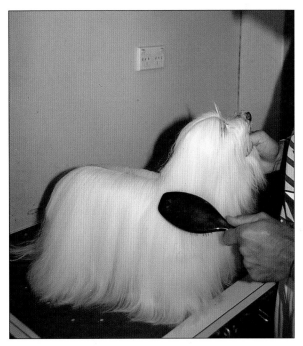
Longhaired breeds, such as the Maltese Terrier, sometimes require professional grooming.

Opposite: Each breed has its own appeal.

Exercise: Generally, the smaller the dog (e.g. Toy Breeds), the less exercise they require. Some breeds, e.g Fox Terrier, Weimaraner, Beagle, Border Collie and Dalmatian, need plenty of exercise for both physical and mental health. Your garden should have adequate space for free exercise; otherwise you will need to spend time each day walking your dog on a lead.

Human contact: Most dogs seek affection, attention and physical contact. It is important for both the dog and its owner to have regular contact with one another. Talking to, stroking, nursing (depending on the size) and playing with the dog provide opportunities for contact.

Training: Your relationship with your dog will be much better if it has some basic training. This can be done at home, or at a local training school where you and your dog can progress to advanced training courses (see p. 51).

Desexing (neutering): If you do not want to have your dog desexed, it is important to take such measures that will prevent it from breeding indiscriminately. Having your dog (male or female) neutered helps to reduce the

Dogs living outside need a suitable kennel in a fenced-off area.

The larger breeds need plenty of exercise.

When your puppy is fully grown, how big do you want it to be!

stray dog problem and generally makes your dog a better companion.

Boarding: If you are going away and cannot take your dog with you, you will need to board it at a kennel or arrange for someone to come daily to the house or apartment to look after it (see Boarding kennels, p. 43).

WHICH BREED TO CHOOSE?

Breeds have well defined characteristics of size, shape, hair length, and temperament.

By choosing a puppy of a certain breed you will have a good idea of what it will look like and what temperament it will have when it matures. Sometimes there is a variation which cannot be predicted. You are advised to discuss with your veterinarian the problems or inherited diseases of any particular breed you are interested in (see Hereditable diseases, p. 38). Crossbred dogs can make ideal companions.

If you choose a crossbred puppy, it is difficult to forecast its size, shape, hair length and temperament when it matures unless you know the parents.

A dog enjoys companionship.

A young puppy, eight weeks of age.

PUPPY OR ADULT DOG?

A mature placid dog may be suitable for an elderly couple who could not cope with a young pup. Beware of the mature dog that is given away as it may have a problem. Enquire carefully as to the reason why the dog is being given away and take it home for a trial period before accepting it.

A young pup approximately eight weeks of age would be ideally suited for a family. The children would benefit from the puppy and its playful antics, and the puppy as it matures would adapt itself to the family and its environment. At this age a puppy will develop a strong bond with you and be easier to train.

MALE DOG OR FEMALE (BITCH)?

Female pups are usually neutered (spayed) at five months of age. They make good companions, are less territorial and usually are more attached to the house. If you don't have your female dog neutered and you don't take any precautions to prevent it breeding indiscriminately, invariably it will become pregnant. Looking after a bitch and her puppies involves a great deal of time and effort and expense on your part. Furthermore, you may be left with some unwanted puppies.

Male dogs are usually neutered (castrated) at the age of six months. With exceptions, they make equally good companions or family pets. Male dogs that are entire tend to roam more if the opportunity is there, are more often involved in fights and car accidents, and being picked up by the dog catcher and placed in the pound.

WHAT TO LOOK FOR

Stand back and look at the pup from a distance. Look for one that is playful, alert, active, outgoing and friendly. Do not select one that is timid, frightened, aggressive or aloof.

Gently pick up the puppy and have a good look at its eyes to make sure they are clear and that there is no discharge or inflammation (redness). Also check to see that there is no discharge from the nose. A puppy that has discharge from the eyes and nose may be incubating distemper (see p. 133).

Check inside the ears, which should be clean and dry. Heavy wax and/or redness inside the ear is often indicative of ear mites (see p. 142).

Carefully pull the lips apart and check to see that the incisor (front) teeth of the upper jaw meet the incisor teeth of the lower jaw when the mouth is closed (level bite), or that the upper teeth fit tightly over the lower teeth (scissor bite). Do not select a puppy where the upper jaw protrudes further than the lower jaw. This is known as an overshot jaw. An undershot jaw is where the lower jaw protrudes further than the upper jaw (see Malocclusion, p. 92), which is desirable in some breeds such as the Boxer.

Also check the puppy's coat, which should be even, soft and shiny. There should not be any hair loss or broken, scaly, scabby skin. The puppy should be clean around the anus. Dirt around the anus, tail or down the back of the hindlegs could indicate diarrhoea due to worms or infection. While holding the puppy you will get an indication of its weight. Avoid choosing a thin bony one , and check to see that the legs are not bowed.

Check for a swelling around the navel (umbilicus) which is known as an umbilical hernia. If prominent, the hernia will need to be repaired surgically at a later date.

HEREDITABLE DISEASES AND DEFECTS OF SOME BREEDS

Once you have made up your mind about which breed of dog you wish to purchase, it is important to select one that is as free as possible from any inherited disease or defect.

It is in the interest of the owner to select a dog that can lead a happy, potentially disease-free life and which will not pass on any significant defect or disease to its progeny, if used for breeding.

A list of popular breeds and their hereditable diseases and defects has been compiled, not with the intention of turning you away from any particular breed, but to make you aware. It is important to note that whilst certain breeds have hereditable diseases and defects , not all dogs within those breeds carry those diseases and defects and therefore do not pass them onto their progeny.

By being aware of this situation and taking the following precautions, you can minimise the possibility of selecting a dog with some inherited defect or disease:

CHOOSING A PUPPY

Stand back and look at the puppies.

Gently examine the puppy more closely.

Look for an alert puppy.

Look for a playful puppy.

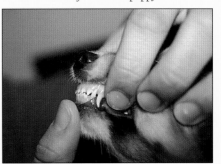

Check that the incisors meet (level bite), or that the upper incisors fit tightly over the lower incisors (scissor bite).

• Ask the breeder if the parents and, or grandparents are free from any hereditable defects. Some defects, such as an umbilical hernia and cleft palate, are obvious to an informed person.

• Consult a veterinarian. Some inherited characteristics, such as hip dysplasia and cataracts, are not obvious at birth and may not be obvious for years. The veterinarian uses manipulative skills and x-ray for the diagnosis of hip dysplasia which can only be diagnosed definitely as the dog matures. In the case of hip dysplasia, ask the breeder if the parents have been certified free of it by a veterinarian.

• Check the puppy or dog's temperament. If one or both parents show signs of an aggressive temperament and the pup or young dog is shy or nervous, it is likely that the puppy or young dog may eventually have a behavioural problem.

• Consult the breed society in your local area. The society should have some idea of the quality of the puppies produced by various registered breeders.

Some inherited diseases and defects have greater significance than others, e.g. intervertebral disc disease is far more significant than an overshot jaw.

BREED	DISEASES AND DEFECTS	SIGNS
Beagle	Ectropion	Turning out of the eyelid resulting in chronic conjunctivitis
	Epilepsy	Fitting: grand mal and petite mal
	Intervertebral disc disease	Back pain Ataxia (wobbliness of the hindlimbs). Partial or complete paralysis.
	Allergic dermatitis	Chronic red, inflamed,irritated skin
	Behavioural abnormalities	Hysteria—sometimes aggressive
Border Collie	Central Retinal atrophy	Degeneration of the retina leading to blindness
	Behavioural abnormalities	Aggressive behaviour
Boxer	Entropion Corneal ulcer	Turning in of eyelid—tears streaming down cheek. Eyelids partially closed.Cloudy cornea. Tears streaming down cheek.
	Heart defects	Poor exercise tolerance. Laboured respiration. Cough. Ascites—abdomen swollen with fluid
	Epulis	Tumour-like growth on the gums.
	Skin tumours Mast cell tumour	A raised swelling of the skin with an ulcerated surface.
	Dermoid cyst	Cyst in the skin
Bull Terrier	Umbilical hernia	A swelling in the region of the navel containing fat and sometimes intestine.
	Deafness	
	Allergic dermatitis	Chronic red, inflamed, irritated skin.
Chow Chow	Entropion—sometimes related to excess loose skin on the forehead.	Turning in of the eyelid with eyelashes rubbing on the surface of the eye—tears streaming down the cheek.
	Displaced tear duct opening	Tears streaming down the cheek.
Cocker Spaniel (American and English)	Ectropion—usually the lower lids.	Turning out of the eyelid -resulting in chronic conjunctivitis.
	Entropion—sometimes related to excess loose skin on the forehead.	Turning in of the eyelids with eyelashes rubbing the surface of the eye—tears streaming down the cheek.
	Cataract	Crystallisation of the lens which becomes cloudy—may lead to blindness.
	Corneal ulcer	Cloudy cornea. Usually a circular break in the corneal surface.
	Glaucoma	Swelling of the eye due to increased pressure within the eye—affects vision.

BREED	DISEASES AND DEFECTS	SIGNS
Cocker Spaniel (cont.) (American and English)	Progressive Retinal Atrophy (PRA)	A disease of the retina causing blindness.
	Cleft palate	A defect (hole) in the roof of the mouth—milk comes out the nose when the puppy sucks on the nipple.
	Umbilical hernia	A swelling in the region of the navel containing fat and sometimes intestine.
	Behavioural abnormalities	Unpredictable, erratic,aggressive behaviour
	Intervertebral disc disease	Back pain Ataxia (wobbliness of the hind limbs) Partial or complete paralysis
Dachshund	Diabetes mellitus— sugar diabetes	Drinking and urinating frequently Ravenous appetite and weight loss
	Intervertebral disc disease	Back pain Ataxia (wobbliness of the hindlimbs) Partial or complete paralysis
	Overshot jaw	The upper jaw being longer than the lower jaw
Dobermann	Deep-set eyes	Conjunctivitis and chronicdischarge in the corner of the eye
	Haemophilia	Defect in blood clotting mechanism — internal bleeding
German Shepherd	Hip dysplasia	Weakness in hindquarters. Awkward gait in hindlegs. Difficulty getting up and jumping
	Anal furunculosis	Discharging sinuses and ulcerated anus.
	Epilepsy	Fitting—grand mal or petite mal
	Behavioural abnormalities	Erratic, aggressive behaviour
Golden Retriever	Cataract	Crystallisation of the lens may lead to blindness
	Hip dysplasia	Awkward gait in the hindquarters. Difficulty in getting up and jumping
Labrador Retriever	Entropion	Turning in of the eyelids with eyelashes rubbing the surface of the eye—tears streaming down cheeks
	Hip dysplasia	Awkward gait in hindlegs. Difficulty getting up and jumping
Pekingese	Entropion	Turning in of the eyelids with eyelashes rubbing on the surface of the eye—tears streaming down the cheek
	Extra eyelashes	Irritates the eye causing blinking and weeping
	Nasal fold— inflammation and infection	Hairs on the nasal fold irritate the eye causing weeping, leading to a moist nasal fold susceptible to dermatitis

BREED	DISEASES AND DEFECTS	SIGNS
Pekingese (cont.)	Corneal ulceration	Closing eyelids; Weeping; Cloudy cornea; Usually a circular break in the corneal surface
	Intervertebral disc disease	Back pain; Ataxia (wobbliness of the hindlimbs); Partial or complete paralysis
	Patella luxation—Dislocating kneecaps	Holds the hindleg off the ground for a short period of time then walks normally—often leads to arthritis
	Umbilical hernia	Swelling in the region of the navel containing fat and sometimes intestine
Poodle (Miniature and Toy)	Facial staining	Reddish-brown stain down cheeks either side of the nose
	Blocked tear duct and Displaced tear duct opening	Tears running down the cheek
	Cataract	Crystallisation of the lens which becomes cloudy and may lead to blindness
	Micropthalmia—a small eye	The eyelids fit poorly around the eye leading to chronic inflammation
	Glaucoma	Swelling of the eyeball due to increased pressure within the eye—affects vision
	Progressive retinal atrophy (PRA)	A disease of the retina causing blindness
	Dry Eye—Kerato Conjunctivitis sicca	The eyeball looks dry and is covered with sticky, tacky pus
	Legg-Calve-Perthes disease—degeneration of the hip joint	Hip lameness and pain
	Behavioural abnormalities	Hysteria
	Patella luxation—dislocating kneecaps	Holds the hindleg off the ground for a short period of time then walks normally—often leads to arthritis
	Extra eye lashes	Irritates the eye causing blinking and weeping
Rottweiler	Entropion	Turning in of the eyelids with eyelashes rubbing on the surface of the eye - tears streaming down the cheek
	Hip dysplasia	Awkward gait in the hindquarters. Difficulty in getting up and jumping
	Osteochondritis dissecans	Drying out and ulceration of cartilage surfaces, mainly of the shoulder and hock joints.
	Behaviour abnormalities	Unpredictable, aggressive behaviour.
Miniature Schnauzer	Cataract	Crystallisation of the lens which becomes cloudy—may lead to blindness.

WHERE TO BUY

There are several sources from which you can obtain a dog.

BREEDERS

If you buy from a breeder specialising in your chosen breed of dog you will be able to see what the pup will look like when it matures by seeing at least one of its parents. You may also be able to get some idea of its temperament.

If you want to buy a pedigreed dog, it is wise to contact the kennel club in your area as it will have a register of member breeders specialising in different types of breeds. Even when buying from a breeder you should be aware of the information given in this section. Always check with the breeder to see if the dog has a vaccination certificate, a record of worming programme and a registered pedigree.

PET SHOPS

Dogs bought from pet shops are usually not pedigreed so you do not know what it will look like when it matures. Often the history of the pup and its parents is unknown. If this information can be supplied, it may give you an insight into the dog's general health and temperament. In some countries, pet shops issue a signed health certificate for the dog you purchase which guarantees a refund of your money within 48 hours if a veterinary examination reveals a serious medical problem.

ANIMAL WELFARE AGENCIES
(ASPCA, RSPCA)

The dogs available are usually abandoned or surrendered by owners for many reasons: behaviour problems, too costly to keep, poor temperament, a medical problem, unsuitable for the family home or lifestyle of the owner.

In the case of puppies that have not been immunised and are admitted into a compound of numerous dogs, there is the danger that they might pick up a virus such as distemper, hepatitis, parvovirus, and kennel cough. These viruses take about ten days to incubate so there is the possibility that you will not see any symptoms until you have had the pup home for a week or so.

NEIGHBOURS

Some family in the neighbourhood has a bitch with puppies. Usually the pregnancy was not planned. At least the mother of the pups is known and often the family has a good idea which dog fathered the pups, so you will have some idea of what they will be like when mature.

As the bitch and its puppies are usually looked after by the family in the family home, they are isolated from other dogs, so generally the puppies are disease free and healthy.

BOARDING KENNELS

It is a good idea to make arrangements well ahead if you are thinking of booking your dog into a good boarding kennel. They are usually fully booked, especially during holiday periods.

To select a good boarding kennel it is wise to find out if it holds a current licence. Kennels in many countries are required to be licensed under such legislation as a Prevention of Cruelty to Animals Act. For the kennel to hold a current licence it has to be checked by some authority such as the Police Department or the local Council.

Do not hesitate to discuss the following with the management:

• Is it a requirement for the dog to have a current veterinary vaccination certificate before being admitted to the boarding kennel? All good boarding establishments demand to see a current vaccination certificate. If your dog is due for a vaccination (see p. 94) around the time of boarding, it is a good idea to have it vaccinated a couple of weeks before it is due to go into the kennel.

• What arrangements does the management have in place for veterinary attention if the dog gets sick while you are away? Leave the name and phone number of your veterinarian in case the dog's health record is required. Leave a contact number in case an emergency arises and the management needs to consult you or someone you have nominated.

• Does the management ask you to sign a contract form at the time of admission? Does it clearly state the responsibilities of both parties?

• Is there somebody continually in attendance at the kennel in case of an emergency?

• What kind of food is given to the dogs and does the management cater for individual dogs that are fussy or require a special diet?

• Ask the management if you can inspect the kennel. If you are refused permission, it may be wise to seek another kennel to board your dog.

During the inspection of the kennel, check that:

• The kennel is clean, tidy, hygienic, with no unpleasant odour, and well organised.

• The dogs in the kennel are healthy, happy, bright and alert.

• The pens are adequate for sleeping, eating, exercising and toileting. The pens should be designed so that individual dogs do not have any direct physical contact.

• The kennel and pens have good security so that your dog cannot escape while you are away.

A good boarding kennel is clean, tidy, hygienic and well organised.

Make sure the pens are adequate for exercise.

• The pens receive good natural light during the day, are well ventilated, dry and insulated from the heat or cold.

Most dogs take a few days to become familiar with and feel at ease in their new surroundings, especially with numerous other strange dogs. Once they realise they are safe and secure, they usually settle in quite well.

IDENTIFICATION

Each year a number of dogs, approximately one in twenty, are reported by owners as having been stolen, lost, or missing. Those that are lost or missing are often injured and end up in a veterinary hospital, animal welfare shelter (e.g. RSPCA, ASPCA), or local government authority's dog pound.

If the ownership of a stolen dog is in dispute, the rightful owner should be able to identify it positively. On the other hand if a stray or lost dog is found, it should carry some form of permanent identification so that the owner can be traced readily and quickly.

METHODS OF IDENTIFICATION

PHOTOGRAPHS

These are of some limited assistance to you in finding your lost, stolen or strayed dog. Many dogs look alike and fit the same description of size, colour, shape and sex. The photograph may be of some use for advertisement purposes or for positive identification by the owner if the dog has some irregular markings.

REGISTRATION TAGS

Some countries or states have passed a law whereby local government authorities require all dogs in their area to be registered and issued with identification tags to be attached to the collar. Some dogs do not wear collars, some lose them and in some cases the tags are so badly damaged that they are not readable.

TATTOOING

This is a relatively simple procedure conducted by your veterinarian. It can be done inside the ear or inside the flank so that it does not cause any disfigurement. If the owner's telephone number was tattooed inside the ear or flank, it would be helpful to the finder when trying to trace the owner. It would also be extremely helpful to the owner if there were any dispute over ownership.

SILICON MICROCHIP IMPLANT (THE TROVAN SYSTEM)

This system involves the painless injection of a tiny microchip implant under the skin. This is done by your veterinarian without the need for sedation or anaesthesia. The missing dog—whether lost, strayed or stolen—if taken to a veterinarian's surgery, animal shelter or dog pound, can be checked immediately with a hand held scanner that will throw upon its screen the dog's registration number. The central animal registry can then be contacted and the owner's name, address and phone number is made available. Such a service allows the missing dog to be reunited quickly with its owner and for the owner to consent to any treatment that the veterinarian feels is urgent and perhaps life saving.

Opposite: This dog is wearing an identification tag attached to its collar.

TRAINING

Puppy training: Bringing home your new puppy—Choice of name
Sleeping box or kennel—Comforters—Puppy pen—Food, water, cleanliness—Toilet training
Making the puppy feel at home—Informal training—Achievement goals
Obedience training: Family dog programme—Basic guidelines
Teaching commands—Teaching tricks

Since early times the dog has been a pack animal subject to the dominance of a pack leader. When a puppy is brought into the family circle the primitive characteristics of a pack animal are still deep seated in its nature. Virtually the family becomes the pack and the owner has the responsibility of assuming the dominant role of substitute pack leader.

Some owners establish their leadership authority on fear, physical cruelty and intimidation whilst others establish it on firmness, kindness, praise, consistency, persistency and patience. The latter approach is recommended to all dog owners. It brings out the best in dog and owner and lays the foundation for a close, lasting relationship. If the owner does not establish leadership authority, the result may be a spoilt family pet with some irritating behavioural habits.

PUPPY TRAINING
BRINGING HOME YOUR NEW PUPPY

It is just like bringing home a new baby. Preparations have to be made beforehand if you want the puppy to settle in with a minimum of fuss and bother and begin its good habit training from 'day one'. Preparations should include:

- choice of name
- setting up a sleeping box or kennel
- comforters
- a puppy pen, if needed
- provision to satisfy the puppy's needs for food, water and cleanliness
- preparations to make the puppy feel at home
- reading literature on puppy training

Make sure training starts as soon as you bring home your new puppy.

Opposite: Training your dog will enhance your relationship with it.

CHOICE OF NAME

A dog's sense of hearing is far more acute than a human's. Its finely tuned ability to hear and distinguish sounds, to associate a particular sound with a particular behavioural act, its desire to please its owner and to be praised are the cornerstones of good habit training.

By using the puppy's name often from the time it arrives home, the puppy will begin to recognise the sound (name) as meaning 'my owner wants my attention'. When you use the name (sound) and the puppy looks at you, praise it immediately with 'Good Girl', 'Good Boy' or 'Good Dog', and as a bonus give it a pat or a rub around the ears or some other friendly touch. This friendly act of the owner, i.e. praising and touching, gives the puppy the feeling that it pleases the owner by giving the owner its attention when it hears its name (sound). With repetition, the puppy falls into the habit of giving attention when a certain sound (name) is made. Bear in mind that in this learning process the dog wants to be praised and wants to please. Use the same praise word or short phrase all the time and remember that there is no room for anger if a mistake is made. If you wish to punish your puppy, never get it to come to you by calling its name. Next time, it won't come. Instead, go to it if it needs to be disciplined.

SLEEPING BOX OR KENNEL

Your young puppy has just been separated from its mother, brothers and sisters; its separation is still in its memory and it misses the warmth, affection and company of its kind.

Before bringing your puppy home, you should have decided whether you are going to let it sleep in the house or in some protected and covered area outside. Keep in mind that if you let it sleep inside with you for a week or two, you are not creating an insoluble problem for yourself when later on you decide to house it outside.

The sleeping box could be made of such materials as plastic, wood, cane, etc., or improvised by using a throwaway cardboard box. It should be large enough to allow for some growth and for the puppy to be able to turn around. It should stand about 5 cm (2 in) off the floor, be draught free, and easy to clean. The entrance should allow the puppy free movement in and out. A suitable covering for the floor of the sleeping box could be a folded newspaper, shredded paper or an old blanket or jumper which could be thrown out or washed when soiled.

When putting the puppy to bed after its evening meal and toilet training, talk to it, letting it know that you are a friend in its new home where sounds, smells and strangers might otherwise give it a feeling of insecurity and bewilderment during the night and result in much whimpering and crying.

The kennel outside the house should be much the

A trampoline bed

same as the sleeping box. Locate it in a spot where it gets a fair amount of sun but not the extremely hot afternoon sun of summer. It should be large enough for the full-grown dog to be able to turn around in it. It should be draught free, off the ground, comfortable inside and easy to clean.

Care should be taken to ensure the cleanliness of the sleeping box or kennel to avoid flea infestation. Check your puppy regularly for fleas, especially around the butt of the tail. Soiled bedding should be removed immediately and replaced.

Some dogs refuse to use the kennel that has been provided. An alternative is the trampoline bed. It has the advantage of being pliant and easy to move and clean.

COMFORTERS

A warm water bottle will give the warmth that will help the puppy to sleep, but try to avoid a rubber one as the puppy's needle sharp teeth may puncture the rubber. A synthetic bone or some such toy, even a teddy bear, may be placed in the sleeping box as a comforter. An old alarm clock ticking away is said to help induce sleep and a coloured tennis ball will provide for some self activity during the day. Do not use smaller balls as they can lodge in the puppy's throat or stomach.

PUPPY PEN

This is similar to a young child's play pen with some kind of waterproof floor such as plastic. It is very useful if the puppy is kept inside the home and is not toilet trained, as it can be supervised all the time. The pen confines the puppy yet allows it some freedom of movement and it frees the owner from constant supervision.

The pen should be just large enough to house the puppy's sleeping box with comforters in one corner, its food and drinking bowls in another, and a sheet of folded newspaper in another for defaecating and urinating; the remainder of the area being for free movement. The puppy should not be able to get out, but it ought to be able to see what is going on outside its pen.

FOOD, WATER, CLEANLINESS

When you bring home your young puppy, follow the diet that it has been accustomed to and only change it gradually if you think a changed diet would be more beneficial for its health (see Feeding and diet, p.77). Putting a puppy on a completely new diet may cause problems such as diarrhoea. Your puppy should have its own feeding and drinking bowl, always kept in the same position, always clean and with fresh water always available.

TOILET TRAINING

Keep in mind that puppies up to 12 weeks old are like babies; when they get the urge, they urinate and defaecate anywhere at any time. In these situations it is senseless to blame the puppy. If blamed, the puppy will associate the blame with urinating or defaecating rather than with where the act took place.

To minimise the incidence of 'relieving accidents' in the house, set up a 'relief station'. A simple one is several sheets of folded newspaper on the floor of the laundry, bathroom, near an exit door or some convenient spot to which the puppy has access from its sleeping quarters. Take the puppy to the 'relief station' after each meal, as soon as it wakes up in the morning, just before putting it to bed in the evening, and at any other time if you think the puppy wants to relieve itself. Remain with the puppy at the 'relief station', encouraging it to urinate or defaecate by repeating some words such as 'Busy, Busy'. When it does its 'Busy' give it praise, using the same phrase you will always use to signify praise and pleasure, e.g. 'Good Dog' or 'Good Girl' or 'Good Boy'. Reinforce the verbal praise with a pat or a tidbit. Imagine your joy when after a few days or weeks your puppy automatically goes to the 'relief station'.

Become aware of and sensitive to signs that the young puppy in the house wants to relieve itself. Signs might be a whimper, restlessness, sniffing the floor or going to the door and giving the owner a look.

When you have established the habit of the puppy automatically using the newspaper indoors as a 'relief station', you may want the puppy to go outside to relieve itself. For a few days place the newspaper near the exit, then outside where it can be seen by the puppy through the doorway, then to a spot in the garden where you eventually want your puppy to relieve itself. After several days the paper in the garden could be dispensed with. Some of the urine will have percolated through the paper into the soil. The puppy sniffing around will identify the spot and continue to use it as its 'relief station.' This will save you time in cleaning up and from carrying dog faeces

into the house accidentally picked up on your shoes.

The repetitious nature of the toilet training programme, its call on your patience and time at all hours, may prompt you to give it away. But don't. Success will come at any time within the first four weeks and you will find it is worth waiting for. In the interim, keep a mop, water, cloth and a mix of white vinegar, detergent and warm water handy for the cleaning up jobs that crop up from time to time.

MAKING THE PUPPY FEEL AT HOME

In providing the puppy with a name, a suitable sleeping box, some comforters, and a comfortable kennel, or a playpen if kept inside permanently , you are taking the first steps to making it feel at home. Both puppies and dogs like to sleep during the day and night; young puppies more so. Reinforce your welcome by showing your new puppy or dog around the house and garden, including the sheds, garage, front and back door, etc. Let it sniff around, explore and discover. Whilst doing so, talk to the puppy or dog, use its name frequently, and stroke and touch it in a friendly way. In short, let it know that you are pleased that it is staying with you.

Extending a friendly hand to the new puppy to make it feel at home.

Puppies love to explore.

INFORMAL TRAINING

From when your puppy first arrives home until it is 4–8 months old, informal training should be associated with its upbringing. The training is mostly unstructured; it arises out of day to day circumstances whenever you see the puppy doing what you want or do not want it to do.

When the puppy is performing a desirable act, e.g. sitting, say the sound (word),e.g. 'Sit', several times while the puppy keeps the sitting position. This will condition the puppy to associate 'sitting' with the sound (word) 'Sit'. At the same time,immediately praise the puppy thereby giving it pleasure and letting it know that you are pleased with what it is doing. The praise cum pleasure reinforces the association of a particular sound (word) with a particular act (behaviour). The praise may be verbal, e.g. 'Good Dog', or a tidbit, or a touch, e.g. a pat, a rub or a shake, or for that matter, all three. Repeat this whenever the opportunity arises. Eventually, the puppy will respond automatically whenever it hears the sound (word) 'Sit', and will sit in anticipation of your praise.

Conversely, if the puppy is doing something you don't want it to do, e.g. scratching at the door, the displeasure in your voice when saying aloud 'No' together with your displeased demeanour will prompt the puppy to sense that it is being blamed—not praised—for its behaviour. After some repetition of the displeasurable association between the sound (word) 'No' and the behaviour, your puppy will desist on hearing 'No' and in time will stop performing the unacceptable act.

Grooming your puppy often provides an opportunity for informal training in responding to the sounds (words) 'Sit', 'Stay', 'Stand'. The release word 'OK' which tells the puppy it need no longer obey can also be introduced informally. For example, when you have shown the dog that you are pleased with it 'sitting' in response to the command 'Sit', say 'OK' and indicate to the puppy, by your tone of voice, facial expression and outflung arms that you no longer want it to sit. The puppy can become familiar with other commands sounds (words) such as 'Bed,' 'Car', 'Stay', 'Come', etc., in the same incidental way.

A training task which should be undertaken in the informal training period, even though it has an air of formality about it, is teaching the young puppy to tolerate and respond to a collar and lead. Depending on the nature of the puppy's acceptance or rejection of the collar and lead, a graded approach to this task should be structured accordingly. If the puppy is living inside the home, that is where the training would begin. If it is living outside, select a quiet area in the garden where there are no distractions. First place around the neck of the puppy a very light collar, perhaps made of linen, light canvas, nylon or leather, just tight enough so that you can place two of your fingers underneath it. If the puppy tolerates it, give praise, and leave it on for a while. Repeat several times in the day, e.g. before meal times. If the puppy fusses with it and tries to remove it, leave it on for several minutes. Later on, repeat the process, giving praise if the opportunity arises and gradually extend the period of time the collar is left on.

After the puppy accepts the collar, tie a small piece of string or nylon cord to it. At this stage the string or cord should not touch the ground when the puppy is running around. When the puppy is accustomed to the dangling string or cord, lengthen it so that it trails on the floor. Again, when the puppy learns to ignore or avoid the trailing cord take it in your right hand and follow the puppy wherever it wants to go. Finally, use the string or cord lead to indicate to the puppy when you want it to stop or walk in another direction. A sharp jerk is often effective in stopping the puppy or directing it to go in another direction. This does not mean engaging in a tug-o-war but it means plenty of patient practice before success is achieved. Remember to reward the puppy's correct behaviour with praise but never blame or show anger with failure. Later, a collar and lead more suited to the dog's height and strength should be chosen.

When the house-trained puppy shows no resistance to the collar and lead, take it for a walk in the garden. When accustomed to that, walk it on the nearby footpath (sidewalk) and later in the park. The puppy in its outings will probably meet some interesting distractions and forget all about the fact that it is on a lead. Don't be disappointed and angry as that kind of initial response is not unusual. With further practice in the new situation, control will be stabilised.

If your puppy sits and refuses to budge when on the lead, coax it to move towards you, saying 'Come' and patting your chest with your right hand; the lead being held in the left (see Heel and Come, pp. 53, 55). If the puppy responds, praise it; if it doesn't, wait a few minutes and try again. If still no response, pick up your puppy and comfort it on the walk back home. Next time try a different location to walk your puppy on the lead. With patience and praise, the puppy will eventually respond.

ACHIEVEMENT GOALS

On completion of the informal training period your puppy should be aware of and accustomed to:

• its name (sound)

• use of collar and lead

• praise sound (word), e.g. 'Good Dog' ,'Good Girl', or 'Good Boy'

• release sound (word), e.g. 'OK'

• displeasure sound (word), e.g. 'No'

• behavioural sounds (words), e.g. 'Heel', 'Sit', 'Stay', 'Come', 'Stand', 'Drop' (the first four commands are more important).

In short, you have made a preliminary start to building up the puppy's sound (word) vocabulary, association of particular sounds with particular behavioural acts, knowledge of those behavioural acts that are acceptable and those that are not, and awareness of your patience, kindness and pleasure in the relationship.

OBEDIENCE TRAINING
FAMILY DOG PROGRAMME

If the suggested informal training of your puppy has been undertaken, your task of formal training, more commonly referred to as obedience training, should be so much easier. Dogs of different breeds, temperament and intelligence learn at a different speed, so that whilst the dog's age of six months may be a good average time to begin your obedience training programme, it is well to remember that some dogs are ready to participate in and respond to obedience training sooner or later than others.

Obedience training programmes vary in extent and emphasis according to the role the dog is expected to play. This is evident in the training of the Sheepdog, Police Dog, Guide Dog, and Security Dog, for example.

For your family dog's obedience training programme, follow the informal training achievement goals. Formal obedience training also includes

Formal obedience training will be easier if informal training of your puppy has been undertaken.

control of the dog when it is on the lead and free.

An owner, with know how, can carry out his or her own obedience training programme, but if the owner is quick tempered, impatient, mean with praise and has not the time nor inclination, it is best done in a group or privately under the supervision of a recommended professional.

Learning is followed by forgetting. It cannot be emphasised too much, that apart from regular revision and practice within the obedience training programme, the owner must follow up with further revision and practice of those commands that the dog is required to remember after the obedience training programme has been completed. If not, the dog's correct response to the commands will fade.

BASIC GUIDELINES

• Keep lessons short, e.g. four ¼-hour lessons are far more productive than a single hour. For a puppy, four 5-minute lessons are better than a single 20-minute lesson.

• Do not give lessons after the dog has had a full meal.

• Lessons should be a happy time for both owner and pup. Always finish with a game.

• Give basic lessons in a quiet area where there are no distractions, such as traffic, other dogs or children at play.

• If you find yourself losing your patience, stop the lesson, but achieve some positive result before you finish, e.g. put the dog into a 'Sit' so that you can finish with 'Good Dog'.

• Keep lessons consistent, regular and interesting.

• Learning does not take place at a steady and even rate; in one lesson the dog may seem to learn a lot; in another lesson, nothing.

• Give commands with firmness and authority, yet with kindness and patience.

• Keep commands simple, i.e. one word only, perhaps two when necessary, e.g. 'Good Dog'.

• Use the same command word all the time. Never use two different words to mean the same thing. This principle should be observed by all family members when giving a command.

• Each command should be clear and distinct and never followed quickly by another.

• Arrange your teaching sessions at the same time and same place each day

• Wait until your dog learns one command before teaching it another.

• Once a command is learnt, revise and consolidate it at the beginning or near the end of each succeeding lesson.

• When the dog is given a command, e.g. 'Sit', it doesn't hear a word; it hears a sound which at first has no meaning. The trainer's task is to teach the dog to realise that the sound (word) has a meaning and that every time it hears that sound (word) it should obey.

• Always use the same tone of voice for the same word. Remember that the dog's hearing is more finely tuned to sound than a human's.

• Your teaching is based on three premises:

1. The dog wants to please you, so when it behaves correctly always give praise and show your pleasure.

2. The dog associates pleasing its owner with performing a certain behavioural act in response to a certain sound (word).

3. **sound (word)** ————>**behavioural act**
   (stimulus) ————————>**(response)**

The response becomes automatic with repetition and practice.

• Dogs have different temperaments, e.g. shy, playful, aggressive, (un)co-operative, and differing degrees of intelligence. Accordingly, the trainer's approach will vary; each dog being treated as an individual.

• Always associate what the dog does correctly with a pleasant experience, e.g. a tidbit, a touch, verbal praise, a show of happiness.

• Never show displeasure if the dog interprets your command badly or wrongly. Many mistakes will be your fault. Try again.

• Only show displeasure if the dog performs an unacceptable act, such as jumping up on you and soiling your clothes. A loud 'No' may be accompanied by some noise, such as a bang or some other reminder, but do not show anger.

• Always praise or blame a dog during an act, never after, as the praise or blame may then be associated with the wrong thing.

• Always secure the dog's attention before giving a command.

Reward is a tidbit.

THE COMMAND 'HEEL'

Ready to heel

'Heel' command, stepping off

Check chain put on correctly

Check chain put on incorrectly

• If the dog is not paying attention, call it by name and use eye contact in the pause before giving the command:

Pause

'Deefa!'————————————————>**'Come!'**

Eye Contact

• Hand signals when used with sounds (words) help with the training and may replace sounds (words) altogether when the training is advanced.

TEACHING COMMANDS

Heel

Your dog is trained to walk on your left side with its chest level with your leg and close to the knee. In training, the collar is in the form of a check chain which is put around the dog's neck so that it is running free. It is important to check this whenever a check chain is used.

The leash or lead is attached to the check chain by a clip and extends in a loose loop across the front of the handler's body so that the dog feels no tension from it. The end of the lead and any slack that has to be taken up to make the loose loop, is held in the right hand positioned in the midline of the body, just below the belt line. The handler's left hand is free to make corrections, provide a prompt or to show praise with a touch.

Begin the heeling exercise with the dog sitting by your left side if it knows how to sit; if not, begin with the dog standing on your left side, its chest level with your left leg (knee). With the dog in position, you may have to attract its attention by calling it by name, e.g. 'Deefa', then pausing for a moment to make sure you have caught its attention.

```
                    Pause
'Deefa'—————————————Attention ————> 'Heel'
```

When sure of its attention, you immediately give the command 'Heel', stepping off with your left foot and walking in a straight line. The dog by your side and with its chest close to your knee, does likewise.

If in walking straight ahead the dog retains its correct position, i.e. it is heeling correctly, repeat the 'Heel' sound several times so that the dog begins to associate its response with the sound of 'Heel'. To reinforce the dog's response, praise it verbally, e.g. 'Good Dog', and physically, e.g. a gentle rub behind the ears with your left hand so that it doesn't disturb yours or the dog's pace or line.

If the dog does not maintain its correct position, corrective action should be taken firmly but kindly. If the dog increases its pace just enough to move forward in

front of you, you may be able to stop that by swinging the end of the lead clockwise in a circle with your right hand so that the end of the lead just tips or misses the dog's nose. If the dog still decides to walk ahead of you, quickly take hold of the lead with your left hand near where it is attached to the clip and jerk (not pull) it back sharply, keeping it more or less parallel to the ground. At the same time that you stop, release the tension on the lead and observe the dog's response, quietly giving it the impression that it has to go your way and not its way. Do not blame the dog, keep your cool and start again.

If the dog drags behind or sits down, the same style of procedure should first be followed. If it refuses to budge, do not turn the exercise into a tug-o-war and pull, pull, pull. Rather, stop the lesson and finish it off on a pleasant note as the dog may be tired or have some other good reason for its reluctance to proceed.

Sometimes a dog will dart to the side having picked up a scent or for some other reason. Apply the same procedure as described for the dog when it walks ahead of you, except if it darts too quickly you may have to give the whole lead a sharp jerk. Another approach is to work your dog close to and alongside a fence. With you on one side of the dog and the fence on the other, it is not so easy for the dog to dart sideways.

Another approach which some handlers have found successful in training dogs that pull away from the heel position, is to grip the lead near the clip with your free left hand and give it a sharp jerk. Immediately turn about to walk a few paces in the opposite direction before stopping and then starting again.

Your first goal is to teach the dog to heel in a straight

THE COMMAND 'SIT'

'Sit' command, with prompts

Responding to the 'Sit' command

Sitting at handler's left side

line. When this is achieved, it is time to practise advanced heeling such as walking in a circle, in and out of people and objects, in different directions turning to the left and to the right, first with, then without the lead and at different times of the day and in different environments.

Sit

With your dog standing beside you in the heel position, shorten your grip on the lead so that the right hand is holding it about where the clip is attached to the check chain. Hold the check chain firmly upwards above the dog's head and place the palm of your left hand with fingers outspread on the dog's rump. Calling the dog by name, get its complete attention, pause, then give the command 'Sit'. At the same time push downward with your left hand and with your right hand jerk the check chain firmly upwards above the dog's head. The firm push on the rump with the left hand stops sideways evasive action and steers the dog to take up the correct position. When the dog sits, release the tension on the check chain and remove the hand from the rump, repeat the command 'Sit' several times, then praise the dog whilst it is still sitting beside you in the heeling position. After some practice, the dog should sit on command without use of such prompts as the hand on the rump and upward jerk of the check chain. Once your dog has learnt to obey the command 'Sit', you can begin and finish the heeling exercise in that position. You should also train it to sit in front of family, friends and later in public. A further extension of the training would be to teach the dog to sit automatically when the owner, heeling the dog, stops to wait for traffic to pass, to talk to a friend, or to rest. The 'Sit' response should also be taught without collar and lead and finally it should be linked to the 'Stay' response even when the owner moves out of sight.

Stay

With the dog sitting at your left side in the position ready to heel, transfer the lead to your left hand and hold it at a convenient spot near the clip so that it is upwards above the dog's head. Give the command 'Stay' as you place the palm of your right hand in front of the dog's nose. Praise the dog if it stays. If it attempts to move, a sharp upward jerk of the check chain with the left hand together with a loud, harsh 'No' should be effective in foiling the attempt. Repeat the 'Stay' command procedure several times and praise any success with a word or touch such as a light stroke under the throat.

The next phase is for you to take a short step with the right foot, more inward than forward, so that you can swivel to turn and face the dog, with your body almost touching the dog's nose. In this position your left hand is holding the shortened lead upward above the dog's head, and the palm of the right hand with fingers extended upward is facing the dog's nose. At the same time, the command 'Stay' is given several times and if the dog is steady in holding its position, return to its side and give praise.

In the next stage, you follow the same procedure except that you take a longer step which, when you swivel turn to face the dog, puts you at arm's length away. This enables you to hold the check chain upwards above the dog's head for control and to give the 'Stay' signal with your right hand, i.e. the palm of the hand and fingers extended upwards facing the dog's nose. If on the command 'Stay' the dog is steady, take another step backward, lengthening the lead without tension and repeating the command several times. If the dog still remains steady in the 'Sit' position return to your standing position alongside the dog and give praise.

In the next lesson revise, and if successful, practise the 'Stay' without the lead, following the same progressive steps as have been followed with the lead. In further lessons you can gradually move further away, and extend the time you keep the dog in the 'Stay' position. Later, the 'Sit–Stay' can be practised in various environments and when convenient the 'Stay' can also be linked with the 'Stand' and 'Drop' commands.

Come

This is a most important command as it may concern the dog's safety. A dog that will not obey the command 'Come' should never be off the lead in public. Whenever you give the command 'Come' always use a happy, encouraging, please-come-to-me kind of voice combined with a hand signal such as patting your chest with the right hand. In teaching the command, do not give the dog a chance to do anything that is wrong. In other words, finely grade the steps of your teaching, make sure the dog knows one step before moving on to the next succeeding one and do not teach in a hurried manner.

Begin your training with the dog in the 'Sit' position, ready to 'Heel', at your side. Holding the lead about midway with your left hand, step forward with your right foot and swivel turn to face the dog, with the left arm raised forward so that there is no tension on the lead. When you have the attention of your dog by saying its name and establishing eye contact, give the command 'Come' in an encouraging voice whilst patting your chest with the right hand.

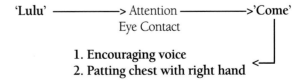

If, at first, the dog does not respond to the command, a slight jerk (not pull) on the lead held in the left hand is

THE COMMAND 'STAY'

Stage one

Stage two

Stage three

Stage four

Stage five

You can link the 'Stay' command with the 'Drop' command

probably all that is needed as you repeat the command 'Come' several times. When the dog comes to you, tell it to 'Sit'. If it does not, repeat the command 'Sit' which you have already taught. After giving it praise, return to the heel position and repeat the exercise several more times, getting it to know what the sound of the word 'Come' and patting the chest means.

The next phase is to increase the distance between you and the dog when facing one another. When you step forward and swivel turn to face the dog, position yourself so that you are holding the lead fully extended but with no tension. Repeat several times the same procedure as for the short lead. In your training always insist that the dog 'Comes' in a straight line towards you. If it does not, use the lead to jerk it back into line. Do not forget to link each successful 'Come' with the 'Sit' position.

The next phase is the intermediate step between using a lead and not using one. When facing the dog,

THE COMMAND 'COME'

The dog is ready and attentive.

Encourage the dog to come.

With your foot on the lead, give the command 'Come'.

With lead removed, stand further away and give the command 'Come'.

The dog is responding to the command 'Come'.

place the extended lead on the ground with your foot on the end of it in case you need to take control of the dog. Keep your left arm in the same position as if you were holding the lead, make sure you have the dog's attention, then give the command 'Come' in an encouraging tone of voice and patting your chest with the right hand. Give the command several times and praise the dog with words and touch when it sits in front of you.

When the intermediate step is successful, move on to the final phase of removing the lead from the check chain and giving the dog practice in coming to you when you are two steps, several steps and then further away. The check chain is left on so that if the dog is distracted during the exercise, the lead can be replaced quickly. As the dog comes to you, particularly as you move further away, remember to see that it still comes in a straight line and that it slows down its pace to sit in front of you, instead of rushing past, bounding around or jumping up onto you, almost knocking you over. Only give praise if the dog comes to sit quietly in front of you.

Stand

When heeling the dog, you probably will have taught it to obey the command 'Sit' or to sit automatically when you stop. On occasions you may want it to keep standing.

If when walking the dog at the heel you want it to stop and stand, slow down your walking pace a few paces before you intend to stop and give the drawn out command 'S-T-A-N-D'. At the same time, place the palm of your open left hand in front of the dog's nose, and even tap it if the dog does not stop. Repeat the command 'S-T-A-N-D' several times and if the dog holds its position, give praise. Repeat the exercise several times until the dog stands on the command and without the use of the left hand as a prompt.

If the approach described is not successful because the dog assumes the 'Sit' each time it stops on the command 'S-T-A-N-D'; then the following approach is suggested.

As you give the command, simultaneously apply pressure to the dog's chest with your right hand, which is holding the shortened lead, and to the offside stifle and nearby groin with your left hand (even just touching it is all that is necessary with some dogs). The whole effect of the pressue is to give the dog the feeling of being stretched upward so that it remains standing rather than going into a 'Sit'. The command 'S-T-A-N-D' is repeated several times and the dog is praised.

Continue heeling and give further practice in the 'S-T-A-N-D', first with, then without, the hand prompts. Praise any improvement and ultimate success.

Later the dog can be trained to 'Stand–Stay' for a longer period, for instance while waiting for its meal to be served, or while you and your friends walk around it, touching, stroking, admiring, and giving praise.

Drop (Down)

This position is difficult to assume, especially by the male dog as it is a form of body language used by dogs to signal submission. Several methods are suggested for training your dog to obey the command 'Drop' ('Down') from the 'Sit' position. Choose one which suits you and the dog.

Method one: Face the dog and crouch or kneel, holding the shortened lead in your left hand and patting or scratching the ground with your right hand where the dog's nose is going to be if it responds to your command 'Drop' ('Down'). The dog may drop to investigate your hand movement; if not, a sudden jerk on the lead with your left hand as you give the command may cause it to drop. If it does, repeat the command several times and praise any success. If the dog fails to respond to this simple method, remain in the same position, then grasp the forelegs and lift them upward and forward to bring them to the drop position, simultaneously giving the command 'Drop' ('Down'). Reward any success with verbal praise or touch.

Method two: Comfortably position yourself on the right-hand side of the dog, grasp the check chain firmly at a

THE COMMAND 'STAND'

Using the hands as a prompt to help the dog respond to the 'Stand' command.

Another approach to the 'Stand' command: apply pressure to the dog's chest and to the offside stifle (knee).

point under the dog's neck with the left hand and push down on it as you give the command 'Drop'('Down'). At the same time, with the right hand, which is holding the shortened lead, scratch or pat the ground in front of the dog where its nose is going to be when it drops. As it drops, repeat the command several time and give praise.

Method three: From the side of the dog, give the command 'Drop' ('Down') as you press downwards on the dog's shoulders with your left hand and take hold of its legs with your right hand to lift them upward and forward to the drop position. Repeat the command several times and praise any success.

Remember, do not continue the exercise if you are aware that the dog is becoming fatigued or is losing concentration.

Link the 'Drop' ('Down') position with 'Stay', 'Heel' and 'Stand' positions and the dismissal 'OK'. Try getting the dog to 'Drop' when it is having a free run with you in open space.

TEACHING TRICKS

In general, the principles and procedures outlined for obedience training, are applied to teaching your dog certain behaviour patterns which are commonly referred to as tricks. Common domestic tricks are Begging, Fetching the Newspaper, Shaking Hands, Catching and Fetching a Ball, Jumping a Hurdle or through a Hoop, Rolling Over or Turning Round (Chasing the Tail).

Such tricks allow the dog to get pleasure in pleasing the owner, make its day more interesting, and give the owner some degree of pleasure and pride in the dog's accomplishments. Rolling Over or Turning Round can be made an interesting form of entertainment for all. The owner asks the spectators to give the dog a little sum, e.g. 2 plus 3, 6 minus 4, etc, and the dog provides the answer by rolling over or turning round the number of times that correspond to the answer. The secret, of course, is that the owner has taught the dog in the training period to start and stop turning round or rolling over by giving a certain signal with the hand or index finger, which the spectators do not observe.

Begin training your puppy from an early age.

THE COMMAND 'DROP'

Method one (simple approach)

Method one (alternative approach)

Method two

Method three

BEHAVIOUR PROBLEMS AND CORRECTION

Causes and influences—A common behaviour problem: straying
Methods of treatment—Strategies used in re-education method
Signs of undesirable behaviour—Correction of problems

Most owners will experience some behaviour problems in their dogs. Many of the problems, e.g. barking, biting, chasing and wandering, are perceived as misbehaviour, whilst other problems, e.g. fear of thunder, are thought to be characteristic of dog behaviour and are tolerated. Some behaviour problems may destroy the goodwill of neighbours or the enjoyable companionship owners have with their dogs. Indeed some problems seem to be serious enough to prompt the owner to give the dog away, place it in a dog's home or have it euthanased.

It is in the interest of all dog owners to have some knowledge and understanding of dog behaviour so that they can cope with problems that may surface from time to time. If you are unable to cope with a particular behaviour problem, consult your veterinarian.

A dog's misbehaviour is often described by such statements as:

'the dog barks all night';

'the dog will not stop digging in the garden';

'the dog is always aggressive to visitors';

'the dog eats dog droppings, horse manure', etc. (Coprophagia);

'the dog strays away from home'.

Some owners treat such signs of misbehaviour by physically punishing the dog. More often, owners threaten the dog verbally in a loud and angry voice. Whilst punishment on the spot may be necessary when the dog misbehaves, its effect is usually only short term, and the misbehaviour will be repeated.

A different approach to misbehaviour is needed; one that promises long term, permanent results. Such an approach is to find the cause of the misbehaviour and treat it accordingly. In identifying the cause, you must do so with caution, e.g. it may not be the judge or another dog in the show ring causing your dog to misbehave; it may be just the general show ring atmosphere.

THE CAUSES OF BEHAVIOUR PROBLEMS

The causes may be found by looking at the influences that shape a dog's behaviour. There are two major influences:

1. the genes that the dog has inherited from its parents and ancestors;

2. the environment in which the puppy lives and develops into maturity.

Genes

The genes are initially responsible for the dog's

• shape, size, colour and sex;

• temperament, state of health and degree of intelligence.

If you observe new puppies in a litter, you may notice that one puppy appears to be shy, timid, sensitive, fearful and retiring; another is happy, robust, and outgoing; and a third is bossy, aggressive and dominant. Of the others, one puppy is excitable, demanding and wanting to make friends; another is more alert, intelligent and sensible;

Simple, aggressive activities, such as nipping, are a form of play.

Opposite: Puppies love to play, but some activities may become undesirable forms of behaviour in the older dog.

whilst another is dull, shows little interest and appears to be a weakling. In short, your observation of a puppy, if discerning, can take you past the obvious, i.e. shape, size, colour, sex and emotional appeal, to an awareness of its temperament, general health and intelligence inherited through the genes from the pup's parents and ancestors.

Environment

The environment in many cases exerts a greater influence on the dog's developing behaviour than does the genetic inheritance. To a large extent the environmental influence determines

- what a dog learns;
- how its temperament develops;
- the dog's general health.

The environment is more than the kennel yard and home lot. The owner and family can play an active role in creating a good, caring environment for their dog by

- treating the dog with affectionate firmness;
- showing interest in the maturing puppy;
- attempting to teach it correct behaviour;
- spending time with it;
- tending to its needs in terms of nutrition, grooming, worming, comfort and hygiene.

In this role, the support of the veterinarian and the professional obedience trainer may also be necessary. (See the chapters on Choosing your puppy or dog, Training, and Health care.)

If the wrong environment is provided, behavioural problems may emerge. For instance:

- A dog may defaecate in the wrong places because it was trained haphazardly to go to a certain spot when it felt the urge.
- A dog may be very possessive of the owner and snarls at anyone who comes near when they are together. The owner may have developed a one-to-one relationship with the dog and is practically with the dog all day and night as the dog has the run of the home and sleeps on its favourite cushion in the owner's bedroom. Needless to say, the dog receives a great deal of affection and when taken out socially it never mixes with other people or animals.
- A dog is savage towards visitors, chases and barks at cats and other dogs because the owner teased and encouraged it to chase and bark savagely as it matured in order to bring out the aggressive attacking instinct.
- An excitable dog, a characteristic evident when it was a young puppy, seems to be getting more excitable, noticeably so when the owner or a friend greets it. The owner when greeting the puppy during the maturing period, may have seemed to get a great deal of pleasure out of stimulating the dog into a frenzy of excitement.

A COMMON BEHAVIOUR PROBLEM: STRAYING

The first step in solving this behavioural problem is to look into the genetic and environmental background of the dog, to search for a possible cause. Questions that might be asked are: Is the dog a male that can scent a nearby bitch on heat? Has it got the roaming spirit of its ancestors in its blood and the feeling that it wants the company of other dogs? Is its environment too small for free running exercise, not secure enough to restrain the dog, and too boring in its simplicity and lack of company? Does the dog not get enough personal praise and friendship at home and seeks it elsewhere?

The answers to questions such as these might reveal the cause(s) of the dog's straying behaviour. If several causes are identified, place them in order of importance so that priorities can be established for the second step, i.e. the method of treatment. In each of the four methods, detailed in the next section, specific reference is made to straying, though the methods are relevant to most behaviour problems.

METHODS OF TREATMENT

There are four well-known methods of treatment:
1. Punishment
2. Veterinary treatment
3. Environment control
4. Re-education

PUNISHMENT

Some owners use this method because its effect is immediate and it requires very little thought. Punishment can range from simple verbal admonishment such as 'No' or 'Naughty Dog', to chaining up, confinement, denying food, and physical punishment which again can range from a brush off with the hand or a tap on the nose, to something brutal which, under any circumstance, is not recommended.

Minor punishment such as the use of a strong vocal 'No', perhaps with appropriate body language, usually is sufficient to stop a dog misbehaving there and then, unless its obedience training has been sadly neglected. You are advised to use the same vocal expression and body language each time the dog deserves such punishment. The dog only learns to understand sound and signs; it does not learn to understand the spoken word. Repetition of the same strong, vocal 'No' sound serves to remind the dog that it must not do that here.

In most cases, because it does not treat the underlying cause, punishment stops the misbehaviour only temporarily. The misbehaviour in the same or in another mode will be repeated. In short, minor punishment is recommended for temporary relief but it is not recommended for some forms of misbehaviour that occur regularly and which the owner wants to terminate permanently.

If punishment is to be given, it must be very closely associated in time with the act. For example, if you punish the straying dog on its return, it will associate its return with punishment—not its straying behaviour. The next time it strays away, it may not return so quickly because of the fear of punishment that it associates with returning. An aggressive, dominant dog, if being punished by you for misbehaviour, may associate you, not the misbehaviour, with the punishment and in a recurring similar situation may show aggression towards you.

If punishment, either verbal or physical, is given, it should be followed by the dog being shown the correct behaviour then being given an opportunity to practise and to be praised for any success.

In the case of the straying dog, take it to the front gate, assuming that is where it escaped, and show it how and where to sit when the gate is open. Open the gate a little and if the dog continues to 'Sit–Stay' without assistance, give it a tidbit and praise it generously. After each success, open the gate a little wider and for a little longer. Reward each successful performance with a tidbit, praise and loving touch. At the end of each lesson take the dog to some place in the garden where you can enjoy a five minute game with the dog, giving it the feeling that home is a good place to be. Let the dog know that you are pleased with it for staying inside, even if the gate is open. If you think the dog is going to dart out as soon as the gate is opened, prevent it from doing so by standing in the gateway and restraining it with check chain and lead.

VETERINARY TREATMENT

This may involve the use of drugs, surgical procedures or behaviour therapy.

In the case of the male dog that strays, the treatment could be in the form of castration (neutering) which in most cases reduces the dog's sexual drive within a month or so from the time of the operation. At the same time, the dog's straying habit of pursuing bitches on heat would stop or be weakened considerably. If you want to keep your male dog entire, your veterinarian may inject the dog with the drug medroxy progesterone acetate to reduce or stop the sexual drive. (The drug will also stop the oestrus of the female dog.) This will also have a desirable effect on such anti-social behaviours as aggressiveness, barking, digging, chewing and excessive urinating. The drug often takes a month before its full effect is evident and it lasts for about five months when, if any regression in its effectiveness is showing up, a top up injection can be given. It has a settling effect without any sedative side effect. Dogs exposed to the drug sometimes put on weight because their appetite is stimulated, their mammary glands may enlarge, and mammary cysts may develop. It is advisable not to use the drug on valuable stud dogs because it may affect their fertility.

ENVIRONMENT CONTROL

Remember that the interpretation of environment is not a narrow one. Apart from the kennel yard, it covers all those persons and facilities that impinge on the physical, emotional, social (the dog is a pack animal) and mental health of the dog.

In the case of the dog that strays, environmental control could embrace making the home environment more interesting:

• Introduce into the home another pet, perhaps a young puppy or kitten either of which should be introduced to the dog gradually and under supervision.

• Spend more time with the dog: take it out more often for walks, introduce it to friends and their pets, play with it and talk to it more often.

• Enrol the dog in an obedience training course, not that obedience training cures a dog of undesirable behaviour patterns but it does give you better control over the dog and this in turn would help to eradicate a behaviour problem.

• Praise and reward the dog more often for good behaviour.

Finally, the confinement area for the dog could be made more secure and if that fails, a complete change of environment might be the answer.

RE-EDUCATION

This method is concerned with training the dog to replace an undesirable form of behaviour with a new desirable form. The desired change in behaviour is brought about by using a suitable strategy. In some cases, success is achieved quickly and in others it takes a much longer time to achieve. Success or failure is determined by such factors as the time and patience that the teacher gives to the re-education, the temperament and mentality of the dog, the nature of the undesirable behaviour and the suitability of the strategy used to change it. If you are not sure of handling this method, but would like to try it, consult your veterinarian for advice.

In the case of the dog that strays, changing the dog's environment to make it feel happy, wanted and contented, and letting it know that you are pleased because it stays home even when the gate is open, is a form of re-education.

However, there are distinct strategies or approaches that are used in the re-education method. The one(s) you choose will depend on the nature of your dog's problem. If you have the dog that strays and it cannot 'Sit–Stay' on command, you would certainly choose the 'Conditioning' strategy to teach it the 'Sit-Stay' as a prerequisite for its re-education.

The common strategies used in re-education programmes are conditioning, reinforcement, counter conditioning, desensitisation, habituation and shaping.

Conditioning

This is a simple strategy to teach the dog to respond in a certain kind of way to a stimulus that it has not responded to before. For example, you are conditioning your dog to respond to the stimulus command 'Sit'. It has never heard the command before and of course it has never responded to it but after a series of practices it does respond by sitting.

$$S \longrightarrow (Practices) \longrightarrow R$$

Stimulus	Response
(Command: 'Sit')	(The dog sits)

At first your dog does not know how to respond to the command, so you should show it how to sit, all the time repeating aloud the command 'Sit'. Assume the heel position and as you give the command 'Sit' place the palm of your left hand with fingers outspread on the dog's rump and push down. At the same time hold the shortened lead above the dog's head and jerk it upwards with your right hand (see Obedience training, p. 51). The use of the hands to help the dog to 'Sit' is referred to as a prompt and as the dog responds with more understanding and competency, gradually reduce the strength of the prompt and the number of times it is given. This process is referred to as fading.

$$S \longrightarrow R$$
$$(Prompt - Fading)$$

When the dog can sit in response to the stimulus without any help, the prompt is faded out completely but may be re-introduced now and then if the dog regresses in the correct response to the stimulus.

Whenever the dog achieves any success in making the response, acknowledge the dog's success with reinforcement.

Reinforcement

There are three general means of reinforcement: food, verbal praise and touch. To the hungry dog, there is nothing more tempting and satisfying than food. The amount given as reinforcement is small; tasty and tantalising. For food to be successful as reinforcement, the dog must be hungry, so do not try to condition the dog after a full meal. Food to a hungry dog satisfies its basic instinctive need to live, to survive.

Therefore, food in the form of a small, tasty morsel or tidbit is given a higher rating level as a form of reinforcement than praise or touch if the dog is hungry.

Verbal praise, e.g. 'Good Dog', should be given sincerely as if you mean it. Touch, such as patting or fondling the dog, shows your affection and that you are pleased with the dog's performance. Verbal praise and touch satisfy the dog's need to be praised and to know that it is pleasing you by its behaviour.

When the desired response to a stimulus appears to be permanently fixed, the food reinforcement is usually faded to leave only verbal praise and touch, and whilst they may be faded a little, they should be used whenever it is appropriate.

Reinforcement is most effective when it is given immediately after the behavioural response, say no later than one second. The reinforcement in essence is a further stimulus to the possibility of the 'learned' behavioural response being repeated next time.

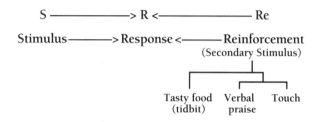

$$S \longrightarrow R \longleftarrow Re$$
Stimulus ———> Response <——— Reinforcement
(Secondary Stimulus)

Tasty food (tidbit)	Verbal praise	Touch

Acknowledge the dog's success in responding to commands with reinforcement—praise, food and touch.

Counter conditioning

This strategy is used when a stimulus is producing an undesirable behavioural response and you wish to substitute a desirable response. For example, your dog barks furiously and angrily at the postman when letters are delivered.

Original Stimulus — Undesirable Response

S ————————————> R
Postman at   Dog barking savagely
letter box   and chasing
                          (Undesirable behaviour)

To counter condition the dog so that it does not perform this undesirable behaviour when it sees the postman, you must pair a stimulus with the stimulus of the postman appearing that is more appealing and compelling to the dog, causing it to behave differently. Nothing is more tantalising and compelling than food to a hungry dog. A tasty morsel (tidbit), as the paired stimulus, is placed in the food bowl and presented to the dog at the same time as the postman appears, on the assumption that having been denied food for the previous 24 hours, it will go to the food bowl rather than chase and bark at the postman. For the first few days the dog may have to be encouraged to go to the food bowl. This procedure is repeated each day and the dog's desirable behaviour is reinforced each time with the tasty tidbit, verbal praise and touch.

Paired Stimulus Situation

Postman at
letter box
S ———————> R <———————— Re
Tidbit in   Dog goes to   ┌────┴─────┐
food bowl   food bowl   Tidbit Verbal Touch
                                      praise

Eventually, the dog's response to the arrival of the postman, will be to go to the food bowl. In short, the dog has been counter conditioned to forget its original response to the postman and to substitute an acceptable response. Depending on how solidly the new substitute response is consolidated, there may or may not be regression to the original undesirable response. If there is, you have to go through the training procedures again.

End Result of Counter Conditioning

S ————————————> R
Postman at   Dog goes to
letterbox   food bowl
                          (Desirable behaviour)

Desensitisation

This strategy aims at reducing or neutralising a dog's sensitivity to a stimulus that arouses an emotional re-sponse, e.g. fear, which finds an outlet in some form of undesirable behaviour. For example, a dog's sensitivity to a loud explosive noise such as fireworks, a thunderstorm or a gunshot is partly genetic and partly a learned experience. The emotional response of fear that the explosive noise evokes may be expressed in one or more of several forms, e.g. whining, howling, barking, running away, hiding, defaecating and urinating.

Desensitisation is made up of several sub-strategies as will be seen in the following example.

Assume that your dog is afraid of the explosive sound of fireworks (crackers), and runs away to hide somewhere, and perhaps urinate. If you wish to proceed with the desensitisation strategy to remedy this kind of behaviour, you would have to carry out preliminary preparations.

First, select a stimulus and response (see (b) below) to pair with the stimulus and response (see (a) below) that are associated with the undesirable behaviour.

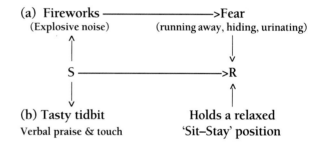

(a) Fireworks ————————————>Fear
    (Explosive noise)   (running away, hiding, urinating)

S ————————————>R

(b) Tasty tidbit   Holds a relaxed
Verbal praise & touch   'Sit–Stay' position

In selecting this pairing, the stimulus in (b), i.e. the tasty tidbit must be more compelling and demanding than the fireworks (crackers) in (a), and the response in (b), i.e. holding the 'Sit–Stay' position must be incompatible with the response in (a), i.e. running away and hiding and perhaps urinating.

If your dog does not already know how to assume a relaxed 'Sit–Stay' response as in (b) then you must teach it (see Conditioning strategy, p. 64, and Training, p.55).

Finally, your preliminary preparation would have to include the provision of a tape recording of the loud explosive noise of fireworks .

After the preliminary preparation, spend time in counter conditioning the dog to take up and hold the relaxed 'Sit–Stay' position whilst the tape recording of the fireworks is being played. The dog is expected not to show any fear (as expressed in running away, hiding and urinating), but should appear relaxed ; for this purpose the volume is turned down to a level that the dog tolerates. Similar procedures are carried out as described in the previous section dealing with the counter conditioning strategy (see above).

Counter Conditioning

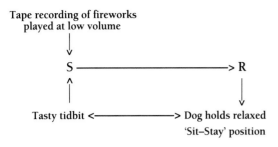

When the dog has been counter conditioned, the actual desensitisation process takes place. The process is begun by playing the tape recording of the fireworks at a low level and for a short period of time that the dog can tolerate and still hold the 'Sit–Stay' position. At first this may need a little experimentation. The dog's desirable behaviour is reinforced with a tidbit and praise. The practice session of course should not take place after the dog has had a full meal. Gradually with each practice, the volume and playing time of the recording of the fireworks is increased, but only to the extent that the dog can tolerate it and hold the 'Sit–Stay' position. If at any stage the dog cannot tolerate it (shows fear, runs and hides), then turn off the sound and comfort the dog. When it is relaxed, turn the sound back to the previous level that the dog could tolerate and proceed cautiously from there.

When the volume and exposure time of the fireworks reaches the point where it duplicates a natural fireworks display and the dog still holds its 'Sit–Stay' position, it is time to introduce your dog to the natural fireworks noise to test the effectiveness of your desensitisation strategy.

Final Desensitisation

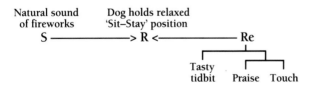

Throughout the desensitisation strategy, reinforcement of correct behaviour is recognised with the tasty tidbit, verbal praise and touch When success is finally achieved, the tasty tidbit may be withdrawn, but verbal praise and touch should continue.

Habituation

This strategy is used for the treatment of some forms of aggression, urination and defaecation, excitement, fear and separation stress, whereby gradual exposure to the stimulus in increasing periods of time eliminates the undesirable behavioural response. It is a far more simple technique than desensitisation.

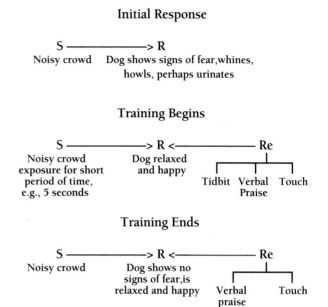

The initial period of exposure to the stimulus is short (perhaps five seconds). Whatever the period of time is, the dog must be able to tolerate the situation without showing any undesirable behaviour.

Immediately after each successful attempt, the dog's good behaviour is reinforced with a tasty tidbit and praise. It is then removed from the stimulus. When it is comforted and relaxed, it is again introduced to the stimulus for a slightly longer time. After each successful response, the exposure time is slightly increased. What the slight increase will be depends on your assessment of the dog's tolerance. If at any time during the habituation process the dog responds in an undesirable way, stop immediately, remove the dog from the stimulus, and comfort it, but do not give it any reinforcement. In the next attempt, go back to the last period of time, which the dog tolerated without showing any signs of undesirable behaviour and start again from there.

When the dog has reached the stage where it tolerates the stimulus for the period of time that you want it to, without showing any undesirable behavioural response, you have successfully habituated the dog to the stimulus concerned.

Shaping

This is a strategy involved in gradually changing an undesirable form of behaviour into a desirable form by introducing and reinforcing a series of slight changes so that each change is more or less the same as, but slightly different from, the one before. The final change in the series is the desirable form of behaviour that you were wanting to establish.

A well-known example is toilet training a puppy. The floor of the puppy pen is first covered with sheets of paper on which the puppy relieves itself, then only half the floor is covered with paper and it is encouraged to relieve on that section, then only one sheet of paper with the puppy's smell of urine on it is left and the puppy is encouraged to use it for relieving.

After that sequence of shaping, the sheet of paper is removed from the pen and placed near the exit door of the home; the puppy can see it and has access from the puppy pen. It is encouraged to eliminate on it, then again the paper is placed outside the door where the puppy can see it and has access.

The sheet of paper is then placed in the garden where the owner wants the puppy to urinate and defaecate permanently.

Finally, the paper is removed but the lingering smell of urine and faeces in the soil guides the puppy to the spot for elimination purposes (see Toilet training, p. 49).

COMMON SIGNS OF UNDESIRABLE BEHAVIOUR

• Fighting, biting, growling, snarling, baring teeth and lifting upper lip, and some forms of barking.

• Urinating and/or defaecating in the wrong places and situations, howling, whining, chewing, digging and destructiveness, some forms of barking.

• Nipping, chewing and mouthing.

• Jumping up onto and licking people.

• Slobbering and restlessness while travelling in cars.

• Dung eating and scavenging.

• Masturbation and mounting.

• Chasing vehicles, bikes, stock etc (see Predatory aggression, p.69).

•Straying (see p. 62).

Fighting, biting, growling, snarling, baring teeth and lifting upper lip, some forms of barking

These are the usual signs of aggression, although there are exceptions. A dog may bark because of separation anxiety (see p. 71), as a means of social communication, as an expression of boredom, or as an expression of joy when it prances around ready to play ball with its owner. Biting that is more of the nipping and tentative kind is sometimes associated with play, particularly the developmental play of the young puppy. Growling and mock fighting can also be observed in developmental play.

The dog signals its aggressiveness in body language, vocalisation and in biting and fighting. Forms of body language are a staring eye, tail up or pointing behind, a tense, alert posture, raised head, hair erection, and bared

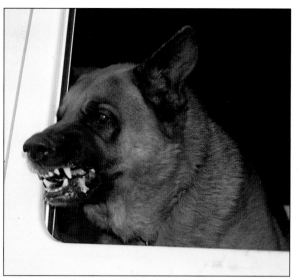

Protective and possessive aggression—note the curled lip and bared teeth.

teeth with lifting of the upper lip. Vocal signs are vicious barking, snarling and growling. In contrast, the submissive dog will accept and look pleased as it is given a friendly greeting, or an affectionate touch, and may approach you in a friendly manner with its tail wagging. It may even urinate. At times the dog indicates its submissiveness by rolling over on its back or to its side, waiting for you to give it some friendly praise or touch, or it allows a dominant dog to stand with head or front leg across its back or neck.

Like humans, some dogs play an aggressive role, others play a submissive role, and some play a role in between. A number of dogs play a changing role according to circumstance.

Whilst your treatment of aggressive behaviour must be immediate—which is why punishment is most often resorted to, and at times unwisely—you must also find the cause and provide a treatment that will secure long term results. To do this, it is necessary to understand the complexities of the aggression concept. Consider the following aspects:

Dominance aggression: A predisposition to dominance in a dog is usually the result of its genetic make up interacting with the environmental learning experiences it encounters. The owner can contribute to a dog's dominant attitude by teasing it and by not controlling the dog's dominance when it shows. The owner may encourage dominance by being a submissive type of person who subordinates himself/herself to the dog's demands. The dog knows it and assumes a more dominant role in the relationship as time goes by. This trait can be observed in the dog that always wants to chase a ball or stick and keeps worrying the owner to throw it. The owner eventually gives in and throws it.

The dominant dog may be of either sex, but is more often male than female. Females that have been spayed appear to be more dominant than bitches and the neutered male is usually, but not always, less dominant. The dominant dog, in order to establish and maintain its dominant status, will resort to some form of aggression if necessary.

Dominance aggression may be directed to other dogs, animals and humans who may be members of the family, visitors or strangers, particularly anyone whose looks and actions appear to pose a threat to the dog's dominance. The dominance aggression may take many forms: barking savagely when a person tries to enter the kennel yard; barking at or attempting to bite some family member or visitor as they approach the house; and curling the upper lip, growling, giving chase and scuffling with another dog that appears to present a threat.

One remedial approach for the aggressive male dog is to have it neutered which in a large number of cases has proved to be successful or partially so. Other approaches are hormone therapy, a change of environment, and re-education. The latter, comparatively speaking, is a long term approach, its ultimate aim being to reverse roles, i.e. for the dog to become submissive and the owner and family members to become dominant.

In re-educating the dominance aggressive dog, counter conditioning supported by habituation and reinforcement strategies would probably be used. Take, for example, the dog that always shows dominance aggression towards a family member who tries to enter the kennel yard. First, the dog is placed on very short rations the day prior to the beginning of the re-education approach and secondly, the family member chooses a tasty morsel or tidbit that would be irresistible to and a stimulus for the hungry dog to come and get it to eat, rather than to bark savagely.

On the first day of the dog's re-education, when the family member tentatively opens the gate of the kennel yard, the dog may respond in one of two ways. It may bark savagely; in this situation the family member just retires and waits till the dog calms down before returning. It may stare and look as if it is on the alert; in this situation the family member would place a small tidbit in the food bowl just inside the gate and retire, verbally praising the dog if it comes to eat it. This would be repeated at mid-day and again in the afternoon before the dog is given a short rations meal in the evening. The next day the same practice would be repeated and if the dog permits it, the family member would step further into the kennel yard, moving closer and closer to the dog with each successful attempt at feeding. Finally, in the next day or so, the dog would be encouraged to come to the family member for its tidbit. If at any stage in this approach, the dog shows aggression, the family member immediately retires with the food and waits until the dog calms down. In the next

session, the family member goes back to the previous step when the dog was not aggressive, thus reinforcing its desirable behaviour before moving on again cautiously to the next step in its re-education.

The counter conditioning is based on pairing the tasty tidbit in the food bowl with the appearance in the

The dog is standing, waiting for the command 'OK'.

'OK' given to eat the food

kennel yard of the family member to whom the dog is aggressive, and as the food is a far more attractive stimulus to the hungry dog than the family member, the dog begins to think more of the food than the family member and so doesn't bark so savagely but goes forward to eat the food. In the end, the dog associates the appearance of the family member with food and welcomes him or her, even if no food is presented.

The habituation is concerned with a gradual increase in the exposure of the family member with the food, both in time and space, so that the dog becomes accustomed to seeing the family member as a food provider and welcomes him or her.

The reinforcement of the dog's desirable behaviour is some satisfaction of its hunger by eating the tasty tidbit and verbal praise being given by the family member at each successful session. When the family member feels safe and secure in the kennel yard, touch could be one of the elements in the reinforcement.

The ultimate hope is that the dog will continue to welcome the family member, even when its food ration is returned to normal and the daily tidbits are faded out to just now and then, with expressions of praise by word and touch being given quite freely.

The final stage in reversing the roles of dominance and submission is achieved when the dog, on command, will take the 'Sit' or 'Stand–Stay' position and wait for the family member to give the further command, 'OK' (see p. 50), before eating its food that has been placed in the food bowl.

Mature dogs, particularly the younger ones, either male or female, will engage in fighting when they meet, if both show dominance aggression and neither submits to the other. To prevent this from happening, when out walking with your dog, always have it on a lead and keep it away from free roaming, dominance aggressive dogs.

If dogs are fighting, it is not wise to try to separate them by hand. In the heat of the fight they might interpret your interference as an act of aggression and will redirect their aggression onto you or may accidentally bite you.

If possible, rather than physically interfering in a dog fight, it is far more effective and less dangerous to give the dogs a hosing of cold water or to throw a coat or rug over the dog's head so that it cannot see. It will stop fighting long enough for you to take control and lead it away.

Possessive and protective aggression: This section does not refer to the protective aggression of a guard dog that has been specifically trained for that purpose.

Possessive and protective aggression are closely linked and when speaking of one, it may include the other. Both of them relate to territory or space, food, favourite objects and family members. The dog that barks at the postman who stops to put a letter in the box is really protecting its territory or property (possessions). Likewise when stran-

A mother will protect her puppies.

gers or visitors enter your lot or home or when a stranger approaches the family baby in the pram or pusher, the dog may show possessive or protective aggression by barking, growling, snarling or biting.

Again, possessive aggression is shown when a dog protects its food from other dogs. A milder form of possessive aggression is shown by some dogs that resist when someone tries to take a ball or stick from their mouth. Have you tried blowing into their eyes to make them drop it? Counter conditioning (see p. 65) and habituation (see p. 66) are recommended as strategies to try first in solving any problem of possessive or protective aggression.

Maternal aggression: Possessive aggression is very strong in the bitch with her newborn pups. It is most often referred to as maternal aggression and is shown when visitors, members of the family and sometimes the owner attempt to come too near or try to touch the new born pups. Warn visitors, especially children, of this characteristic of the bitch with her new born. If the owner is faced with maternal aggression, the strategies of shaping and habituation could be applied to achieve a more acceptable form of behaviour.

Predatory aggression: A dog normally barks aggressively when chasing the postman on his bike, a car or another dog. This act is referred to as predatory aggression and is possibly linked with a dog's strong hunting instincts that have been passed down in the genes. There is also an element of dominance aggression in the act of a dog chasing animals and humans who appear to be running away.

After dogs were domesticated, the drive to chase and hunt in some breeds was channelled into a form that was helpful to humans in their work and recreation. Two very good examples of this are the modern day sheep and cattle dogs, which, if living in modern suburbia, transfer their drive to chase such moving objects as cars, bikes, trucks, etc. To train out of these dogs and other breeds the drive to chase, which has been bred into them for centuries, is a difficult task and meets with mixed success.

The following suggestion involves the elements of counter conditioning, habituation and punishment. It has been tried and found to be successful by some owners.

Tie a lengthy piece of rope (6–8 m, 18–24 ft long) to the dog's collar. Let the dog chase (response) a moving car (stimulus) and just at that moment before the rope is fully extended, shout the command 'No' and give a sharp jerk on the rope. The dog will tumble over and feel some hurt (incompatible response). Gradually the dog will respond to the word (sound) 'No' because of its association with hurt and will stop in the act of chasing the car. When this happens, praise the dog. Next, with the dog in the 'Sit–Stay' position, give the command 'No' as a car goes by. If the dog attempts to chase, restrict it with the lead; if it doesn't, give it a tidbit and/or praise by word or touch. In doing this, you are reinforcing a form of desirable behaviour that you want the dog to substitute for the undesirable behaviour. In your approach, you are showing the dog what to do as well as what not to do. Your correction is positive.

Eventually your standard of training should be such that if your dog is on the lead with you or is running free, it will not chase a car, etc. If it shows the slightest sign of giving chase, your command of 'No' should be sufficient restraint. Use a variety of moving vehicles in the training sessions.

Pain or fear of pain aggression: Pain or fear of pain may elicit aggressive behaviour, even in a submissive dog. The dog that is fearful usually exhibits a slinking posture, with ears back and tail between the legs. The dog may pant, urinate and have a rapid heart rate. In its fear, the dog may run away, hide, submit by lying down, turn on its back or side, cringe or if it feels cornered and threatened, it may turn aggressive.

An owner inflicting pain through physical punishment of a dog may find it fearful at first but as the punishment and pain build up to an intolerable level, the dog may turn on the owner, growling, snarling, barking and ready to bite. (A veterinarian in the surgery when palpating a patient may sometimes finds the dog savagely turning on him or her with a snap or bite, because of the pain unconsciously inflicted.)

The dog in being exposed to these kinds of 'learning' experiences, can become conditioned to being aggressive to the owner or veterinarian. Furthermore, that aggressiveness can also be transferred to anyone who raises an arm even to pat the dog, or who, vaguely resembling the veterinarian, approaches the dog in the surgery environment to speak to it or give it a pat. Implanted in the dog's mind is an association of pain with a raised arm or a person in the surgery environment, and hence the aggressive response.

Punishment offers no solution for the problem. Undesirable behavioural responses to fear are sometimes wrongly interpreted by owners as misbehaviours and the dog is blamed or punished for being naughty. Instead, fear is the cause for which re-education involving counter conditioning (see p. 65) and desensitisation (see p. 65) is recommended.

Urinating and/or defaecating in the wrong places and situations, whining, howling, chewing, digging and destructiveness, and some forms of barking

Dogs showing one or more of these characteristics may be:
• improperly house-trained;
• suffering from a disease;
• in a state of fear;
• in a state of intense excitement and extending a submissive greeting;
• performing the natural act of marking;
• suffering from separation stress.

The immediate thought that comes into the minds of many owners is to punish when they observe their dog doing something which they consider is wrong or see the damage that the dog has caused. Some owners have been known to take such drastic measures as rubbing the dog's nose in the urine or faeces with the thought, 'That will stop it'. But it does not! The cause is still there so the dog will either do it again and avoid the owner, do it in another place, or substitute some other misbehaviour for that particular form. Punishment—but not so drastic or as cruel as the one mentioned (perhaps an angry shout of 'No' or isolation)—may be used to support any treatment decided upon. But remember that punishment must be given there and then when the dog is caught in the act so to speak. It is useless to punish some time after the act because the dog does not then associate the punishment with the crime. Identification of the cause of the wrongdoing and the subsequent appropriate treatment is the correct approach to the problem.

Improperly house-trained: A dog is properly house-trained if it urinates or defaecates in a designated area such as on newspaper left in the bathroom or laundry for that purpose or in some spot in the garden. Dogs that do not do this but void indiscriminately in the home or garden have been improperly trained or not trained at all (see Toilet training, p. 49). Of course, there may be other reasons a dog is urinating and defaecating in the wrong places and they must be taken into consideration before reaching a definite conclusion on what is the contributing cause.

Suffering from a disease: If the dog urinates in the wrong places and situations, it may be caused by:

Urinary incontinence (see p. 179);

Cystitis (see p. 137);

Diabetes (see p. 138).

If the dog defaecates in the wrong places and situations, it may be caused by:

Faecal incontinence;

Diarrhoea (see pp. 139,195);

Constipation (see p. 136);

Spinal disease.

In a state of fear: Fear of sudden explosive noises such as thunder, lightning, an alarm bell ringing, or fireworks exploding may cause the dog to run away, hide, pant, tremble, whine and its pulse rate to rise. These behaviours are regarded by most owners as being natural signs of fear, and they accept them as such. The same owners do not accept urination and defaecation in the home, due to the same cause, as similar natural signs of fear but regard them as forms of misbehaviour. As stated before, punishment in these cases serves little purpose. Counter conditioning and desensitisation would be the approach recommended for a re-education programme (see p. 63).

In a state of intense excitement and extending a submissive greeting: When a dog greets its owner or a close friend who has been absent for some time or who is returning home after a day's work or outing, it may become highly excited, particularly if encouraged by the owner or friend's style of greeting. It will prance and jump about and may urinate. Sometimes in its excitement, instead of leaping for joy, it will assume a submissive posture, approaching with head down, tail down and wagging, spasmodically urinating, even lying down and turning over on its back, to show the returning owner or friend that it is pleased to see them. A dog may also become highly excited when playing, and urinate.

Excitement urination usually occurs more frequently in the younger rather than in the older dog. Maybe the lesson to be learned from this is to do nothing if your young dog urinates when excited and does no harm. Let time solve the problem. Another approach is to subdue the excitement in the dog's greeting or play. This can be done by adopting a low profile in any game and in any greeting. Counter conditioning the dog to adopt the 'Sit' position when it greets its owner or a friend and to wait until it is praised or fondly petted before being released from the position, is a strategy that can be used in subduing the greeting excitement to prevent urination.

Performing the natural act of marking: Marking urination against telephone poles, walls, tree trunks, etc., takes place outside the home where it is regarded as natural behaviour. It also takes place inside the home, on furniture, walls, etc., particularly if some new change has just taken place, such as a new carpet laid, new furniture installed, or a new baby or puppy is brought home. In this situation, though it is still a natural behaviour, it is most often regarded as misbehaviour .

Marking which is characteristic of the male dog over 12 months of age is generally interpreted to be a ritual that is performed to mark the male dog's territory although there may be other connotations.

Marking in the home is objectionable because of the urine stain and smell that it leaves behind. Some of the treatments recommended are castration, hormone therapy, changing the dog's environment, isolating it from the home and familiarising it with the carpet, the furniture or the new arrival so that it feels that it has no need to mark.

Whatever approach you adopt to solve the problem, if the dog happens to be inside the home and is about to mark or is marking a piece of furniture, you can support your approach with mild punishment such as by yelling out loudly and angrily 'No'. This punishment does not cure the dog; it only stops the act there and then. The dog may perform it later on when you are not looking.

Suffering from separation stress: This problem is caused by the dog being separated from its owner or member of the family for whom it shows a very strong attachment. The separation may be due to the absence of the person concerned and the dog is left inside or outside the home by itself. Or the separation may be due to a family decision that whilst the dog in the past has been allowed in the home it will never be allowed inside in the future. The stress placed on the dog, whether outside or inside, may be expressed in one or more forms of undesirable behaviour such as whining, howling, some forms of barking, digging, chewing, destructiveness, urinating and defaecating. Indoors, the destructiveness may take the form of tearing curtains and lounge chairs, scratching furniture, walls and doors, and ripping and chewing the carpet, as well as urinating and defaecating. Outside, it may be scratching doors, digging holes in the garden or elsewhere and also urinating and defaecating. Other annoying forms of behaviour such as whining, howling and barking may be apparent.

The dog may greet the returning owner with a depressed or sad look which the owner, seeing the damage, interprets as a 'guilty' look. The usual and immediate reaction of the owner is to take the dog to the scene of the 'crime' and punish it. The dog, of course, then associates the punishment with the owner's return and not with the damage that has been done. The punishment does not achieve its purpose, and may make the dog more frightened of its owner.

To avoid any damage to the home when the family is absent, you could confine the dog to the kennel yard, but this may not be practical. The best approach would be to put the dog on a re-education programme (see p.63), employing the strategies of counter conditioning and habituation, with perhaps some support from medication if recommended by the veterinarian.

In using the habituation strategy, simulate the usual preparation for going away (out) and returning. The absence time would be very short, say a minute. On returning, if the dog has not commenced separation stress misbehaviour, give the dog a tasty tidbit and praise it verbally and with stroking. Repeat this procedure for a number of sessions each day—say ten, or more if possible. Each time a session is successful the absence time should be extended gradually but never for so long that the dog cannot tolerate it and resorts to its old forms of misbehaviour. If this does happen, stop the session, comfort the dog, and in the next session, revert to the previous time period of absence that the dog could tolerate. When you have consolidated that, move on to the next graded step with caution. When the dog can tolerate a five minute or more absence without misbehaving, you can assume that with further habituation practice, the good behaviour period will extend.

The dog that is suffering from separation stress because it is no longer allowed inside the home could be treated in a similar fashion.

One of the causes of separation stress is that the owner–dog relationship becomes so close that other people and animals are excluded from it. Be careful to see that the dog's social environment always extends beyond a 'twosome'.

Nipping, chewing, mouthing

What is regarded by many owners as a form of aggression in puppies up to about six months of age, and which many owners tolerate, is the chewing and mouthing of shoes, clothing, the biting of furniture, and the nipping and clamping of their jaws on to a person's trouser legs, socks, dress, stockings, shoes, fingers and ankles.

These kinds of simple, aggressive activities, that are also directed to other pups and dogs, are providing learning experiences and growth development through a form of play.

The activities should not be encouraged, especially by teasing, as they may become fixed in the dog's behaviour pattern, and later on, as the dog matures, will be regarded as undesirable behaviour. Redirect the dog's behaviour away from persons and furnishings to objects and play things that will provide it with plenty of opportunity to nip, mouth and chew. Tug-o-war with a piece of rope, chase and fetch ball games, a plastic bone to chew are a few examples of what can be provided to redirect the dog's behaviour. Make up simple little games to engage it in play. If it resorts to the undesirable behaviour, stop it with a loud 'No' accompanied by suitable facial and body expressions. Do not punish with the hand as the pup

might interpret the raised hand as the beginning of a play activity and nip it as it comes near. Praise the pup if it is playing with the toys you have provided or if it is standing or sitting quietly near the shoes, curtains, etc., that it damaged on previous occasions.

Jumping up onto and licking people

This problem involves two undesirable acts, namely, jumping up onto you and attempting to lick either your face or hands.

From the age of about eight weeks, puppies in litters like licking each others' faces and other parts of the body. This genetic behaviour is sometimes transferred to attempts to lick the hands and faces of humans. To train the puppy out of the habit, bend over or get down on your knees so that your face and hands momentarily are exposed on the same level as and near the pup's face. If the pup does not attempt to lick you when you are in that position, give it a tasty tidbit, and praise either by word or touch, to let it know that you are pleased with its response. After each successful training session, slightly increase the exposure time of your face and hands. When your dog takes no further interest in licking your hands and face, it is time to stop your training sessions and check to see if the dog behaves in the same way in day-to-day activities. This is using the habituation strategy to solve your dog's problem. If at any time during the training sessions, the dog licks or attempts to lick your face or hands, a loud 'No' should be sufficient to stop it. Comfort the dog and in the next scheduled training session, revert to the previous time exposure which was successful. Consolidate it before moving on cautiously to the next step.

Your dog jumping up on family members or visitors may cause you some embarrassment. Do not become angry, as the dog may be showing its pleasure in seeing the person and is trying to get into a face licking position or it may be trying to show its dominance. If a dog does jump up onto you, give a loud 'No' command and brush it away with your leg if it is a small dog; if it is a large dog, sharply raise your knee into its chest. This should discourage the dog and cause it to return quickly to the standing position. If there is no further attempt to jump up on to you, praise the dog, letting it see and know of your pleasure as it stands before you. The type of punishment suggested should be accompanied by showing the dog how to behave, e.g. to walk to you, to stand or sit in front of you. The punishment alone is negative; showing the dog how to behave is positive and with counter conditioning or habituation the undesirable response could be replaced with a desirable one.

Another approach that may eliminate the undesirable behaviour is to place the dog on a long lead, and ask a friend, who the dog invariably jumps up onto, to stand a short distance away and encourage the dog to run

Opposite: Discourage a large dog jumping up onto you by sharply raising your knee into its chest.

Waiting for the command to enter

Command 'In' given to enter car

towards him or her. As it is about to jump up onto the friend jerk the lead so that the dog tumbles over and at the same time angrily shout 'No'. Immediately show the dog the correct behaviour in meeting a friend while on the lead and then without the lead. Praise any success. With further counter conditioning, the undesirable behaviour should be replaced with the acceptable one, which of course should be praised every now and then.

Slobbering and restlessness while travelling in cars

Some dogs love travelling in cars, others are extremely restless, suffer anxiety, slobber, whine, and are car sick. Car travel training can prevent these problems from arising.

First, introduce the dog to the car. Let it snoop and sniff inside and outside the car while you keep repeating the sound (word) 'Car' so that sooner or later the dog associates the sound with the object, car. Show the dog how to sit on a rug in the car with the window partly down. The dog begins to learn that the rug is for it to sit on whenever it enters the car. Turn on the engine and talk to the dog, praising its good behaviour. If the dog's reaction appears to be quiet and calm, take it for a short drive, praising it while it remains calm. If it becomes restless, slobbers, etc., stop the car, calm the dog and make it feel happy. Let that be the end of the lesson. What you are doing is conditioning the dog to enjoy riding in the car,

mainly through the strategy of habituation.

Progressively, as the dog tolerates the car drive, the distance and time can be increased. Restrict food and water intake before departure according to the length and time of the car journey. During a long journey, make stops for light exercise, water, and relief.

Train your dog to enter and leave the car calmly and to sit on its rug. The sound (word) 'Stay' could be the command word used to indicate to the dog not to enter the car nor to scramble in wildly when the door is opened. The command sound (word) 'In' could indicate to the dog to enter. Again the release sound (word) 'OK' could be used for the dog to start getting out after the door is opened. Similar conditioning strategies could be adopted for the dog entering and leaving the home when a door is opened, rather than it rushing in or out and knocking someone over in the process.

If you find that your dog continues to be car sick, restless and slobbering, despite your car travel education programme, refer your problem to your veterinarian.

Dung eating and scavenging

The abnormal eating of animal manures, such as dog, cat, horse and cow manure, is technically referred to as coprophagia. Some say it is due to a lack of an enzyme, others say it provides some nutrient, such as a vitamin, that is missing from the dog's diet and others say that dogs, which do not have the usual social contact with humans are more prone to coprophagia. If you do not know the cause, the old saying 'Prevention is better than cure' should apply if your dog presents this problem.

Keep the dog's kennel yard and play area free of dung and when walking the dog in the park or street keep it on a lead, if it has not been obedience trained. If you notice your dog smelling or about to eat any faeces or manure, a loud 'No' accompanied by any other noise you can make may be sufficient to deter it. If so, immediately give the dog praise to let it know that it has pleased you. In time, this type of punishment may support your efforts to stop the dung eating habit. Changing the dog's social and physical environment and diet may help solve the problem.

Scavenging, which is usually associated with predatory dogs raiding garbage bins, is an annoying form of behaviour. If you have received complaints about your dog, check the security of your yard, your dog's nutrition programme and the quantity and palatability of the food given to the dog. If you are a complainant, check the security of your garbage, or try commercially available dog repellants or household products, such as menthol-eucalyptus based cough suppressants, phenol or pepper lightly sprinkled over the top of the garbage bin.

Masturbation and mounting

Masturbation is a natural behaviour for the dog to relieve itself of its sexual frustration due to not having opportunities to mate with bitches. Mounting of other dogs and the mounting of children and adults is also a natural attempt for dogs to release their sexual drive. It is more noticeable in the young mature male dog between the age of one and five years.

Mounting could cause an embarrassing situation and any such kind of behaviour should be nipped in the bud by distracting the dog's attention with a loud noise, a loud 'No' or mild punishment. Keep in mind that success achieved with this kind of intervention is short lived. Consult your veterinarian for a long term solution which may be a choice of hormone therapy or castration.

Castration is the removal of the testicles, which are the source of testosterone, the male sex hormone that is responsible for the dog's sexual drive. After the operation, it takes about one month for the testosterone in the system to dissipate.

The distinctive black spots and white coat of the Dalmatian make it an eye-catching breed.

HEALTH CARE

Feeding and diet—Grooming—Teeth care
Vaccination programme—Worms and worming

The old adage 'Prevention is better than cure' applies just as much to dogs as it does to humans. A healthy, happy dog results from the owner establishing certain routines, some carried out on a daily basis, others periodically.

Any preventative programme of health care for your dog, if it is to be positive, must involve the veterinary surgeon. It is a good idea to contact the veterinarian of your choice to find out about such matters as hours of attendance, night calls and what to do in an emergency. Then, if your first visit to your veterinarian is a hasty one, perhaps arising from an emergency, you are well prepared for it. Get to know your veterinarian as he or she can be most helpful, not only in the services provided but also in the advice offered.

The following guidelines for daily and periodic dog care are set out for owners, breeders and others who show a serious concern for the dog's health.

FEEDING AND DIET

It is very important at an early age (eight to ten weeks) to expose your puppy to a wide variety of foods so that it does not become addicted to any one type, which, unknown to the owner, may be one that does not cover the puppy's complete nutritional requirements and might put its health at risk. Once a dog develops an addiction for a certain type of food, it can be very difficult, and sometimes impossible, to change it over to another type of diet.

The nutritional requirements of dogs vary according to individual needs and are determined by such factors as maintenance, growth, exercise, pregnancy, lactation, disease and age. The basic ingredients of any sound nutrition programme are proteins (amino acids), carbohydrates, fats, vitamins and minerals.

The diet fed to your dog should supply all the nutritional requirements, as well as being attractive and

This Boxer looks healthy and happy.

Opposite: A healthy, shiny coat results from good nutrition, health care and grooming.

These puppies are feeding under the watchful eye of their mother.

palatable to the dog and economical, convenient and aesthetically pleasing to the dog owner.

TYPES OF DOG FOOD

MEAT

This is a good source of protein as well as being highly palatable. However, dogs cannot live on a meat diet only. Meat is very high in phosphorus and very low in calcium, and does not contain enough iron, magnesium, copper, sodium or iodine. The ratio of calcium to phosphorus in the dog's diet should be in the order of 1.2–1.4 calcium to 1.0 phosphorus. Meat diets have a calcium to phosphorus ratio of approximately 1:20. Dogs, especially those four to six months of age, fed only on a meat diet develop a disease called nutritional secondary hyperparathyroidism (see p.169). Meat should not exceed 20–25 per cent of the dog's total diet.

Dogs on a meat diet only may have an iodine deficiency which can give rise to a thyroid gland abnormality (see pp. 157,158).

MILK

This is a good source of protein, fat, vitamin A, vitamin D, vitamin B12, calcium, phosphorus, potassium and io-dine. In the wild, when puppies are weaned from their mother, they never drink milk again. Once puppies are weaned, milk is not necessary for their growth or mainte-nance of a healthy state. Even bitches feeding a litter of suckling puppies do not need it. Many dogs older than 12 weeks of age cannot metabolise milk and consequently suffer from diarrhoea, because they lack an enzyme called lactase.

Those dogs that do have the lactase enzyme and can drink milk without developing diarrhoea may be fed milk as part of their diet.

LIVER

This is a good source of protein. It is very high in phosphorus and vitamin A, low in calcium, and a good source of vitamin B1, niacin, choline and cobalt.

During pregnancy and lactation, the bitch can de-plete her store of vitamin A by up to 50 per cent. During that period it is recommended to occasionally feed her liver.

FISH

This is a good source of protein, magnesium, iodine and selenium. Raw fish contains an enzyme called thiaminase, which destroys vitamin B1 (thiamine). Cooking the fish will destroy the thiaminase enzyme. Thiamine or vitamin B1 deficiency leads to brain damage. Early signs are not eating, weight loss, vomiting and weakness of the hindquarters, followed by irritability, wobbliness and walking with nails extended and the head and neck bent downwards. Excess fish can result in the diet being high in unsaturated fatty acids.

EGGS

These are an excellent source of protein, vitamin D, vitamin B12, choline, sulphur and iron. Raw egg white contains an enzyme which destroys biotin. Biotin deficiency causes dry, flaky skin and dry hair. Raw egg yolks are not a problem. A cooked egg is an excellent source of protein for the dog.

KIDNEY

This is a good source of protein, very high in phosphorus and very low in calcium. It is also a good source of vitamin B1 (thiamine) and cobalt. Dogs fed on a kidney diet only develop a disease called nutritional secondary hyperparathyroidism (see p. 169).

BONES

These are a good source of calcium, phosphorus and copper. Chewing on a bone is a good exercise that helps to maintain healthy gums and removes plaque and tartar from the teeth. The risk with bones, though only slight, is that they may become caught in the teeth or throat or may cause a blockage of the intestine if swallowed. Brisket bone when ingested is broken down into a sandlike material and may cause severe constipation.

VEGETABLES

Green vegetables such as lettuce, cabbage and cauliflower are not of much value to the dog because of high water–fibre content and poor palatability.

Some dogs may eat cooked vegetables from which they obtain some vitamin A and B.

Potato, carrots and turnips fed raw are not very palatable and are poorly digested by the dog. Cooking improves their palatability and digestibility. They are a source of energy and some vitamin A. Peas and beans are a good source of protein and energy and most of the B vitamins. Most legumes contain complex carbohydrates and simpler sugars which are resistant to digestion and pass into the large intestine where they are fermented by bacteria producing flatus or intestinal gas.

MINERAL–VITAMIN SUPPLEMENT

If the dog is on a complete diet, that is, one which covers all of its nutritional requirements, then the addition of a mineral–vitamin supplement may be harmful. This ap-

plies particularly to excess vitamins A and D, calcium and phosphorus. If not harmful, the additional mineral-vitamin supplement may be of no benefit whatsoever.

A mineral–vitamin supplement should only be fed to the dog if the diet is deficient in those areas or if it has some metabolic problem or disease. Seek the advice of your veterinarian.

When purchasing a mineral-vitamin supplement, it is important to ensure that it contains the whole range of vitamins and minerals in correct balance. Read the label carefully. It is not sufficient for it to list what is included in the contents of the container; the precise quantity of each vitamin and mineral should also be included. Only then can you evaluate the quality and economic value of the product.

Minerals

Calcium and phosphorus: Calcium is found in bones, milk, cheese and bread. Phosphorus is found in bones, milk, cheese and meat.

The metabolism of calcium and phosphorus is linked with vitamin D. They are the major minerals and vitamin involved in the formation of bones and teeth. Calcium is involved in the blood clotting mechanism and in the transmission of nerve impulses. Phosphorus is involved in numerous metabolic processes of the body. The ratio of calcium to phosphorus in the diet is of great importance (1.2–1.4 to 1.0). Imbalance of the ratio, especially if the calcium level is much lower than phosphorus, leads to nutritional secondary hyperparathyroidism (see p. 169).

Potassium is found in meat and milk. It is essential for muscle metabolism, fluid balance and nerve transmission. Naturally occurring deficiencies are rare due to the wide distribution of potassium in foods. A deficiency results in muscular weakness, poor growth, as well as heart and kidney abnormalities.

Sodium chloride is found in salt and also in cereals. Sodium chloride (common salt) plays a major role in fluid balance. Excessive sodium in the diet may be associated with hypertension in the dog.

Magnesium is found in cereals, green vegetables, bones and fish. It plays a role in muscle and nerve function, bone formation, fluid balance (sodium and potassium metabolism) and in many enzyme systems of the body. Dietary deficiency is unlikely but is characterised by muscle weakness and convulsions.

Trace elements

Iron is found in eggs, meat, cereals and green vegetables. It is essential for haemoglobin formation and subsequent oxygen transport throughout the body. Iron deficiency results in anaemia, associated with signs of lethargy and poor appetite. Iron in excessive amounts is toxic and causes loss of appetite and weight. The ferrous irons are more readily absorbed than the ferric irons.

Copper is found in meat and bones. It is associated with the function of many enzyme systems and is linked with iron metabolism. Copper deficiency is associated with anaemia and bone abnormalities.

Excess dietary copper can lead to anaemia and in some breeds of dogs such as the Bedlington Terrier, Dobermann Pinscher and West Highland White Terrier, it can lead to hepatitis and cirrhosis of the liver.

Manganese is found in many foods. It plays a role in many enzyme systems. A deficiency affects growth and reproduction as well as fat metabolism. Excess manganese can cause poor fertility and anaemia.

Zinc is found in meat, and many other foods. It plays a function in enzyme activity and protein synthesis. Zinc availability to the dog is adversely affected by a high dietary calcium and phytic acid which is found in cereals.

Zinc deficiency is a cause of poor growth, depressed appetite, shrinkage of the testicles, weight loss and poor skin and coat condition. Zinc is relatively non toxic.

Iodine is found in fish, vegetables, dairy products and salt. It plays an essential role in the production of thyroid hormones. Deficiency of iodine results in increased activity of the thyroid gland (see p. 157) in an attempt to compensate for the iodine deficiency. Signs of iodine deficiency are swollen thyroid gland, skin and hair abnormalities associated with lethargy, and reproductive failure in the bitch.

Excess iodine can impair the production of the thyroid hormone and cause thyroid gland malfunction. (See pp. 157,158.)

Selenium is found in cereals, fish and meat.

Selenium deficiency causes degeneration of both skeletal and cardiac muscle. Excess selenium can be highly toxic.

Vitamins

Vitamins are divided into a fat soluble group and a water soluble group. Fat soluble vitamins (A, D, E and K) are stored in the body fat whereas water soluble vitamins (B complex) are not and have to be replaced more frequently.

Fat-soluble vitamins

Vitamin A: The dog can obtain its vitamin A requirement from the yellow pigment of plants called carotene. B—carotene is converted to vitamin A mainly in the intestine. Vitamin A is found in milk, butter, cheese, cod liver oil and liver. Vitamin A is essential for vision, growth and health of skin cells, bones and teeth. Vitamin A deficiency causes numerous eye disorders, such as dryness of the eye, conjunctivitis (see p. 135), ulceration of the cornea (see p. 146), and thickening and hardening of the skin.

Excess vitamin A can cause painful changes in the bones and gingivitis (see p. 150) associated with the teeth falling out.

Vitamin D: This is found in cod liver oil, eggs, dairy products margarine and meat. Vitamin D in the small intestine aids in calcium and phosphorus absorption as well as playing a role in regulating the level of calcium and phosphorus in the blood. Vitamin A can be produced by the effect of ultraviolet light on compounds in the skin.

Vitamin D is essential in the young dog for bone development and growth. A deficiency of vitamin D causes rickets.

Excessive amounts of vitamin D can cause calcification of the soft tissues, deformities of the teeth and jaw.

Vitamin E: This is found in green vegetables, cereals and margarine. Its function is closely linked to the trace element selenium.

In the presence of a high level of polyunsaturated fatty acids, the requirement for vitamin E increases. Vitamin E linked with selenium plays a role in maintaining the cell membrane.

Deficiency of vitamin E is associated with degeneration of the muscles, reproductive failure and an adverse effect on the immune system. The function of vitamin E is not completely understood. Excess of vitamin E may be harmful but is not considered to be as dangerous as is an excess of vitamins A and D.

Vitamin K: This is found in green vegetables, meats and cereals (vitamin K is manufactured by bacteria in the intestine). It plays an important role in the blood clotting mechanism.

Vitamin K deficiency rarely occurs naturally but if drug induced, such as in the extended use of antibiotics, it leads to haemorrhage.

Vitamin K in excess does not appear to have harmful effects on the dog.

Water-soluble vitamins

Thiamin (Vitamin B1): This is found in offal, whole grains, peas and beans. It can be destroyed by cooking or by an enzyme found in fish called thiaminase. Thiaminase in fish is destroyed by cooking.

Thiamin plays a role in carbohydrate metabolism. Thiamin requirement is dependent on the carbohydrate content of the diet. Dogs with a thiamin deficiency stop eating, show signs of disorder of the nervous system, weakness, and may die from heart failure. It is unlikely thiamin excess will cause toxicity.

Riboflavin (Vitamin B2): This is found in most foods and is essential in carbohydrate metabolism. A deficiency is associated with small testicles, and eye and skin disorders.

Some riboflavin may be manufactured by bacteria in the intestine. The amount produced by this method is not adequate to cover the dog's requirements so it is essential that riboflavin (vitamin B2) be supplied in the dog's food.

Toxic effects from excess thiamin are not known.

Pantathenic acid: This is a vitamin found in most foods. It plays an essential part in carbohydrate, fat and amino-acid metabolism.

Signs of a deficiency are depression, reduced appetite, failure to grow, hairloss and diarrhoea.

Toxic reaction due to excess is unknown.

Niacin (Nicotinic acid): This is a vitamin found in cereal grains, legumes, meats and liver. It plays a role in the metabolism of all the major nutrients.

Signs of deficiency are not eating, an inflamed, ulcerated mouth, black tongue, bad breath, weight loss and diarrhoea.

Toxic reaction to excess is unknown in the dog.

Pyridoxine (Vitamin B6): This is found in meats, vegetables and cereal grains. It is involved in enzyme systems associated with nitrogen and amino-acid metabolism.

Pyridoxine requirement is dependent on the protein content of the diet.

Signs of a deficiency are weight loss, anaemia, dermatitis and hair loss.

In excess, it is not considered to be highly toxic.

Biotin: This is a vitamin found in meats, legumes and vegetables. Dogs on a balanced diet produce their daily requirement by bacterial synthesis in the intestine.

Antibiotics can produce a biotin deficiency by destroying the intestinal bacteria which produce the vitamin.

Raw egg white contains a protein called avidin which binds with biotin to render it unusable. Avidin is readily destroyed by heat, so eggs fed to your dog should be cooked.

Signs of a biotin deficiency are scaly dermatitis. Toxic reaction to excess is unknown.

Folic acid: This is a vitamin found in green vegetables, legumes and some grains. Dogs on a balanced diet produce their daily requirement by bacterial synthesis in the intestine.

Signs of a deficiency are loss of appetite, lethargy and anaemia.

Antibiotics, by destroying the bacteria that produce folic acid, can cause a deficiency.

Excess folic acid administered orally is not toxic.

Cyanacobamalin (Vitamin B12): This is found in meat, eggs and dairy products. Its function is closely linked with folic acid.

Vitamin B12 deficiency results in anaemia and nerve degeneration. Research conducted on the dog for vitamin B12 deficiency is incomplete.

Choline: This is found in a wide variety of plant and animal materials, liver, grains, legumes and egg yolk.

A deficiency of choline causes kidney and liver dysfunction. The effects of excess are unknown.

Ascorbic acid (Vitamin C): This is not required in the diet as the dog is able to manufacture its own requirement of ascorbic acid (vitamin C).

WATER

Water plays a vital role within the body. It is the major constituent of blood, is involved in temperature regulation and essential for digestion. Water represents approximately 50 per cent of the dog's body weight.

The dog can live without food for weeks, but depending on the dog's health and the climatic conditions, it may die within hours or days if water is not available.

Water is lost from the body via expired air (the dog pants to regulate body temperature), faeces, urine and to a limited extent in sweat from the pads.

Water intake is from drinking water and food. Water is also produced from the chemical breakdown of nutrients within the body. Dry dog food may contain less than ten per cent water whereas moist food (canned) may contain more than 80 per cent water.

Water requirements vary according to the climatic conditions, the dog's health, whether or not it is pregnant or lactating, and the water content of the food eaten.

WHAT SHOULD YOU FEED YOUR DOG?

If you wish, you may feed your dog a home-cooked meal, commercial pet foods (canned, semi-moist or dry), or a combination of all three. Needless to say, a meal prepared at home can be time-consuming, and you will need to know the dog's nutritional requirements and what foods provide the necessary proteins, fats, carbohydrates, vitamins and minerals to satisfy those requirements.

Your dog may reject a meal you have prepared because it is not palatable, or it may select the meat only and leave the rest.

Commercial preparations are palatable, easy to use, readily available and reasonably priced. Some provide a complete and balanced diet while others need to be supplemented if the dog is to obtain all its nutritional requirements. When buying commercial pet food, read the label carefully to check if the food is complete or incomplete. Well-known brands of commercial dog foods are made by reputable companies and what they claim on the label must conform to legal requirements.

CANNED FOOD

There are numerous varieties of canned foods that are attractive, palatable, nutritious, economical and convenient. They consist of a mixture of meats and cereals with all essential vitamins and minerals added. Read the label carefully to make sure that it is a complete and balanced dog food. If the dog food is incomplete, it will require supplementation.

Feed your dog a variety of canned foods to prevent it from developing a taste for one type and refusing all others. When feeding your dog a number of different types, mix them thoroughly together, otherwise it may eat the one it prefers and leave the others.

If 80 per cent of the dog's total diet is made up of a complete and balanced canned food, it will not suffer nutritionally if the other 20 per cent is made up of table scraps, meat or other highly palatable titbits.

DRY FOOD

Dry food comes in various shapes and sizes, from flakes to a biscuit-type form. Check the label to ensure that it is a complete dog food. If it is, the dog can live a healthy life on the dry food diet only.

The dog's requirement for water increases with dry food. Make sure that fresh water is always available. Dry foods contain salt, which increases the voluntary water intake. They should be introduced gradually so that the dog can adjust its drinking habits. If your dog is drinking very little water, the dry food can be moistened before feeding.

SEMI-MOIST FOOD

This food is usually in the form of cubes, chunks or mince contained in a sealed packet. Check the label to ensure that it is a complete dog food. These foods are made with a variety of ingredients including meat, meat by-products, vegetable protein concentrates, cereals, fats and sugars.

FEEDING ROUTINE

When puppies are eight weeks old, they can be fed canned, semi-moist, and/or dry food. Four small meals a day are best for the young puppy. At four months the meals should be reduced to three a day; at nine months to two a day; at twelve months to once a day (for those owners who have a very busy schedule, feeding the dog once a day is quite satisfactory, except in special cases, e.g. dogs in work or lactating bitches).

It is a good idea to feed the dog at the same place and time each day.

How much to feed?

The amount of food required daily by a dog varies according to such factors as breed, growth, maintenance, exercise, lactation, pregnancy, environment and disease. Some dogs require more food than others; some require less. A young dog, active and playful, would require more food than an old mature dog of the same breed that spends most of the day lying around.

If your puppy or young or adult dog is healthy (in good condition with good skin and coat, alert, active and neither too fat nor too thin), but
• leaves some of its food, even though it is palatable, then you are feeding it too much;
• eats all of its food either quickly or slowly, but is still too thin, then you need to give it more;
• eats all of its food but looks fat, is slow to move and appears lazy, then maybe you are feeding it too much;
• eats all of its food, is steadily growing and shows a normal weight gain, then you can assume that you are feeding it the correct amount.

DIET CHART			
WEIGHT OF DOG	CANNED FOOD	SEMI-MOIST FOOD	DRY FOOD
lb / kg	680 g cans per day	250 g packets per day	per day
2–11 / 1–5	½	⅓–⅔	50–100 g ½–1 cup
13–22 / 6–10	½–1	⅔–1	100–200 g 1–2 cups
24–55 / 11–25	1–2	1½–3	200–400 g 2–4 cups
57–110 / 26–50	2–3½	3–5	400–700 g 4–7 cups

The figures in the diet chart set out the approximate daily food requirements of your dog and can only be used as a guide. In general, a young puppy with the same body weight as a non-working adult dog, requires about three times more calories for the energy it expends in growth. Active breeds vary greatly in weight from 1.5 kg (3.3 1b) to 118 kg (259 lb). There is also a wide range in the activities of the dogs. Food requirements vary according to both body weight and activity.

WEANING

Weaning usually begins at three to four weeks of age but the precise starting time will depend on the size of the litter, the bitch's milk supply and when you want the puppies to go to their new home(s).

As a starter, use puppy canned food mixed with water to form a paste. Smear some of the food around the puppies' mouths or entice them to suck the food from the end of your finger. Once they show interest, introduce them to a flat dish or saucer containing the food.

Initially, they walk in the food and make a mess but soon they get the idea of lapping it up. Once this is achieved, increase the consistency of the food to a more solid nature.

Four small meals a day are best for young puppies.

Provide the puppies with water or milk in a dish, but be careful as some may develop diarrhoea from cow's milk. If so, use a low lactose milk formula.

After a week, the puppies should be eating puppy canned food readily from a bowl. It is a good idea to feed them four times a day. At this young age the pups should be exposed to a wide variety of taste and texture in foods, as some dogs become addicted to the one type of food as they mature. In time, if you discover that the diet to which the dog has become accustomed does not cover all its nutritional requirements, it may be difficult to get it to change and accept a more balanced diet.

If the bitch wants to feed them all the time during the weaning process, remove her from the puppies while they are being fed solid food. The puppies should be completely weaned over a four-week period, so that at eight weeks of age they are self-sufficient and ready to go to their new home.

By removing the puppies from their mother for periods during the weaning, the bitch's milk production will decrease, so that when the puppies are fully weaned at eight weeks of age, she will not have uncomfortable, swollen mammary glands full of milk.

PREGNANCY AND LACTATION IN THE BITCH

Pregnant bitches require extra food in the last third of pregnancy for the rapid growth of the foetuses during this period. Increase the volume of food at this stage by 25 per cent, otherwise the bitch will metabolise her own body tissue and lose weight.

Bitches that are lactating require extra food for milk production and to make up for the loss of nutrients in the milk suckled by the puppies. If she is not fed adequate amounts of good quality food, her milk supply will decrease and the puppies will suffer (see pp. 77,81,191).

WORKING DOGS

Working dogs vary enormously in the type of work they do, for example, compare the work of a sheep dog to that of a guide dog for the blind. Not only the type of work but also the conditions under which they work vary greatly, for example, compare sledge dogs working in sub-zero temperatures to a sniffer dog used for drug detection at an airport.

Working dogs need more calories in their diet to provide extra energy. Their diets will vary according to the amount and type of work and prevailing climatic conditions. Food for working dogs should be concentrated, palatable, nutritionally balanced, and highly digestible.

The dry and semi-moist foods are more concentrated than canned food. Fats and soluble carbohydrates are the main source of energy. Diets high in fat must be balanced with protein, vitamins and minerals.

Feed only a small meal prior to working and feed the dog its major meal after work, giving it time to settle down before eating.

Water should be made available during the working period.

Large amounts of dietary fibre in the diet such as vegetables are not beneficial due to low digestibility and palatability.

SPECIAL HEALTH PROBLEMS RELATED TO DIET

CALCIUM–PHOSPHORUS IMBALANCE

The ratio of calcium to phosphorus is important for good bone formation and skeletal development. Meat only diets are high in phosphorus and low in calcium, iodine, magnesium and some vitamins, which leads to nutritional secondary hyperparathyroidism (see p. 169).

Dogs (particularly puppies) that are on high meat

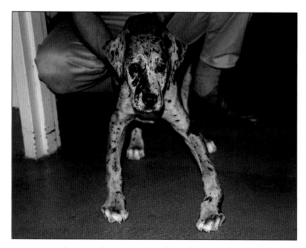

High meat diets can cause bowed legs in the dog.

diets have such problems as poorly formed bones, bowed legs, an overall stunted appearance, lameness, joint pain, deformed spinal column and pelvis. The bones are very susceptible to fracture.

The dog's diet should be changed to one based on complete and balanced canned, semi-moist and/or dry food. Add calcium to the diet daily for about a month in the form of calcium carbonate, gluconate or lactate at the rate of one tablet or one teaspoon of powder per 5 kg of body weight. It is most important that the calcium supplement does not contain any phosphorus such as calcium phosphate because the imbalance in the calcium–phosphorus ratio will not be rectified.

DIABETES (See p. 138.)

DIARRHOEA (See pp. 84, 139, 195.)

Some dogs, once they are older than 12 weeks, do not produce the lactase enzyme in the intestine. Lactase is essential to digest lactose in milk. Dogs deficient in lactase develop diarrhoea when given milk, due to fermentation of lactose by bacteria in the intestine. In these cases, do not give the dog milk or dairy products.

Dogs with diarrhoea should be fed a fat-free diet while they have the complaint and until their faeces (motions) return to normal. Boiled chicken, lean grilled meat, grilled fish and boiled rice are relatively fat free. Reduce the volume of food by two-thirds. Fresh water should be readily available.

DIETARY ALLERGY (See p. 140.)

GASTRIC DILATION (BLOAT)

This is a life threatening condition occurring more frequently in deep-chested dogs, such as Great Danes and Basset Hounds. The exact cause of the condition is unknown. In most cases it is associated with eating rapidly a large volume of food (often dry), or eating bones or other foreign material, such as horse manure. Exercise, excitement and drinking large volumes of water are often associated with this condition.

Signs

• attempting to vomit

• severe abdominal pain

• bloated stomach (the gas-filled stomach when tapped with the fingers has a drumlike sound)

• refusing to move

• salivating and/or panting

• initially excited and distressed, then as shock sets in becomes depressed.

This is an emergency situation. For treatment see your veterinarian immediately.

WORKING DOGS

Working dogs need extra calories for energy.

Sledge dogs working in sub-zero temperatures.

Prevention

• Feed the dog three or four small meals per day.

• Do not feed dry food to susceptible dogs. Add water to moisten the dry food thoroughly before serving.

• Do not give bones to the dog or allow it access to garbage.

• Avoid excitement or exercise before or after meal times.

KIDNEY DISEASE (See p. 159.)

The kidneys filter waste products from the blood, and when diseased they either stop filtering or do so inadequately. Waste products then become concentrated in the blood and have a toxic or poisoning effect on the dog.

There are diets specifically formulated with reduced amounts of high quality protein, sodium and phosphorus. By reducing the amount of protein, the amount of waste product in the blood is reduced for the kidneys to filter. Excess sodium and phosphorus have a detrimental effect on kidney function.

Do not feed eggs, meat or cheese to the dog.

HEART FAILURE (See p.151.)

OBESITY (See p. 161.)

PANCREATITIS (See p. 169.)

Pancreatic insufficiency is a decrease in the secretion of a number of digestive enzymes produced by the pancreas. It leads to poor digestion of food, weight loss, harsh coat, and pale, soft, foul smelling faeces. The dog's ability to digest fat is poor.

Your veterinarian will prescribe oral preparations containing digestive enzymes and a diet specifically formulated with high quality nutrients and a low fat content and which is more readily digested and absorbed.

SICK DOG WITH POOR APPETITE

Make sure the dog's diet is complete and balanced. In addition, there are specially designed vitamin–mineral supplements which also should be given. They contain the whole range of vitamins, minerals and trace elements in correct balance. When purchasing these supplements, read the label carefully. It is not sufficient for them to list what is included in the contents; the precise quantity of each vitamin, mineral and trace element should also be included. Only then can you evaluate the quality and economic value of the product.

These supplements can be administered by injection, or orally in a tablet, powder, liquid or paste form.

Feed the dog small amounts of food frequently, three to four times a day. Give foods with plenty of flavour and odour. Warm the food, as this makes it more appetising and heightens the flavour and odour. Hand feeding will often encourage a sick dog to eat.

If the dog does not eat or drink for two days, contact your veterinarian as the dog will start to dehydrate, which will exacerbate the illness. If the dog is dehydrated but will still drink, an electrolyte formula can be purchased from your veterinarian to add to the water to help overcome dehydration. If the dog refuses both food and fluids, it may be fed with a syringe, stomach tube or an intravenous drip administered by your veterinary surgeon.

GROOMING

Dogs, unlike cats, devote little or no time to grooming themselves and therefore need more attention from owners, especially the longhaired breeds.

The average owner can attend to the day-to-day grooming needs of the dog; the information in this section is structured for that purpose. For specialised grooming techniques, the owner is advised to consult the professional grooming salon, a person with an experienced background, or information contained in books dealing specifically with dog grooming.

Dog hair, unlike human hair, does not continue to grow. In the dog, the follicle from which the hair grows and is nourished, eventually becomes dormant and the hair growth stops. After some months of dormancy, the hair falls out. The cycle is then repeated with the follicle producing a new hair.

Longhaired breeds require more grooming than shorthaired breeds.

Opposite: Washing the dog can be an activity for the whole family.

Other factors which affect the growth, quality and loss of hair are:
• Genes (e.g. the Old English Sheepdog grows a long coarse coat, whereas the German Shorthaired Pointer grows a very short fine coat)
• Vitamins
• Hormones
• Parasites
• Disease
• Environment (coat development is stimulated by decreasing daylight hours, not by a drop in temperature)

HAIR LOSS OR SHEDDING THE COAT

People living with dogs in the house often notice and complain about the amount of hair the dog sheds. Shedding of hair is a normal process; dogs are covered in hair, and they have a lot more hair to shed than humans.

If a dog is losing large amounts of hair but is replacing it so that the coat looks healthy, then the hair loss can be regarded as normal.

Some breeds of dogs such as the German Shepherd, Samoyed and Chow Chow have a long outer coat with a short woolly undercoat. The undercoat may be shed unevenly giving the dog a patchy, moth-eaten appearance. Some owners are unnecessarily alarmed by the moth-eaten appearance of their dog and think the dog has some disease affecting the coat.

Heavier shedding of the coat in spring and summer is not due to a change in temperature but is due to the increase in daylight hours. Consequently, house dogs exposed to lengthy periods of artificial light throughout the year shed their coat all the year long.

Dogs living outdoors in very cold climates develop heavy coats that serve to protect them from the elements. Coat growth is stimulated by the decrease in daylight hours, not by the drop in temperature.

GROOMING EQUIPMENT

The grooming equipment required will vary according to the breed of dog and whether you wish to groom your dog yourself or have it done professionally at a dog grooming salon.
• Short, pure bristle brush—to brush shorthaired dogs.
• Short, flexible wire bristle brush—to brush longhaired dogs.
• Pointed scissors—to trim hair and deknot long hair.
• Cotton buds—to clean ears and control bleeding if nails are cut too short.
• Nail cutters—designed to cut the nails of dogs.
• Ferric chloride—to control bleeding if nails are cut too short.

Grooming equipment

• Cotton wool balls—to clean eyes.
• Wide-toothed comb—to comb out knots in longhaired dogs.
• Insecticidal rinse or shampoo—one recommended for dog use.
• Baby shampoo or medicated shampoo—one recommended for dog use.
• Powder—talcum powder or flea powder for dogs.
• Towel or suitable drying cloth.
• Grooming table—a solid table with a non-slip surface.
• Hound glove—to use on shorthaired dogs to give a polished finish.
• Electric clippers—for certain longhaired breeds such as poodles and schnauzers.

COAT CARE

Grooming keeps the coat clean, prevents matting of the hair, stimulates circulation, and removes loose hair.

Longhaired dogs need their coats combed and brushed daily to prevent the hair becoming matted. Mats tend to form behind the ears, around the neck, under the belly, along the sides and in the tail. Dogs that are badly neglected can develop matted hair practically all over the body which looks and feels like a thick dense carpet. Once this happens, these dogs are impossible to groom with a brush or comb. Loose hair sometimes catches around the teeth of longhaired dogs, causing gingivitis (inflammation of the gum, see p. 150), and an unpleasant odour to come from the mouth.

BRUSHING AND COMBING

Start grooming your puppy at about three months of age so that it becomes accustomed to the feel of the brush and/or comb. Don't be too vigorous, otherwise the puppy will resent being groomed. Most dogs enjoy being brushed and combed and grooming your dog at an early age makes your task much easier as the dog gets older.

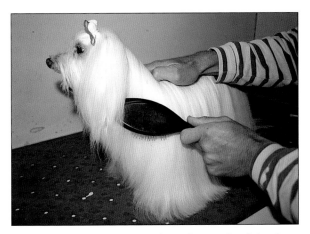

Groom longhaired dogs every day with a wire bristle brush.

Shorthaired dogs should be brushed twice weekly using a brush with flexible wire bristles or short natural bristles. Brush the hair in the direction it falls. Dogs often resent having their face brushed. In these cases wipe the face with a moist cloth. If brushing the face, be careful to see that you do not accidentally damage the eyes.

Longhaired dogs should be groomed every day using a short flexible wire bristle brush and a wide tooth comb.

Comb the hair away from the body to remove any small knots, followed by a thorough brushing in the direction that the hair falls. Knots that cannot be combed out may be teased out or broken down by using a pair of pointed scissors followed by combing. If the knots cannot be teased out or broken down with scissors then they can be very carefully cut out. To do this cut a few hairs at a time just under the knot until it is free, otherwise if you try to cut out the knot impatiently, you may take out a section of skin with the hair.

It is impossible to groom long haired dogs which have large areas of hair badly matted. The best method is to get your veterinarian to sedate or in some cases anaesthetize the dog so that the matted hair can be shaved off with electric clippers.

WASHING

Dogs require regular washing to keep them clean and to prevent skin problems from developing, especially if they live in a warm climate. Where ticks and fleas are prevalent, dogs should be washed weekly in dog shampoo followed by an insecticidal rinse. Dogs with a very strong body odour usually have a skin problem (see p. 176). If the odour condition does not improve with washing, see your veterinarian for advice and treatment. Many dog owners are concerned about washing their dog too much, thereby removing natural oils from the skin and coat. It is my experience that most skin problems of dogs presented at my hospital are due to insufficient washing.

The frequency of washing will vary according to the breed and climate, but generally a dog should be washed once a week during summer, once every two to three weeks in spring and autumn (fall) and at the beginning and end of winter.

Some dogs hate water so it is a good idea to start washing them at about three months of age so that they become accustomed to it. The best place to do the washing is in a large laundry tub. Do not place the puppy in a tub full of water or under a jet of water from a tap; it will become frightened and may be impossible to handle. To begin with, the water should only be about 5 cm (2 in) deep. Large dogs that are difficult to lift or hold in a tub can be held securely on a lead and washed outside, using a hose with the water running gently.

Begin by gradually wetting the dog's coat until it is saturated then apply sufficient dog shampoo to achieve a good foaming lather as you gently massage the shampoo into the coat. Use only shampoos recommended for dogs

WASHING THE DOG

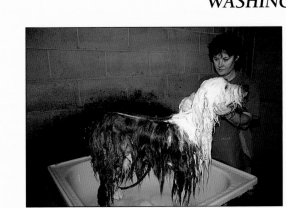

Apply dog shampoo and massage well into the coat.

Rinse the dog thoroughly with clean water.

and if unavailable use baby shampoo. Only shampoo the head if it is necessary. Be careful to see that no shampoo gets into the eyes or ears.

Once a good foaming lather is achieved, rinse the coat thoroughly and repeatedly with clean water. Using your hand, squeeze the water out of the coat. If washing the dog in a tub, lift it onto a bench and towel dry it. The drying process may be completed with a hair dryer. It is important with long haired dogs to comb and brush the hair as it dries, to prevent knots forming.

Immediately after being washed and dried, your dog may roll in the dirt or garden and spoil the effect of your hard work in washing it. To prevent this happening, after you towel dry your dog, take it for a brisk walk on a lead or lock it in a tiled area for a period of time.

EYE CARE

Healthy dogs, except those breeds with a flattened face such as the Pekingese, Bulldog and Pug or longhaired breeds such as the Maltese and Yorkshire Terrier, rarely if ever require their eyes to be cleaned.

The longhaired breeds with flattened face often have tear ducts that are kinked or too narrow and do not allow tears to flow down the duct and out the nose. Instead, the tears flow out of that corner of the eye closer to the nose, causing a wet stain in the hair on either side.

Tear staining may also be due to excessive tear production caused by entropion, i.e turning in of the eyelid with the eyelashes rubbing on the surface of the eyeball (see p.144), or by conjunctivitis (see p.135).

Long hair close to the corner of the eye near the nose can act like a wick. Carefully clipping the hair short in this area will help to keep the area dry and prevent staining.

If tear staining continues, consult your veterinarian who may flush the tear ducts under a general anaesthetic; if the tear ducts are narrowed or blocked due to the flattened shape of the face, flushing will not improve the situation.

Your veterinarian may prescribe an antibiotic (tetracycline) which will eliminate the reddish stain produced by the tears. If the eyes require cleaning, use a moist cotton wool ball.

EAR CARE

Check the inside of the ears regularly for dirt, wax and foreign matter, such as grass seeds. Like humans, some dogs produce more wax in their ears than others. Wax is a suitable breeding ground for ear mites, bacteria, fungi and yeast. The wax also can irritate the dog and cause partial, temporary deafness if it blocks the ear canal.

If there is no sign of dirt or wax, do not clean the ears. Overzealous cleaning irritates them and sets up an infection.

To clean the ear, take hold of it in such a way that you expose the inner side. With a cotton bud moistened in diluted peroxide or in a special cleansing agent obtained from your veterinarian, clean carefully in and around the folds of the ear as well as the opening of the ear canal. Be careful not to push any wax or dirt deeper into the canal thereby compounding the problem.

Some dogs, such as Cocker Spaniels, have floppy ears with long hair. The heavily weighted ears do not allow for good air circulation inside the ear flap and canal. A warm, moist, waxy environment with poor air circulation is an excellent breeding ground for bacteria, fungi, yeasts and ear mites (see p. 142).

Develop the practice of daily grooming to prevent the hair on the ears becoming knotted. Better still, clip off the hair on the ears regularly. The clipping makes the ears lighter, allows for better air circulation and helps prevent ear infections.

Dogs that have hair growing in the ear canals (e.g. Poodles), should have the hair plucked regularly to prevent ear infections. Otherwise, the hair mats with the wax produced in the ear canal to form a plug. The plug then makes the ear canal very susceptible to infection, commonly known as otitis externa (see p. 141). If there

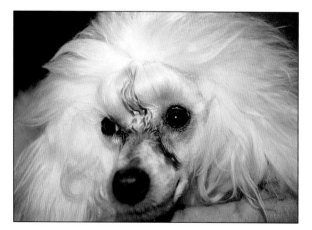

Facial hair stained by tears

Clean the dog's ear carefully with a moistened cotton bud.

are signs of the dog scratching its ear, holding its head to one side, redness inside the ear or of discharge in the canal, seek your veterinarian's advice.

NAIL CARE

Dogs wear down their nails during their daily routine by walking, running, hunting or working.

Some breeds of dog, e.g. the Bassett Hound, grow very long nails partly because of the shape of their paws. They require regular nail cutting.

Dogs that are sedentary, old or confined inside a carpeted apartment or house should have their nails checked regularly, especially those of the front paws. If the nails are not checked regularly they could grow too long, sometimes growing in the shape of a hook and back into the pad causing lameness and infection.

The degree of difficulty met in cutting the dog's nails depends on the temperament of the dog and on the owner having a suitable pair of nail clippers designed for dogs. Scissors or human nail clippers are not satisfactory and if used tend to split the nail. It is important to get a good view of the nail so that you can identify the quick which contains blood vessels and nerves. If you cut the quick, it

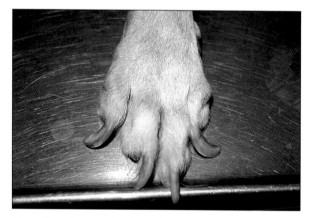

Check the nails regularly. This old dog's nails have grown too long.

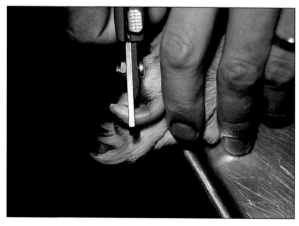

Identify the quick before cutting the nails.

will hurt the dog and the cut may bleed freely for a short time. It is easy to identify the quick in the dog's white nails. The quick is the pink coloured tissue inside the nail. Cut the nail a short distance from where the quick ends. If the nail bleeds after cutting, apply pressure with a cotton bud for a few minutes. Ferric chloride applied to the bleeding nail will stop the bleeding almost immediately.

Cutting the nails will not prevent the dog from damaging furniture in the home or scratching your person if it jumps up on you. If possible, give the dog ready access to the garden where its scratching can do no real damage.

The nail can only be cut back so far because of the limitations imposed by the quick. After cutting, there is a reasonable length of nail still protruding which can cause damage. The only way to stop this behaviour is by training or re-education (see p. 63).

TEETH CARE

The dog is a predator which uses its canine teeth (fangs) to catch and hold its prey. The incisor teeth (front) are used to tear the flesh off its prey and the pre-molar and molar teeth (back) are for masticating the food in preparation for digestion. The dog usually masticates the food to reduce it to pieces of a size that can be swallowed.

ERUPTION OF TEETH

Like humans, the dog has two sets of teeth in a lifetime: the temporary or deciduous set (milk teeth) and the permanent set. The teeth erupt through the gum in pairs; when one incisor appears on one side of the jaw, the corresponding incisor appears on the other side.

Temporary teeth begin erupting between the 2nd and 3rd week after birth, the first to appear being the incisors. By the 6th to 8th week all temporary teeth have erupted. The total number of temporary teeth is twenty eight.

Eruption of the permanent teeth occurs from the 3rd to 7th month. The total number of permanent teeth is forty two.

The time of eruption of temporary and permanent teeth can help you determine a dog's age up to about seven months. Beyond this stage, the dog's teeth (unlike horse's teeth) are of no help in determining age. Puppies do not appear to have any real discomfort when cutting their temporary or permanent teeth.

TEETH PROBLEMS

Displacement of teeth

This usually occurs with the incisor teeth. The teeth may be rotated, crossed, backward or forward. Displacement may be the result of a decrease in the size of the jaw leading to overcrowding. This condition is seen in the smaller

TIME OF ERUPTION OF TEMPORARY TEETH			
TEETH	**NUMBER**		**TIME OF ERUPTION**
Incisors	Top Jaw	6	2 to 6 weeks
	Bottom Jaw	6	
Canines	Top Jaw	2	2 to 6 weeks
	Bottom Jaw	2	
Molars	Top Jaw	6	4 to 8 weeks
	Bottom Jaw	6	

TIME OF ERUPTION OF PERMANENT TEETH			
TEETH	**NUMBER**		**TIME OF ERUPTION**
Incisors	Top Jaw	6	3 to 5 months
	Bottom Jaw	6	
Canines	Top Jaw	2	4 to 6 months
	Bottom Jaw	2	
Pre-Molars	Top Jaw	8	4 to 6 months
	Bottom Jaw	8	
Molars	Top Jaw	4	5 to 7 months
	Bottom Jaw	6	

breeds and may be due to selective breeding. Consult your veterinarian when the dog is about six months of age. Sometimes displacement of teeth is possible to rectify by using orthodontic techniques.

Supernumerary teeth

This is reasonably common in the dog, especially the smaller breeds, e.g. the Miniature Poodle. The incisors and canine teeth are more commonly involved.

The permanent teeth erupt alongside the temporary ones. The temporary tooth or teeth remain firmly embedded in the gum leaving the dog with extra teeth. This usually occurs in the upper jaw on both sides more frequently than in the lower jaw. Food collects between the teeth, causing plaque and tartar to form on the teeth and the gum to become inflamed; this condition is associated with unpleasant odour from the mouth.

If the temporary teeth are still firmly embedded in the gum by the age of eight months, see your veterinarian who will distinguish the temporary teeth from the permanent ones, give the dog a general anaesthetic and then extract them.

Malocclusion

Undershot jaw: The normal occlusion or bite is one where the upper and lower incisor teeth meet when the mouth is closed. The common malocclusion seen in the brachycephalic dogs, i.e those with a pushed in face, is the undershot jaw, where the lower is longer than the upper jaw. It is common and considered acceptable in the Pekingese, Boxer and Bulldog breeds.

Overshot jaw: The overshot jaw or parrot mouth, i.e. where the lower jaw is shorter than the upper jaw is unacceptable in any breed. This condition is seen more commonly in those dogs with long noses, such as Dashchunds and Collies. The incisor teeth of the lower jaw may press on the tissue covering the palate. If so, consult your veterinarian.

Broken teeth

The canine teeth, as they are long, tapered and more exposed, are prone to being chipped or broken. The common causes are fights, falls and automobiles.

If the end of the tooth is chipped or broken, it usually remains healthy. The sharp jagged edge of the tooth may irritate the lip causing an ulcer. In these cases, the dog is given a general anaesthetic and the end of the tooth is filed to make it round and smooth.

If the fractured tooth becomes discoloured, the pulp cavity is exposed, the gum at the base of the tooth is inflamed or it is causing the dog discomfort, then the tooth including root should be extracted under a general anaesthetic.

Erosion and discolouration of dental enamel

Erosion can be due to the dog contracting distemper before the permanent teeth erupt or puppies born from bitches being fed diets deficient in fat soluble vitamins A, D, E and K during their pregnancy. (See Feeding and diet, p. 77.)

Staining of the enamel can be caused by administering tetracycline antibiotics to puppies before their permanent teeth erupt.

Once the enamel is eroded or stained, it is a permanent blemish.

Plaque and tartar

Dogs carry large numbers of bacteria in their mouth because they have no oral hygiene and lick their skin and fur. The bacteria develop on food particles in and around the teeth and combine with saliva to form plaque. Plaque is a yellow-brown scum which eventually becomes calcified to form a hard cement-like mass called tartar. Tartar is found mostly on the outside of the canine, pre-molar and molar teeth at the junction of the tooth with the gum. The gum over a period of time recedes from the tooth; eventually the tooth becomes loose and falls out.

TEETH PROBLEMS

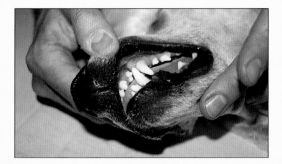

A rotated upper incisor tooth

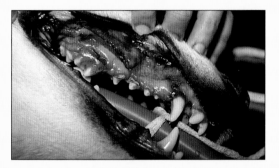

Plaque and tartar on teeth

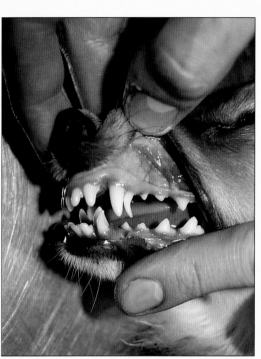

A permanent canine erupting alongside a temporary tooth

Undershot jaw

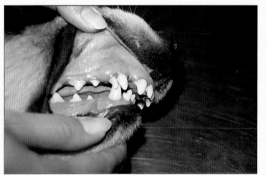

Overshot jaw

Signs: Drooling saliva, bad breath, reluctance to eat hard food, difficulty closing the jaw if tartar build up is excessive and rubbing the mouth on objects or with a paw.

If you pull the lips back, you notice a yellow brown scum or a hard, cement like brown substance stuck to the canine, premolar and molar teeth at the tooth–gum margin. The odour from the mouth is offensive.

Treatment: See your veterinarian who will give the dog a general anaesthetic, provided it has not eaten or drunk for eight hours and will remove the plaque and tartar with an ultrasonic scaler. After all the tartar is removed, the teeth are polished to provide a smooth surface which slows down the re-formation of plaque.

The teeth cannot be scaled properly unless the dog is anaesthetised. If the gums are inflamed or infected (gingivitis) they are treated at the same time. After the tartar is removed, the teeth are inspected and any loose, decayed or broken teeth are extracted.

Cavities caused by decay are not common. If a tooth cavity is extensive, extraction is the preferred method, otherwise the cavity can be filled.

Prevention: The dog's diet should include:

• dry dog food—its hard crunchy nature has an abrasive effect on the teeth helping to remove some of the plaque;

• strips of meat—so that the dog has to chew the meat into

suitable sized pieces for swallowing;

• bones with meat on them—to encourage chewing. This is likened to a person eating an apple; it has a cleansing effect on the teeth and massaging effect on the gums.

The temperament of some dogs will allow you to clean the teeth using your finger covered with gauze dabbed in bicarbonate of soda. Rub the tooth firmly, concentrating on the area of the tooth near the gum. Some dogs may allow you to use a child's toothbrush. Dogs will not tolerate the taste or foaming action of toothpaste.

No matter what you do, eventually the plaque and tartar will build up so that a check up by your veterinarian every six to 12 months followed by ultrasonic scaling if necessary is the best way to maintain the health of your dog's teeth and gums.

VACCINATION PROGRAMME

Young puppies are temporarily protected for a maximum period of 16 weeks against many diseases by the antibodies received through their mother's first milk (colostrum). The young puppy will respond to vaccination when these maternal antibodies decline to a sufficiently low level. The decline may occur at any time in the six to 16 week period after birth. The time of decline varies from puppy to puppy even if they are from the same litter.

The only effective method of preventing your puppy from catching a viral disease is vaccination.

Vaccines stimulate the puppy's immune system to produce antibodies against specific viruses. The antibodies remain in the bloodstream for varying periods of time; it is important that regular booster vaccinations are given throughout the dog's life.

Vaccination at six to eight weeks, 12 to 14 weeks and 16 to 18 weeks of age will ensure that the puppy is protected over that period.

About 50 per cent of puppies have low levels of maternal antibodies at six to eight weeks of age. If these puppies are not vaccinated until they are 16 weeks of age, they will have no protection against the viruses from approximately six to 16 weeks of age, and they run the risk

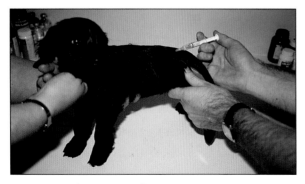

A young puppy having its vaccination

of catching a viral infection unless they can be completely isolated from other puppies or dogs during that period.

Immunity after vaccination may take up to ten days to develop.

VACCINES

CANINE DISTEMPER VACCINE

This is a modified live virus vaccine.

Vaccination procedure

Puppies: Vaccination at six to eight weeks, 12 to 14 weeks and 16 to 18 weeks.

Adults: An annual booster vaccination.

Bitches: Vaccination of pregnant bitches with modified live virus vaccine is not recommended. A bitch that has a regular annual booster vaccination before pregnancy occurs will produce a high level of antibodies in the first milk (colostrum). Providing the pups suckle soon after birth, they will have strong temporary immunity.

Modified live measles virus vaccine is an alternative to the modified live distemper vaccine—to be given to puppies at six weeks of age. The modified live measles virus vaccine has been used for many years with variable degrees of success. This vaccine is not recommended for use in puppies over 16 weeks of age and should not be used in breeding bitches.

If the live measles virus vaccine is used at six weeks of age, it should be followed by the modified live distemper virus vaccine at 12 and 16 weeks of age to provide good immunity against the distemper virus.

INFECTIOUS CANINE HEPATITIS

There are two types of this vaccine, either killed or modified live virus. The latter acts more quickly to give protection and immunity lasts longer.

In the past, a small percentage of dogs given the modified live virus vaccine developed a blue haze of the cornea (surface of the eye). Certain manufacturers claim that their vaccine does not cause blue eye.

Vaccination procedure

Puppies: Vaccination with either killed or modified live virus vaccine at six to eight weeks, 12 to 14 weeks and 16 to 18 weeks.

Adults: An annual booster vaccination with either killed or modified live vaccine. Modified live vaccine is not recommended for use in pregnant bitches.

CANINE PARVOVIRUS

There are two types of this vaccine, killed or modified live virus. It is suspected that the protection from the killed vaccine may only last for six months.

Vaccination procedure

Puppies: Vaccination with either killed or modified live vaccine at six to eight weeks, 12 to 14 weeks, and 16 to 18 weeks.

Adults: An annual booster with the modified live vaccine or a six monthly booster if the killed vaccine is used.

The use of modified live vaccine for pregnant bitches is not recommended. An annual booster with the modified live vaccine before pregnancy occurs should provide breeding bitches with a high antibody level in the first milk (colostrum). Providing the puppies suckle soon after birth, they will have a strong temporary immunity.

CANINE PARAINFLUENZA VIRUS

This virus is commonly known as kennel cough. The vaccine is a modified live virus.

Vaccination procedure

Puppies: They are given the modified live vaccine at 12 to 14 weeks, and 16 to 18 weeks.

Adults: Adult dogs should be given a booster vaccination annually. It is not recommended for use in pregnant bitches.

A secondary infection caused by the bacteria *Bordatella bronchiseptica* often occurs with the parainfluenza virus.

A bordatella vaccine is available and can be given at the same time as the parainfluenza vaccine.

LEPTOSPIROSIS

This disease can be dangerous to humans. Dogs living in areas where domestic and wild animals are known to have the disease should be vaccinated.

The vaccine is a killed form of the bacteria.

Vaccination procedure

Puppies: Vaccinated at nine, 12 and 15 weeks of age.

Adults: An annual booster vaccination.

RABIES VACCINE

Rabies is a viral disease of warm blooded animals and is transmitted by biting. It can be transmitted to humans by a bite from a rabid dog. The disease in most cases is fatal.

Rabies occurs worldwide except in Australia, Ireland, Japan, the Netherlands, Norway, New Zealand, Sweden and the UK.

The vaccine is a modified live virus which is not available in countries that do not have the disease.

Vaccination procedure

Puppies: Vaccinate at three to four months of age.

Adults: Booster vaccination at 12 months of age, then once every three years.

TETANUS VACCINE

Tetanus is not common in dogs, therefore they are not routinely vaccinated. The disease is caused by a bacteria, *Clostridium tetani*. There is a killed vaccine, Tetanus toxoid, which can be administered to pups older than four months. Two vaccinations a month apart then a booster annually is necessary for protection.

WORMS AND WORMING

All dogs have worms, and puppies have a higher worm burden than mature dogs. Worms in dogs can be transferred to humans and may be dangerous. It is very important to ensure that your dog is worm free, not just for the dog's health but also for the health of yourself and family, especially young children.

The dog is subject to many types of worms. The four most common intestinal worms are discussed in this section. For Heartworm, a parasite of the heart and blood vessels, see p. 152.

HOW DOGS GET WORMS

ROUNDWORM

Orally: Puppies less than three months of age can swallow eggs which develop into larvae in the small intestine. The larvae migrate through the intestinal wall, liver, and diaphragm, into the lungs, where they pass up the trachea and are swallowed back down into the stomach and thence to the small intestine where they develop into a mature worm. This process takes approximately five weeks.

Dogs older than three months develop an immunity which prevents the larvae from developing into mature adults. The larvae lie dormant in the dog's tissues.

Through the mother's uterus: Some dormant larvae in the bitch's tissues become active in the last two weeks of pregnancy, and penetrate the uterus to infect the unborn puppies. The puppies can have adult round worms in the intestine as early as three weeks of age.

Through the mother's milk: Some dormant larvae in the mammary glands become active and are ingested by the pup when suckling milk from its mother.

Through the mother cleaning the pups: The mother licking and cleaning the pups swallows larvae which develop into mature worms. The adult worms produce eggs which are passed in the mother's droppings, contaminating the immediate area, and are a source of infection to the pups. Infestation of the bitch with adult worms does not last for any length of time because of the immunity the bitch has developed.

From vermin: Rats or mice which have dormant larvae in their tissues are a source of infection if eaten by a dog.

COMMON TYPES OF WORMS				
WORM		LENGTH	COLOUR	SHAPE
Roundworm	Toxocara canis	10–18 cm	White	Slender, with tapered ends
Hookworm	Ancylostoma caninum Ancylostoma braziliense Uncinaria stenocephala	10–20 mm	White	Thin, with tapered ends
Whipworm	Trichuris vulpis	4–7 cm	White	Whiplike—named after its shape
Hydatid tapeworm	Echinococcus granulosus	5 mm	White	Flat with a broad tail segment
Flea tapeworm	Dipylidium caninum	(i) Up to 50 cm	White	(i) Flat, made up of segments
		(ii) 5 mm segments	White	(ii) Segments look like flattened grains of rice.

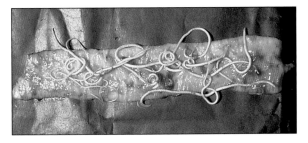

Roundworm in intestine

From the contaminated environment: The adult female roundworm produces large numbers of eggs. When shed into the environment, they can survive for many months.

HOOKWORM

Orally: The eggs or larvae are swallowed and attach themselves to the mucous membrane lining the small intestine and develop into an adult worm within two to three weeks.

Through the skin: The larvae penetrate the skin and migrate through the tissues to the small intestine.

From the mother's milk: Some dormant larvae in the mammary glands become active and are ingested by the pup when suckling milk from its mother.

Through the mother's uterus: Some dormant larvae in the mother's tissues become active during the latter stages of pregnancy and penetrate the uterus infecting the unborn puppies. The puppies can have adult hookworm as early as two to three weeks of age.

From vermin: Rats or mice which have dormant larvae in their tissues are a source of infection if eaten by a dog.

From a contaminated environment: The adult female hookworm produces large numbers of eggs which can survive for months when shed into the environment.

WHIPWORM

Orally: Eggs are picked up from a contaminated environment or hair while grooming and are swallowed. The eggs develop into larvae penetrating the small intestine and they migrate to the large intestine and mature into adults. This process takes about three to four months.

From a contaminated environment: Eggs shed into the environment can last for years.

TAPEWORM

There are five species of dog tapeworm. The two that occur most commonly and are of major importance to humans are the flea tapeworm and the hydatid tapeworm.

FLEA TAPEWORM

Orally: Tapeworm segments contain eggs which are released when the segment ruptures or disintegrates in the intestine, around the dog's anus or in the environment.

Flea larva ingest the tapeworm eggs. The flea larva develops into an adult flea which if caught by the dog and swallowed, is digested freeing the tapeworm egg. The egg develops into a mature tapeworm in the intestine. Puppies four to six weeks of age can have mature tapeworms.

HYDATID TAPEWORM

Orally: The adult tapeworm in the dog sheds eggs in the dog's faeces. Eggs ingested by sheep, goats, cattle, pigs and kangaroos develop into small cysts, penetrate the mucous membrane lining the intestine and are carried via the blood stream to the liver and occasionally to the lungs or brain where they develop into hydatid cysts.

The dog becomes infected by eating uncooked offal infected with hydatid cysts. Each cyst can produce vast numbers of adult worms in the dog's intestine.

TYPES OF WORMS AND HYDATID TAPEWORM LIFECYCLE

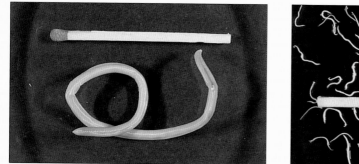

Roundworm

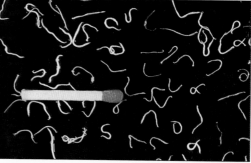

Hookworm

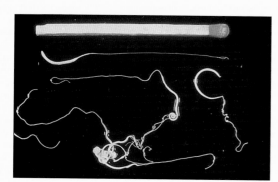

Whipworm

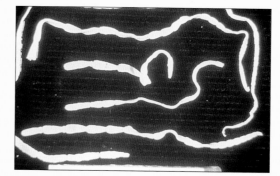

Tapeworm

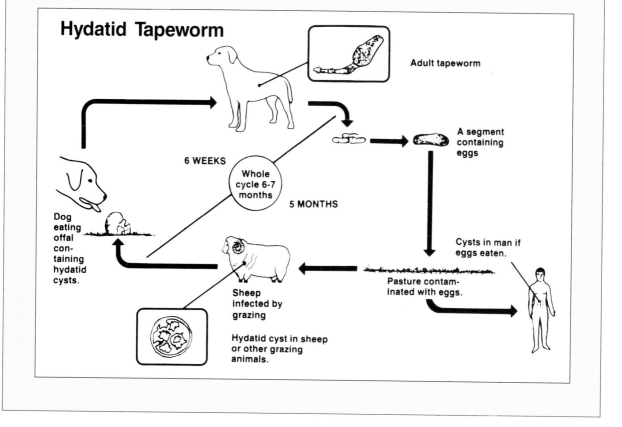

Hydatid Tapeworm

Adult tapeworm

A segment containing eggs

6 WEEKS

Whole cycle 6-7 months

5 MONTHS

Dog eating offal containing hydatid cysts.

Cysts in man if eggs eaten.

Pasture contaminated with eggs.

Sheep infected by grazing

Hydatid cyst in sheep or other grazing animals.

ROUNDWORM AND FLEA TAPEWORM LIFECYCLES

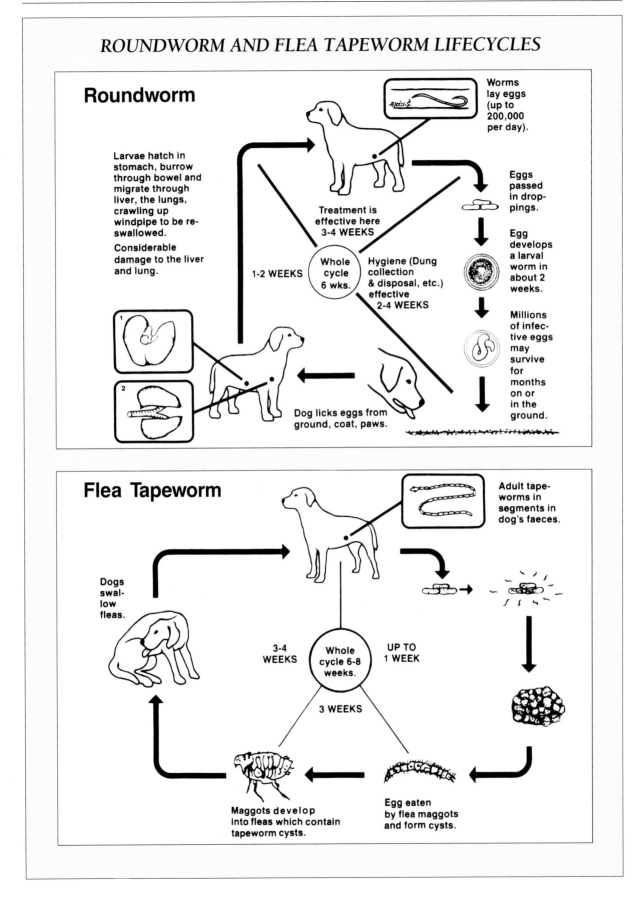

Roundworm

Larvae hatch in stomach, burrow through bowel and migrate through liver, the lungs, crawling up windpipe to be re-swallowed.

Considerable damage to the liver and lung.

Worms lay eggs (up to 200,000 per day).

Treatment is effective here 3-4 WEEKS

1-2 WEEKS

Whole cycle 6 wks.

Hygiene (Dung collection & disposal, etc.) effective 2-4 WEEKS

Eggs passed in drop-pings.

Egg develops a larval worm in about 2 weeks.

Millions of infec-tive eggs may survive for months on or in the ground.

Dog licks eggs from ground, coat, paws.

Flea Tapeworm

Adult tape-worms in segments in dog's faeces.

Dogs swal-low fleas.

3-4 WEEKS

Whole cycle 6-8 weeks.

UP TO 1 WEEK

3 WEEKS

Maggots develop into fleas which contain tapeworm cysts.

Egg eaten by flea maggots and form cysts.

WHIPWORM AND HOOKWORM LIFECYCLES

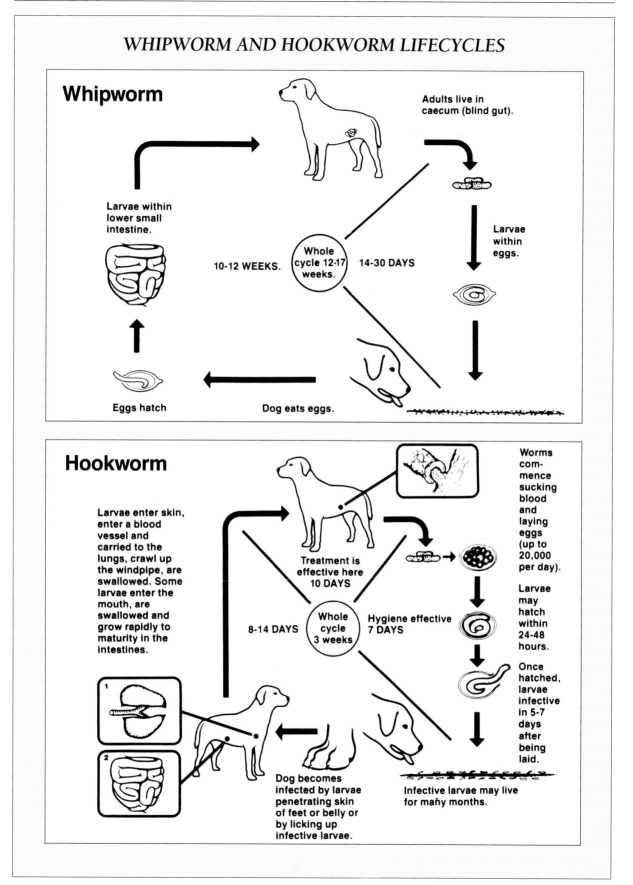

Whipworm

Adults live in caecum (blind gut).

Larvae within lower small intestine.

Larvae within eggs.

Whole cycle 12-17 weeks.

10-12 WEEKS.

14-30 DAYS

Eggs hatch

Dog eats eggs.

Hookworm

Larvae enter skin, enter a blood vessel and carried to the lungs, crawl up the windpipe, are swallowed. Some larvae enter the mouth, are swallowed and grow rapidly to maturity in the intestines.

Worms commence sucking blood and laying eggs (up to 20,000 per day).

Larvae may hatch within 24-48 hours.

Once hatched, larvae infective in 5-7 days after being laid.

Treatment is effective here 10 DAYS

Whole cycle 3 weeks

8-14 DAYS

Hygiene effective 7 DAYS

Dog becomes infected by larvae penetrating skin of feet or belly or by licking up infective larvae.

Infective larvae may live for many months.

The hydatid tapeworm causes little damage to the dog but it creates a problem and can cause economic repercussions if it is found in the offal or carcase of intermediate hosts such as sheep, cattle or pigs which must be condemned. If humans ingest hydatid tapeworm eggs, cysts can develop which may be life threatening (see p. 96).

SIGNS OF WORMS

These are fairly obvious and include weight loss, pot belly, dull harsh coat, inflamed skin, poor appetite, tail rubbing, anal scooting along the ground, lethargy, abdominal pain, diarrhoea, anaemia (pale mucous membranes around eyes and gums), coughing, and in heavy worm infestations, you may observe worms in the dog's faeces or vomit.

Signs or symptoms alone do not necessarily indicate that a dog has worms. Numerous other health problems, such as poor nutrition, teeth and gum problems, may give rise to similar symptoms. Even healthy-looking dogs may have worms.

WORM EGGS

The female round, hook and whip worm lay eggs in the intestine of the dog, and they are passed into the environment via the dog's faeces. The mature tapeworm segments contain eggs which are released when a segment ruptures or disintegrates in the intestine or in the environment. Each of these four types of worms—round, hook, whip and tape—has a distinct type of egg so that the egg found in the faeces indicates the type of worm in the intestine. Also, the number of eggs found in the faeces gives an approximate indication of the number of worms in the intestine.

In the case of tapeworm infestation, look for segments in the faeces or in and around the dog's anus.

Worm eggs are microscopic, and positive diagnosis can only be made in the veterinarian's laboratory.

TREATMENT

If you suspect your dog has worms, there are various courses of action that you can take.

• Seek your veterinarian's advice and diagnosis on the signs and symptoms evident in the dog.

• Have the dog's faeces tested in the veterinarian's laboratory to find out if your dog's condition is due to worms. If worms are present, your veterinarian can identify them, give an estimate of the number present, and prescribe appropriate treatment.

• Worm the dog with a worm preparation and wait to see if it improves. This is not as advisable as the two previous approaches because it may take some time before you can expect a change, and during that time your dog's condi-

tion may deteriorate if its condition is due to some cause other than worms.

METHODS OF WORMING

Palatable worm syrup is usually used with young puppies, three to six weeks of age, because it is easier to administer than other worm preparations. Worm syrups containing pyrantel cover round and hook worm which are common to young puppies.

Worm syrup can be mixed with the food or milk or put directly into the mouth.

Tablets when put in the food either whole or crushed, are often rejected. In most cases, you can assume that the dog has not eaten the tablet and therefore is not wormed.

Placing a tablet over the back of the tongue is a quick, direct and effective method (see Administration of medication, p. 117).

Bear in mind that whatever the method you have chosen to administer the worming preparation, it does not automatically follow that the dog is worm free.

• Some worms have developed a resistance to certain worming preparations.

• Worming preparations are only effective against adult worms. The migrating, immature larvae in other areas of the body at the time of worming are not affected and consequently mature into adult worms.

• A worming preparation may be very effective against one type of worm and partially or not at all effective against other types.

WORMING PROGRAMME

Start worming the puppies at two, four, eight and 12 weeks of age, then again at four, five and six months. Worm the mother when the puppies are two and four weeks of age. The reason for worming puppies so frequently is because they usually have a heavy worm burden and numerous migrating larvae. The repeated worming kills not only the adult worms in the intestine, but also those that develop from the migrating immature larvae.

Once the puppy is older than six months of age, worm it every three months throughout its life. Make sure you use an effective worming preparation. If you follow this worming programme, you can assume that your dog is worm free and is therefore healthy and poses no threat to the health of yourself or your family.

A worming preparation that is effective against all intestinal worms should contain Praziquantel, Febantel and Pyrantel Embonate.

Bitches should be wormed two weeks before going to a breeding establishment for mating, two weeks before whelping and two and four weeks after whelping.

This is to ensure the bitch is worm free and to

help prevent the puppies being infected by the bitch.

Dogs going to a boarding establishment should be wormed two weeks before boarding and two weeks after returning home.

WORM PREVENTION

Take the following precautions against worms:

• Remove the faeces daily from the dog's environment, burn or wrap securely and place in the rubbish bin.

• Wash the dog thoroughly and groom it regularly to minimise accumulation of worm eggs in the dog's coat.

• Clip the hair away from the anus of longhaired dogs to minimise contamination of the hair with faeces and worm eggs.

• Avoid crowding too many dogs in one area. Overcrowding results in heavy contamination of the environment with worm eggs, greatly increasing the risk of infection and reinfection.

• Keep your dog(s) flea free, as the flea plays a part in the tapeworm lifecycle (see p. 96).

• Restrict your dog's hunting drive and eradicate rodents. This will help to prevent hook and round worm infection.

• Roundworm and hookworm eggs can survive for long periods in moist, warm surroundings. In a breeding or boarding establishment, runs with a concrete base that can be thoroughly cleaned and kept as dry as possible will help to prevent infection or reinfection.

RISK TO HUMANS

The usual worms that infect humans, especially children, are not to be confused with dog worms.

Humans can pick up the dog's roundworm eggs from the environment or from the dog's contaminated hair and transfer the eggs via their unclean hands to the food that they place in their mouth. The roundworm eggs are swallowed and develop into larvae in the human's intestine. The larvae migrate through the intestinal wall into the liver or lungs and may stay there. In small numbers they may not cause any obvious damage but in large numbers the damage caused to the liver or lungs could be quite severe. Whilst it is rare, larvae migrating to the optic nerve of the eye have been known to cause blindness in that eye. The migrating larvae of the roundworm in humans are known as visceral larvae migrans. Migrating larvae in humans are not affected by routine worming preparations.

Hookworm larvae can penetrate the skin causing it to become red and itchy. This condition is more common in humans in tropical areas.

Flea tapeworm is not uncommon in children and is due to the accidental ingestion of fleas. It is not particularly dangerous.

It is thought that whipworm is not a risk to humans, although it is not certain.

The adult hydatid tapeworm is not a problem in Britain; it occurs mainly in Australia and New Zealand. It has little effect on the dog, but it poses a serious threat to humans, especially those living in rural areas. Dogs in rural areas are more exposed to uncooked offal. Eating offal infected with hydatid cysts can produce vast numbers of adult worms in the dog's intestine which in turn produce thousands of worm eggs that pass out in the dog's faeces. Humans accidentally and unknowingly ingesting hydatid tapeworm eggs, can develop cysts in the liver, lung or brain which may be life threatening.

To prevent hydatid tapeworm:

• worm the dog every six weeks with a preparation containing Praziquantel;

• never allow dogs to eat offal, especially sheep offal which is the most common source of infection;

• dispose of any sheep carcases or offal by burning or deep burying;

• prevent country and farm dogs from roaming and scavenging;

• feed dogs commercial canned and dry food;

• wash hands thoroughly after touching dogs and before eating or handling food.

In general, to minimise the risk to humans associated with dog worms, take the following precautions:

• worm dogs frequently with correct worming preparation (see Methods of worming, p. 100);

• do not fondle dogs with the face or kiss them;

• thoroughly wash your hands after handling, cuddling or caressing dogs and before eating or handling food;

• keep dogs out of bedrooms and kitchens;

• practise strict flea control on the dog and in the environment;

• wear shoes when walking on soil contaminated by dog faeces.

Humans, especially children, are susceptible to some dog worms.

WHEN TO CALL YOUR VETERINARIAN

Call immediately—Call same day—Wait 24 hours before calling

For dog owners who are uncertain about when to call their veterinarian, the following information will serve as a guide.

CALL IMMEDIATELY

- *Birth difficulties*

    No pup appears after straining for 30 minutes; if after straining for a period of time, the bitch gives up; if part of a pup appears, e.g. head, but nothing else appears after 20 minutes of straining.

- *Burns*

    Often difficult to assess the depth and extent.

- *Choking*

    Appears distressed; extends head and neck; salivates; coughs; paws at the mouth.

- *Collapse or loss of balance*

    Overreaction to external stimuli; depression; staggering/knuckling over; walking in circles; down/unable to get up; general muscle tremor; rigidity; paddling movements of legs; coma.

- *Continual straining*

    Attempting to defaecate (pass a motion) or urinate with little or no result.

- *Difficulty in breathing*

    Gasping; noisy breathing; blue tongue.

- *Heavy bleeding*

    From any part of the body; will not stop; apply pressure to stop the bleeding on the way to the veterinarian.

- *Injury*

    Severe continuous pain; severe lameness; cut with bone exposed; puncture wound especially eye, chest or abdomen.

- *Itching*

    Continual uncontrollable scratching, biting, tearing at the skin; skin broken and bleeding.

- *Pain*

    Severe, continuous or spasmodic.

- *Poisoning*

    Chemical, snake, spider or plant—retain for veterinarian to identify type of poisoning.

- *Urine*

    Obvious blood in the urine.

- *Vomiting and/or diarrhoea*

    Evidence of blood; putrid, fluid diarrhoea.

CALL SAME DAY

- *Abortion*
- *Afterbirth*

    If retained for eight hours.

- *Breathing difficulties*

    Laboured breathing; rapid and shallow breathing with or without cough.

- *Diarrhoea*

    Motion fluid and putrid.

- *Eye problems*

    Tears streaming down cheeks; eyelids partially or completely closed; cornea (surface of eye) cloudy, opaque or bluish-white in colour.

An eye injury

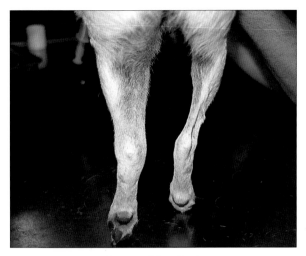

A hot, painful swollen leg

• *Frostbite and/or hypothermia.*

   Low body temperature usually associated wlth sub-zero temperatures.

• *Injuries*

   Not urgent, but liable to become infected; a cut through full thickness of skin which needs stitching; puncture wound in leg or head; acute sudden lameness.

• *Itching*

   Self mutilating; biting; scratching; hair loss; skin red and inflamed.

• *Mismating*

   Termination of an unwanted pregnancy can be done safely and harmlessly within 24 hours after intercourse.

• *Not eating*

   Depressed; in conjunction with other signs such as laboured breathing, diarrhoea, lying down, pain.

• *Swallowed object*

   Better to assess early, rather than wait until a possible life threatening situation develops.

• *Swelling*

   Hot, hard and painful or discharging.

• *Vomiting*

   Evident on a number of occasions; associated with some other symptom such as lethargy.

WAIT 24 HOURS BEFORE CALLING

• *Diarrhoea*

   No indication of abdominal pain; no sign of blood; no straining.

• *Itching*

   Moderate; no damage to the skin by self-mutilation.

• *Lameness*

   Ability to bear weight on leg; not affecting eating or other functions.

• *Not eating*

   No other sign or symptom.

• *Odour*

   Unpleasant odour, other than a soiled coat.

• *Vomiting*

   On two or three occasions; no other symptoms.

These Basset Hounds are enjoying the outdoors.

Opposite: A German Shepherd

FIRST AID

*First aid kit—Approaching, handling and assessing an injured dog—Allergic reaction
Resuscitation—Bleeding—Choking—Fish hook in lip—Fit or convulsion—Fracture
Heatstroke—Hypothermia—Paint on coat—Poisoning—Puncture wound—Shock
Snake bite—Spider bite—Tick poisoning*

Injury and accidents to dogs appear to be fairly common, possibly because of their inquisitive nature and exuberant approach to life, often disregarding any danger.

FIRST AID KIT

- Antibiotic powder
- Antiseptic wash (e.g. chlorhexidine)
- Hydrogen Peroxide 3%
- Mercurochrom
- Paraffin oil
- Roll of cotton wool
- Roll of adhesive bandage 2.5 cm (1 in) wide
- Roll of gauze bandage 2.5 cm (l in) wide
- Scissors
- Thermometer
- Tincture of Iodine
- Tweezers

APPROACHING AN INJURED DOG

Approach an injured dog with caution as a dog frightened or in pain can give you a nasty bite.

Before handling the injured dog check to see if:

- it is conscious or not;
- there is any obvious blood on the dog or ground nearby;
- there are any obvious wounds or broken bones;
- its breathing appears to be normal or laboured, rapid and shallow;
- it shows an aggressive reaction to your approach.

HANDLING AN INJURED DOG

If the dog shows no reaction to your approach, rub the back of your hand behind its ears and then turn your hand to take a good handful of the scruff of the neck. This grip gives you good control of the dog, particularly its head, and prevents you from being bitten when moving it.

A pressure bandage applied to control bleeding from the ear.

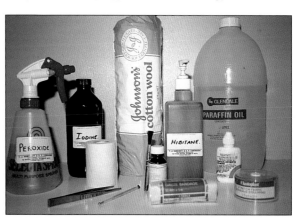

A first aid kit

If the dog reacts to your approach by growling or snarling, or drawing away with its ears back, do not touch it. Instead, to stop the dog biting you, make a muzzle with about one metre (3 ft) of any material suitable to make a strong loop (e.g. tape, gauze bandage, tie, nylon stocking). With the material make a closed loop with a half knot—continue talking reassuringly to the dog—then quickly slip the loop over the dog's muzzle and pull it tightly so that the half knot of the loop is on the top side of the nose. With each hand holding an end of the material make

*Opposite: Injury and accidents seem to beset dogs, possibly because of their inquisitive
nature and exuberant approach to life, often disregarding any danger.*

107

MUZZLING A DOG

Step 1: Make a closed loop with a half knot and slip over the dog's muzzle.

Step 2: Make another closed loop with a half knot and pull tightly so the half knot is under the jaw.

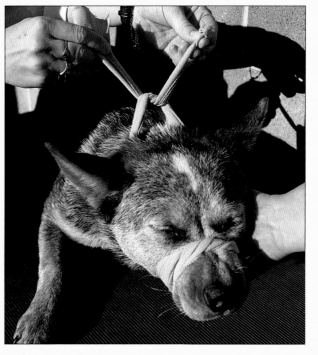

Step 3: Complete the muzzle by tying in a tight bow behind the dog's ears.

another closed loop with a half knot, slip it over the dog's muzzle, and pull it tightly so that the half knot is under the jaw. Complete the muzzle by tying the two ends of the material in a tight bow (for quick release) behind the dog's ears.

This will enable you, with the help of an assistant if necessary, to lift the dog into the car without being bitten, and to take it to your veterinarian.

If you are unable to put the dog in the passenger section of the car, it is all right to put it in the boot where it will not suffocate nor cause any injury to the driver or passengers if it panics.

ASSESSING THE INJURED DOG

Look at the colour of its gums. If pale or white, the dog is probably suffering from shock or blood loss. Take the dog to the veterinarian immediately. If the gums are pink, it is a good sign that there is no major blood loss externally or internally.

Carefully run your free hand over the dog's body, looking and feeling for a wound, swelling or painful area. Check the movement of the limbs and note if there is pain, swelling, a grating sensation, a floppy limb irregular in appearance, or the dog itself cannot move one or more limbs. These indicate that the limb, pelvis or spine may be broken (fractured) or the joint dislocated. In such cases, or if the dog is unconscious, take it to the veterinarian.

If everything seems to indicate that the dog is sound, prop it up on its four legs and encourage it to walk. If it flops down; walks on three legs and carries the fourth; limps; staggers; refuses to move; cries frequently as if in pain; or breathes in a laboured, panting fashion; wrap the dog in a blanket to keep it warm and to counteract shock, and take it to your veterinarian immediately.

ALLERGIC REACTION

Being inquisitive, dogs usually investigate something moving in the garden with their nose or front paw. In the event of a bite or sting, the first thing you will notice is a swollen face or paw and the dog rubbing its face with its paw or against some object. If the paw is swollen, the dog may bite it to relieve irritation. Usually it is difficult to determine what caused the allergic reaction. If the dog is not distressed and the swelling is small and local, investigate the swollen area for a sting or bite mark and apply a commercial preparation such as calamine lotion. If the swelling is extensive and the dog is distressed, take it to your veterinarian.

RESUSCITATION

If the dog is in a state of collapse, not breathing, and perhaps has a blue tongue, apply resuscitation.

• Check the mouth for any food or foreign body obstructing the airway. If the dog is small, take it by the hindlegs, hold it upside down and shake it vigorously to dislodge the obstruction. Lay a large dog on its side and check the mouth; use your fingers or a pair of long nosed pliers to clear any obstruction.

• Turn the dog on its right side, tilt its head backwards, and keep its mouth closed.

• Place a piece of cloth (handkerchief) over the dog's nose. This allows the air to pass through, but is more cosmetically acceptable to the operator.

• With your mouth to the nose of the dog, breathe quickly into the nose five times.

• If breathing restarts, keep the dog under observation.

• If breathing does not resume, check the dog's heartbeat by placing your thumb on one side and fingers on the other side of the chest just below its elbow.

• If heartbeat present, keep applying mouth to nose resuscitation at the rate of one breath every three seconds (20 breaths to the minute) until breathing is restored.

• If heartbeat absent, apply cardiac compression. If the dog is small, place thumb and fingers as formerly described. If the dog is large, place the heel of your hand over the dog's heart just behind its elbow. The force of the compression should be sufficient to massage the heart but will vary in relation to the size of the dog.

• If one person present, give 20 cardiac compressions followed by two breaths into the nose. Repeat at rate of four sequences per minute.

• If two persons present, one gives six cardiac compressions followed by the other giving one mouth to nose breath. This synchronised sequence is repeated at the rate of 12 sequences per minute.

• Check the heartbeat after one minute, then after every two minutes. If the heartbeat returns but breathing is absent, continue with mouth to nose resuscitation until breathing is restored.

If breathing and heartbeat do not resume after ten minutes and the gums and tongue are blue, the pupils of the eyes are dilated, and there is no blinking of the eyes when the cornea (surface of the eye) is touched with the finger, the dog is dead.

BLEEDING

Do not panic and just stand and watch a dog bleed to death. Immediately apply direct pressure on the wound and stop the dog from moving around.

If the dog is bleeding freely from a wound, two persons are needed to assist. One to take hold of the dog firmly, the other to control the haemorrhage (bleeding).

If the blood is slowly oozing from the wound, apply direct pressure to the site by means of a piece of clean gauze or sheeting held between the fingers. Don't dab or wipe the wound; this tends to promote further bleeding. Hold the pressure on the wound for ten seconds, then remove the hand holding the gauze or sheeting and evaluate the depth and breadth of the wound. If the bleeding recommences apply further pressure.

If the blood is flowing freely, take a wad of gauze or suitable absorbent material and apply heavy pressure to the wound with your clean hand. If you press too hard the dog may resent it. Over the wad of gauze wrap firmly, but not too tightly, a 2.5 cm (1 in) wide adhesive bandage and

CONTROLLING BLEEDING

This dog is bleeding freely from a wound

Apply heavy pressure with gauze wad.

Firmly apply adhesive bandage.

leave it in place for about 30 minutes. Remove the bandage and evaluate the wound. Do not use cotton wool as small, fine fibres tend to collect in the wound, acting as a foreign body and slowing down the healing process.

In cases of arterial bleeding, the blood is normally bright red and spurts out with a pulsating action. Apply heavy pressure with gauze in hand directly over the site of the bleeding. Then wrap a 2.5 cm (1 in) wide adhesive bandage tightly around the gauze. Not only does the bandage apply pressure, but it also immobilises the edges of the wound, thereby helping to stop bleeding. Keep the dog calm and quiet, preferably wrapped in a blanket. Leave the bandage in place and take the dog to your veterinarian.

If the blood is coming through the bandage, do not remove it; apply more adhesive bandage over the top.

If the dog is bleeding from an inaccessible area such as inside the nostrils, restrict its movement then apply cold to the area in the form of ice packed in a towel or some suitable container. When a pressure bandage to control haemorrhage of a limb is left on for any length of time, always check the limb below the bandage. If it is swollen, cold to the touch or does not react to pain when pinched then remove the bandage immediately and if necessary apply a new bandage less tightly.

Tourniquets are not recommended. They are often difficult to apply and, if applied incorrectly, can accentuate rather than retard blood loss.

CHOKING

If the dog is choking, one or more of the following signs may be evident:
- retching;
- mouth open (dog does not appear to be able to close it);
- saliva dribbling from the mouth;
- dog clawing at the mouth with its front paws.

These signs often indicate that a foreign body is stuck in the throat, or across the roof of the mouth and between the teeth. If the dog is breathing reasonably freely, take the dog to your veterinarian immediately.

If the dog is on the verge of collapsing and its tongue is going blue, wedge something (e.g. the rubber handle of a screwdriver) between the molar teeth on one side of the mouth. Quickly inspect between the teeth, the roof of the mouth and in particular the back of the throat for a foreign body. With your fingers or a pair of long nosed pliers, carefully pull the tongue out. This may reveal a foreign body over the back of the tongue. Remove it with the pliers or, if the dog cannot close its mouth and bite your finger, get your finger behind it and lever it out. The same applies to a foreign body in the roof of the mouth.

If you are unable to remove the foreign body, and providing that you can lift the dog, take hold of its

Bleeding from the nose

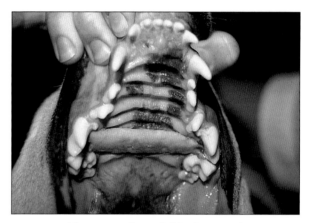

A bone across the roof of the dog's mouth

hindlegs to hold it upside down. Shake it vigorously to dislodge the foreign body and clear the airway. This action often stimulates the dog to breathe. If its tongue is still blue, apply artificial resuscitation (see p. 109).

FISH HOOK CAUGHT IN THE LIP

Do not try to push or pull the hook. If the dog is quiet and the barbed end of the hook is protruding through the lip, seek the help of an assistant who will hold the dog by the scruff of the neck to control movement of the head. With a pair of pliers, cut through the hook between the barb and the skin, allowing the rest of the hook to be removed relatively easily.

If the dog is agitated or the barbed end of the hook is embedded in the lip or mouth, seek veterinary assistance.

If you notice a fishing line or thread disappearing into the dog's mouth, open the mouth, and if it appears to disappear over the back of the tongue, pull the line or thread gently. If it will not budge, do not persist with the pulling and do not cut the line or thread. The line could be very useful to the veterinarian to locate the hook or needle and assist in its removal. Take your dog immediately to your veterinarian.

FIT OR CONVULSION

Usually the dog is lying on its side unconscious, paddling with its legs, champing its jaws, frothing at the mouth and twitching. Though you may be concerned that the dog will swallow its tongue, do not try to take hold of it, as you may be badly bitten by the unconscious dog champing its jaws. Observe the dog, but do not touch it. Touching the dog while it is having a fit may aggravate and prolong the fit. Usually the fit lasts for a minute or two and then the dog recovers, although it may seem a little disorientated temporarily. Once it has recovered, make an appointment to see your veterinarian.

If the dog continues fitting beyond five minutes, take the dog to your veterinarian immediately. If there is a break in between fits, pick up the dog holding it by the scruff of the neck with one hand, supporting its body with the other hand. Place it gently into the car quickly and quietly. If the dog is impossible to handle, call your vet.

FRACTURE

The majority of fractures (broken bones) in the dog involve the limbs, pelvis, lower jaw or spine.

To avoid being bitten when handling a dog with a fracture, try not to increase any pain or trauma it may be suffering (see p. 107).

Because the limbs are angular, particularly the hindlimbs, it can be difficult to apply a splint to immobilise the fractured limb and to prevent pain and further damage.

When a dog fractures a limb it usually holds the leg off the ground indirectly immobilising and protecting it.

The sudden onset of one or more of the following signs may indicate a fracture:

• swelling;

• pain;

• holding the limb off the ground;

• limb at an odd angle;

• collapsing in both hindlimbs, but able to move them;

• unable to move the hindlimbs and no response to pinching the toes (indicates spinal injury).

Fracture of a limb

Be careful when handling a dog with a fractured limb as it may bite because it is in pain (see p. 107).

If a forelimb or hindlimb is fractured, pick up the dog by placing one hand under the neck and the other hand under the abdomen. This method enables the dog to be lifted without causing further hurt to the fractured leg.

Fracture of the spine

If the dog cannot use its hindlimbs and there is no pulling away of the limbs when pinching the toes, suspect a middle to lower spinal injury.

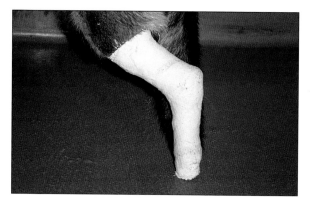

Plaster cast on a fractured hindleg

If the dog cannot use the forelimbs and/or hindlimbs and there is no response to pinching the toes, suspect a neck injury.

If the dog is lying quietly, place a flat board beside it. Take the dog by the scruff of the neck and gently pull it on to the board. If a board is not available, place a blanket beside the dog and gently pull it by the scruff of the neck onto the blanket. With a person holding each corner of the blanket, it can be used as a sling to lift and carry the dog.

Transport the dog to the veterinary hospital with minimal movement of its spine to prevent any further damage to the spinal cord.

MOVING AN INJURED DOG

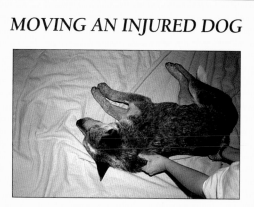

Gently pull the dog onto a blanket by the scruff of the neck.

Use the blanket as a sling to lift the dog.

If the dog cannot use its hindlimbs, but is trying to drag itself around using its forelimbs, restrain it by holding and talking to it or by placing it in a suitable box.

HEAT STROKE

Dogs can only regulate their body temperature by panting; they have no sweat glands. They are inefficient at getting rid of body heat, especially in hot weather; whereas they are efficient at retaining body heat and can tolerate very cold conditions.

The common causes of heatstroke are being locked in a car in very hot weather or confined in a poorly ventilated area and left in the sun.

The signs of heatstroke in the dog are:

• panting with mouth open gasping for air;

• distressed;

• often unable to stand;

• moving about in an agitated and uncontrolled fashion;

• gums are deep red.

Immediately cool down the dog by wetting it thoroughly with cold water and placing it in front of a fan or air conditioner. When the dog appears to have recovered, remove it from in front of the fan and place it in a cool, shady area with easy access to water.

If the dog after ten minutes does not appear to be responding to treatment, contact your veterinarian. Prolonged heatstroke can lead to coma and death or brain damage.

Do not leave your dog confined in a poorly ventilated area in summer, e.g. in a car. In very hot weather provide the dog with a cool, shady area and access to water.

LOW BODY TEMPERATURE
(HYPOTHERMIA)

In cold conditions, a healthy dog should not suffer from hypothermia. It is mainly seen in the newborn, geriatric or sick dog (see Care of newborn puppies, pp. 191, 196).

PAINT ON THE COAT

It is important to remove paint from the dog's coat, otherwise it will more than likely lick the hair and ingest some of the paint.

Water-based paints while still wet can be removed from the coat by thorough rinsing with water.

Oil-based paints while still wet can be very carefully wiped from the surface of the coat using a cloth dampened with the appropriate paint solvent, e.g. turpentine. *Under no circumstances allow the solvent to contact the skin.* Immediately after wiping the paint off the hair, wash the affected area with warm water and soap and rinse thoroughly to get rid of the solvent, otherwise it will inflame the skin causing the dog to scratch violently and lick it

vigorously, with the possibility of being poisoned (see Poisoning, below).

If the oil or water-based paint has dried, remove it by carefully cutting away the affected hair.

POISONING

Many dogs are not very careful about what they eat and they tend to gulp their food down rapidly. Consequently, they are susceptible to being poisoned by eating a bait, i.e. food which has been deliberately laced with a poison with the intention of killing the dog.

Because of their inquisitive and hunting nature, dogs are also likely to be bitten by poisonous snakes or spiders. Dogs can be inadvertently poisoned by deliberate or accidental contamination of their coat with insecticides, disinfectants, paint, tar and other toxic substances. The poison may be absorbed through the skin or by ingestion when the dog cleans itself by licking its coat.

The fact that many dogs spend much of their life confined to their owner's home reduces their exposure to many poisons, although there are numerous household disinfectants, cleaning agents, insecticidal sprays, herbicides and pesticides which, if ingested, are highly poisonous. Fortunately most of these products are unpalatable and it is very unlikely that the dog would ingest them.

Most countries have poison information centres with information on hundreds of thousands of potentially poisonous substances. Always have a contact phone number listed in an accessible place in case of emergency.

If your dog is ill, you can only suspect the dog is poisoned unless you have actually observed the dog eating, drinking or coming into contact with a poisonous substance.

GENERAL RULES FOR
TREATMENT OF POISONING

1. Initiate treatment immediately you are sure that the dog has been poisoned.

2. Induce vomiting if:

• **you are sure** that the dog has eaten some poisonous substance;

• **you are sure** the poisonous substance is not petrol, kerosene, turpentine, alkali or acidic cleaning fluids, or corrosive material such as paint thinners;

• **the dog is conscious and able to vomit** (if the dog is semi-conscious or unconcious when induced to vomit, it may inhale some of the vomitus into the lungs causing death by asphyxiation or by inhalation pneumonia).

• Induce vomiting by administering:

10–20 ml (2–4 teaspoons) of salt solution (3 teaspoons of salt to half a cup of warm water); or

Syrup of Ipecac. Average adult dog dosage is 2 ml per kg (2.2 1b) of the dog's body weight.

3. If the hair and skin is contaminated with a poisonous substance, wash the dog with warm water and soap. Then rinse the dog thoroughly and repeatedly with water.

4. If the dog is convulsing intermittently, wait until it stops then carefully pick it up by the scruff of the neck with one hand and support it under the chest and stomach with the other hand. Take it to your veterinarian immediately.

5. If the dog is convulsing continuously, try to protect the dog from injuring itself and phone your veterinarian. Be careful to avoid being bitten.

6. Contact your veterinarian and take the dog there as quickly as possible. Take the container of suspected poison with you to aid in identification of the poison and antidote.

Recovery depends on the type of poison, amount of poison in the body, the period of time lapsed after poisoning and before treatment is started, and whether or not a specific antidote is available.

PUNCTURE WOUND

Dogs fighting may bite one another and inflict a puncture wound with their canine teeth. The common sites for puncture wounds are the neck, limbs and back.

If you hear or see your dog fighting, check your dog carefully, feeling and looking for a puncture wound, a painful spot, or blood matted in the hair. Invariably, these puncture wounds become infected because of the large number of bacteria in the dog's mouth. Often the puncture wound looks clean and neat whereas the tissues under the skin can be badly torn, and smouldering with infection.

If you find a puncture wound, carefully clip the hair away from the hole, clean the area with 3% peroxide and dab the wound with tincture of iodine. If the puncture penetrates through the full thickness of the skin into the tissues underneath then take your dog to your veterinarian. He will treat the dog with an antibiotic to clear up the infection and prevent it developing into a more serious infection or abscess.

SHOCK

Shock is a term used to describe a state of collapse following many forms of serious stress such as a car accident, massive haemorrhage, heavy fall, overwhelming infection (septicaemia), intussusception (intestinal blockage) and dehydration. The symptoms can vary depending on the cause and may include depression, prostration (lying down), rapid breathing, pallor of the gums and conjunctiva (membrane around the eye), and cold to the touch.

Take the dog to your veterinarian immediately, but in the meantime:

• keep the dog warm, but not too warm (maintain the normal body temperature; warmth can be overdone, accentuating the shock if the dog becomes too hot);

• control any bleeding (see p. 109);

• keep the dog calm and quiet.

SNAKE BITE

In most instances of snake bite, you will probably not see the dog get bitten and will not know if the snake was venomous or non-venomous. If you do witness it, try to visualise a good description of the snake or capture or kill the snake for identification purposes. In many cases of snake bite you will find the dog in a stunned state, staring with unblinking eyes and lying on its side or chest with little movement of its limbs. Take the dog to your veterinarian immediately.

In cases where you see the dog bitten on a leg, apply a broad bandage with firm pressure over the bite and about five centimetres either side of the fang marks. Keep the dog quiet and immediately take it to your veterinarian. The purpose of the pressure and immobilisation of the dog is to slow down blood flow from the site of the bite and to minimise spread of the poison.

Do not apply a tourniquet as they can be difficult to apply and if applied incorrectly, they can aggravate the problem. Do not cut the skin at the site of the bite as this will increase the blood supply to and from the bite, helping to spread the poison. If the dog is bitten in an area which cannot be readily bandaged (e.g. the face), apply ice to the site of the bite to constrict the blood vessels in the area and prevent spread of the poison. Take the dog to your veterinarian immediately.

There are anti-venoms available, some of which are effective against a number of different types of snake poisons. The veterinarian will treat the dog according to its symptoms.

SPIDER BITE

In most cases, you will not witness the dog being bitten by a spider. If in your presence the dog cries out, and appears to be in pain, and you see a spider in the vicinity of the dog, you may assume that it has been bitten. Collect the spider in a sealable container and take it with the dog to your veterinarian. The spider will be identified by the veterinary surgeon, and if it is a poisonous variety the dog will be kept under observation and treated according to symptoms as they develop.

If you are not aware of what has bitten your dog or even that it has been bitten, but you notice that it appears to be in a state of shock, take it to your veterinarian immediately.

TICK POISONING

(See p. 177.)

SPECIFIC TREATMENT FOR POISONS GENERALLY FOUND IN THE HOME AND GARDEN			
POISON	SOURCE	SIGNS	TREATMENT
Acids	Battery acids	Burns on skin and mouth; vomiting may contain blood; shock.	If on skin, wash with warm water and soap, and rinse thoroughly and repeatedly with water. If ingested **DO NOT** induce vomiting; give sodium bicarbonate in water and contact your veterinarian immediately.
Alcohol— Methylated spirits	Dog may be encouraged to drink alcohol.	Depression; wobbling; vomiting; collapse.	Give water; keep dog warm; contact your veterinarian.
Anti-freeze (Ethylene glycol)	Used in automobile radiators; some dogs like taste, will seek out and drink.	Wobbling; vomiting; depression; convulsions; coma.	If sure that dog has ingested anti-freeze, induce vomiting; take dog to your veterinarian who will inject ethyl alcohol to block effect of anti-freeze and administer further supportive treatment.
Arsenic (vermin, poisons, insecticides, herbicides)	Ingestion of grass sprayed or rodents poisoned with arsenical preparations; licking fur covered with insecticidal or herbicidal spray.	Salivating; thirsty; vomiting; fluid diarrhoea with blood; abdominal pain; collapse; death.	Induce vomiting in early stages (see p. 180); contact your veterinarian immediately who will administer antidote.
Aspirin (Acetylsalicylic acid)	Usually administered by owner without veterinary advice to alleviate pain or discomfort — a single large dose or a series of small doses can be poisonous.	Signs vary according to period of time during which dosage administered — include poor appetite; depression; pale gums; vomiting; blood-tinged vomitus; staggering; falling over.	If recently administered, induce vomiting; give sodium bicarbonate (baking soda) solution by mouth; contact your veterinarian.
Barbiturates, Sedatives, Anti-depressants	Sleeping tablets; valium.	Depression; wobbling; coma.	In early stages, induce vomiting; contact your veterinarian.
Benzine hexachloride (Lindane, Dieldrin, Aldrin, Chlordane, Gammexane)	Insecticidal rinse for dogs in concentrated form.	Agitated; restless; twitching; convulsions; coma; death.	If no sign of convulsions, wash with soap and water and rinse thoroughly; contact your veterinarian.
Carbon monoxide	Automobile exhaust fumes — dog exposed to fumes if kept in garage.	Legs wobbly; breathing difficult; gums and mucous membrane around eyes (conjunctiva) bright pink.	Remove dog from poisonous environment to fresh air; if unconscious, give artificial respiration (see p. 109); contact your veterinarian immediately who can administer oxygen directly to lungs with an endotracheal tube and give a respiratory stimulant.
Chlorine	Concentrated powder or tablet used in swimming pools — chlorinated swimming pool water is not poisonous.	Weeping red eyes; salivating; red mouth; ulcerations of mouth and tongue; vomiting; diarrhoea.	Rinse eyes and mouth with water; encourage dog to drink water; contact your veterinarian.
Kerosene	Heating fuel and cleaning fluid has a burning effect on dog's skin; dog licks affected area, thereby ingesting kerosene orally.	Red, inflamed skin; vomiting; diarrhoea; possible convulsions; inflamed and ulcerated tongue.	Wash the dog's skin with soap and water; give it 20-30 ml (2 tablespoons) of olive oil; contact your veterinarian.
Lead	No longer used in paint manufacture, but some old houses still covered with lead paint; soil around lead mines polluted with lead; dog becomes poisoned by licking its coat contaminated with lead.	Poor appetite; weight loss; vomiting; anaemic; diarrhoea. Depending on degree of lead poisoning, dog may show signs of hyperexcitability, convulsions, depression, blindness, paralysis, coma.	Lead poisoning shows up over a period of time; consult your veterinarian who will confirm lead poisoning by a blood or urine test and will treat your dog with an antidote as well as for any presenting symptoms.

SPECIFIC TREATMENT FOR POISONS GENERALLY FOUND IN THE HOME AND GARDEN			
POISON	SOURCE	SIGNS	TREATMENT
Metaldehyde	Snail and slug poison in powder or pellet form; dogs like the taste and actively seek it out.	Tremor; salivation; diarrhoea; wobbling; convulsions.	If dog observed at time of ingestion, induce vomiting; contact your veterinarian immediately; recovery rate very good.
Oil, grease	Dog lying under a motor vehicle or accidentally falling into a container.	Covered in grease or oil; depressed.	Wash with warm water and soap; if unable to remove oil or grease, see your veterinarian.
Organo-phosphate carbamate	Snail and slug poison in pellet form; some dogs like the taste and will actively seek it out.	Tremor; salivation; diarrhoea; wobbling; convulsions.	If observed at time of ingestion, induce vomiting; contact your veterinarian immediately; recovery rate very good.
Paracetamol	Household pain reliever; may be administered to dog by owner.	May appear hours to days after ingestion. Include lethargy; gums may range from pale (anaemic) to yellow (jaundiced) to bluish; difficult breathing; swelling of lips and face.	Induce vomiting if recently ingested; contact your veterinarian.
Phenol (carbolic acid)	A potent disinfectant; poisonous to dogs by ingestion or absorption through skin; after skin contact, dog may ingest by licking the contaminated hair and skin.	Dog smells of phenol; vomiting; diarrhoea; severe abdominal pain; shock; collapse.	Remove phenol from hair and skin with soap and warm water; give 20–30 ml (2 tablespoons) of olive oil by mouth; contact your veterinarian.
Strychnine	Rat poison; often used deliberately to poison animals with a bait.	Restless; twitching; general stiffness; convulsions with head and neck arched and limbs stretched out; convulsion can be set off by a touch or noise, become continuous, followed by death.	If dog has ingested strychnine, but shows no symptoms, induce vomiting immediately. If showing symptoms, take to veterinarian immediately. In transit, do not touch dog or make a noise. If dog dies, strychnine can be confirmed by chemical analysis of stomach contents.
Thallium	Rat, cockroach and ant poisons; dog can be poisoned by eating poisoned rat.	Vary according to amount ingested and period of time it is in dog's system. Redness of skin followed by a crust, peeling, and hair loss; starts on ears and lips, progresses to head, feet, limbs and body. Further symptoms are weight loss; vomiting; diarrhoea; wobbling; convulsions.	Veterinarian can confirm by testing for thallium in urine. If dog has just swallowed thallium, induce vomiting; see your veterinarian who will administer a drug to bind thallium and prevent its absorption through intestine.
Turpentine (turps)	Paint solvent, wrongly used to remove paint from dogs hair or to dab on tick embedded in skin. Never use turps on dog's hair or skin as it can poison by absorption through skin.	Red, inflamed skin; dog vigorously licks skin affected by turps; vomiting; diarrhoea; abdominal pain; restlessness; hyperexcitable; wobbly, coma.	Wash skin and hair with soap and water, rinse thoroughly; see your veterinarian.
Warfarin	The dog may eat the poison itself or eat a dead rat that has been poisoned with warfarin, which stops blood from clotting.	Lethargy; pale gums and membrane around eye; weakness; laboured breathing; may be signs of haemorrhage in gum tissue; collapse; death. Signs may be slow to develop and vary according to time and amount ingested.	If recently ingested, induce vomiting; treat for shock (see p. 113); see your veterinarian who can administer an antidote; recovery rate very good.

ADMINISTRATION OF MEDICATION

*Palatable tablets, powders and granules—Liquids—Pastes
Eye ointments and drops—Ear drops—Injections*

There is nothing more worrying and frustrating than your dog refusing to take its medication. If the medication is not administered correctly, the dog's condition will not improve and may even worsen, and in most cases the medicine is wasted. If the dog's condition is serious and you find it impossible to administer medication to the dog, call your veterinarian who will medicate the dog in a professional manner. If the treatment needs to be given frequently, it may be preferable to hospitalise the dog.

Whether the medicine is given orally, by stomach tube, or by injection, depends upon the type of medicine and its palatability, the condition and temperament of the dog, and the temperament of the owner.

The following is a guide on how to administer medication efficiently and successfully.

PALATABLE TABLETS, POWDERS AND GRANULES

With the food: Dogs are very suspicious of any foreign materials, such as tablets, that are introduced into their food. There are chewable tablets, powders and granules that are flavoured to make them palatable. These can be hand fed or mixed thoroughly in the food.

UNPALATABLE TABLETS

Via the mouth and over the back of the tongue: Most tablets are unpalatable, so it is reasonable to assume that if you place one (whole or crushed) into the food, the dog will avoid eating it. The surest way of knowing the dog is getting the tablet is to place it over the back of the tongue. Before you can do this, however, you must know how to open the dog's mouth.

Opening the dog's mouth

Move the dog into a small room such as a laundry and shut all the doors. If the dog is small, put it up on a bench at a comfortable height. If you cannot open the dog's mouth by yourself get someone to hold the dog firmly to stop it moving away from you.

Take hold of the dog's upper jaw between your fingers and thumb. Tilt the dog's head back so that it is looking towards the ceiling. Using the middle finger of your other hand, press the lower jaw down to open the mouth wider. Do not try to open the mouth too wide as the dog will become distressed.

Placing the tablet in the mouth and over the back of the tongue

1. Using a pill popper: With the tablet placed in the pill popper, quickly and smoothly pass it into the back of the mouth and press the plunger to release the tablet over the back of the tongue. It is important to release the tablet over the back of the tongue. If it is put on the front of the tongue the dog will spit the tablet out. The most common cause of failure is due to not putting the tablet far enough over the back of the tongue. Do not be afraid of pushing the tablet into the windpipe because once you push a tablet into the back of the mouth it triggers off a swallowing reflex. Keep the dog's head tilted so that it is looking at the

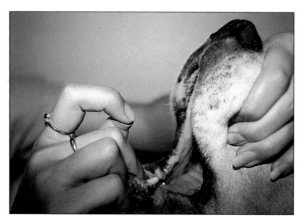

Administering a pill using the fingers

ceiling. When you see the dog lick its upper lip with its tongue, the tablet has been swallowed.

2. Using the fingers: With the tablet between your thumb and index finger, open the mouth wider by pushing the lower jaw down with your middle finger. Drop the tablet onto the back of the tongue, then with your index finger quickly push the tablet over the back of the tongue. Remove your finger before the dog closes its mouth. Keep the dog's head tilted back until the tablet is swallowed. Massaging the throat will stimulate swallowing.

3. Using a spoon: Place the tablet on a teaspoon and open the dog's mouth wider by inserting the spoon into the mouth and pressing firmly down on the lower jaw. Push the spoon into the mouth, tilting it to release the tablet onto the back of the tongue. Then use the spoon to push the tablet over the back of the tongue. Keep the dog's head tilted back until the tablet is swallowed.

LIQUIDS

Hold the dog's upper jaw with one hand and tilt it slightly backwards so that the liquid will run towards the back of the throat rather than towards the open mouth (lips). Holding a syringe or eye dropper in the other hand, slowly dribble the liquid directly onto the tongue. If the dog does not swallow, tilt the head back a little more and dribble more liquid onto the tongue. If you tilt the head back too far, the liquid may flow into the windpipe causing the dog to cough and splutter.

Alternatively, tilt back the dog's head, hook your finger into the corner of its mouth and pull the cheek out slightly to form a pocket. Slowly dribble the liquid into the pocket allowing sufficient time for the dog to swallow.

If the taste of the liquid is unpleasant, the dog may salivate profusely, causing saliva with most of the liquid to dribble out of the mouth.

Using a stomach tube: Stomach tubing an adult dog should be left to your veterinarian as it takes professional knowledge, skill and restraint. For stomach tubing puppies, see Orphan puppies (p. 193).

PASTES

Paste usually comes in a syringe. You can administer the paste directly from the syringe onto the tongue. The paste adheres to the surface of the tongue and is swallowed. If it is unpalatable, the dog will salivate, causing a mixture of paste and saliva to pour from the mouth.

EYE OINTMENTS AND EYE DROPS

Generally, two people are required: one to hold the dog, the other to administer the medication. If the dog is held too tightly, it will struggle and may become aggressive. If held too loosely, it will tend to move about and escape

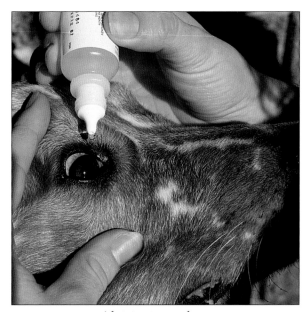

Administering eye drops

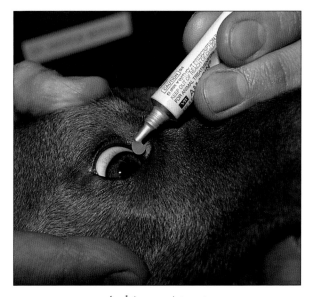

Applying eye ointment

from your grasp. The person holding the dog should tilt the head back slightly. The person administering the drops holds the eyelids apart with the index finger and thumb and puts two eye drops directly onto the eyeball. Keep the head tilted back for 20 seconds, otherwise the dog will drop its head forward, the eyedrops will roll out and be wasted.

Many eye ointments are designed to be solid at room temperature and to melt at body temperature. Pull the lower lid down with the thumb and lay a strip of eye ointment inside the lower lid along its full length. Then close the eyelid and the ointment will melt forming a film over the eyeball and conjunctiva. Alternatively, pull the upper eyelid up and lay the ointment under it.

EAR DROPS

One person holds the dog firmly while the other person administering the drops takes hold of the ear with the index finger and thumb of one hand and pulls it towards the other ear. This helps to open up the inside of the ear and makes the opening of the ear canal obvious. Squeeze four to six drops into the ear canal. Continue to hold the ear tightly, otherwise the dog will shake its head vigorously spraying the drops everywhere. With your free hand massage gently below the ear to work the drops down the ear canal.

If the dog is fidgety, do not worry about trying to count the drops, just put the nozzle of the container in the ear canal and give it a squirt. Stop when you see the drops starting to well up out of the dog's ear canal.

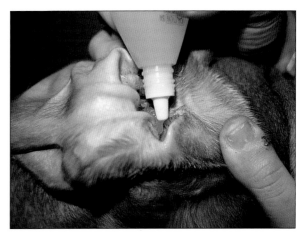

Administering ear drops

INJECTIONS

Some drugs can only be administered by injection. It is almost impossible to administer drugs to some dogs orally because of their temperament; injection is a viable alter-native. Because of the serious nature of their illness, some dogs respond better and more quickly if the drug is administered by injection.

Take your dog to your veterinarian who will administer the injection quickly and efficiently.

A Shetland Sheepdog and her pups

DISEASES AND HEALTH PROBLEMS A–Z

General signs of illness—Specific diseases and health problems A–Z
Causes—Signs—Treatment—Prevention

Dogs are creatures of habit and any variation or departure from their normal habits should be viewed with suspicion. It is advisable to develop the habit of following a routine checklist in assessing your dog's health. In doing so, you may become aware of a health problem in its early stages, which you may be able to treat, or if not, to refer the problem to your veterinarian before it becomes too serious.

GENERAL SIGNS OF ILLNESS

A health checklist should at least include the following:

ACTIVITY

Dogs range from being slow and languid to being very active and alert. Observe what is the norm for your dog. If it is normally very active and suddenly one day it is inert and lying around, indications are that something is wrong. If your dog is normally lethargic, it may be difficult to pinpoint its inactivity as indicating something is wrong.

APPETITE

Loss of appetite is one of the first signs of illness. If your dog has eaten very little compared with what it usually eats or has not eaten anything at all, try to find a logical explanation for it before calling your veterinarian. Keep in mind that some dogs can be fussy about their food so check its palatability and whether or not there has been any change in quality or type. If your dog continues to be off its food for 24 hours and you cannot find any logical explanation for it, call your veterinarian.

COAT

A dog's coat will vary according to its breed, the time of year, housing, grooming and washing.

If the coat is dry, harsh, broken, sparse, mottled, patchy, matted, knotted, or wet in a local area because of excessive licking, it is usually a sign of illness.

CONDITION (WEIGHT)

A dog's condition (weight) varies with diet, exercise and breed. Condition can also vary within a breed: some dogs may be well muscled, others may be fat or thin. A thin dog is not necessarily an unhealthy one. A dog on the same ration doing the same amount of exercise will remain at a certain weight for years. If suddenly or over a short period

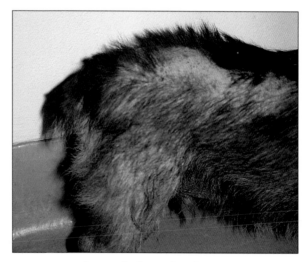

A sparse, broken and patchy coat.

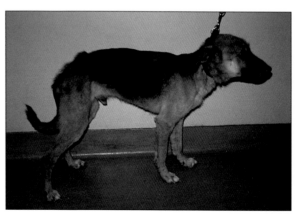

Severe weight loss

of time it loses weight, the change in condition should alert you to check the dog carefully.

Weight loss, especially in association with some other sign, such as poor coat, diarrhoea, poor appetite or lethargy, is indicative of a health problem.

DEMEANOUR

Demeanour in different breeds and in individual dogs varies tremendously. A sharp change in demeanour, such as from being quiet to excited, alert to dull, placid to aggressive or relaxed to restless, is a sign that should alert you to the fact that the dog may have a health problem.

DROPPINGS (FAECES)

Some dogs are modest about their toilet habits and you may never see them in the act of defaecating (passing their droppings) or any evidence of their faeces (droppings). If you happen to notice your dog defaecating, observe it and inspect the faeces.

If the faeces contain worms, mucus, blood, undigested food, or are small in volume, hard, fluid-like or black, white or yellow, then a health problem is indicated. If your dog is straining excessively for a lengthy period of time or more frequently than usual and is passing nothing or just some small amounts of hard faeces or fluid-like faeces, it is a sign of illness.

When female dogs urinate or defaecate they adopt the same position. This may mislead owners when they observe their dog straining frequently or for longer periods than usual. They may think their dog is constipated when in reality it has a bladder infection or perhaps a blockage of the urethra.

EARS

A health problem may be indicated if there is a sign of discharge, redness, swelling, scratching, rubbing, shaking, a heavy build up of wax from the ear, if the dog is holding its head to one side, or if one ear flops down when both ears should be erect.

EYES, NOSE, MOUTH

Call your veterinarian if:

• a discharge from these areas is excessive in volume and/ or yellow in colour;

• odour from the mouth is foul and offensive;

• the mucous membrane lining the eyes, nose and mouth (normally glistening pink in colour) is white, yellow, bluish or brick red.

RESPIRATION

Coughing or rapid, shallow, heavy or noisy respiration is abnormal and requires veterinary attention.

SKIN

The state of the skin may be a telltale sign of illness especially if it is broken, red, dry, scabby, scaly, tight when pinched or there is evidence of raised lumps.

TEMPERATURE

A normal thermometer can be used to take the temperature of a dog. Make sure you shake down the mercury before using it. Insert the thermometer for two-thirds of its length via the anus into the dog's rectum so that the bowl of the thermometer rests against the rectal wall. Leave the thermometer in position for approximately one minute.

If the dog's temperature is outside the range of 37.8° to 39.2° Celsius (100° to 102.5° Fahrenheit), contact your veterinarian.

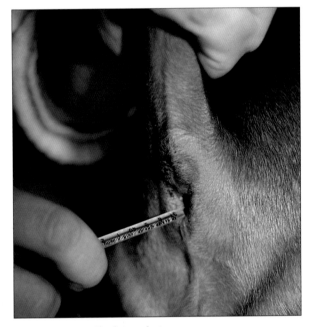

Checking a dog's temperature

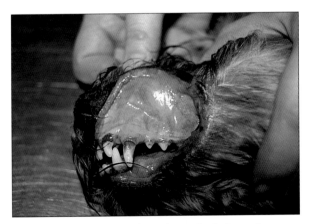

Yellow mucous membrane lining the dog's mouth

The third eyelid can been seen in the corner of the dog's eye.

THIRD EYELID

This is also known as the nictitating membrane. The third eyelid plays an important role in cleaning the surface of the eye (cornea). The Harderian gland, which is attached to the inside of the third eyelid, is part of the tear production system. For these reasons the third eyelid should only be removed as a last resort.

If you look carefully, the third eyelid, in most breeds, can only just be seen in the corner of the eye near the nose. In some breeds it cannot be seen at all and in other breeds, such as the Bloodhound, it is obvious.

Protruding third eyelids in both eyes often indicate that the dog is suffering from some generalised illness. A protruding third eyelid in one eye is usually indicative of a problem associated with that eye or it may be a congenital defect. The exposed border of the third eyelid is usually pigmented. Some dogs have the border pigmented in one eye and not in the other, giving the dog an asymmetrical look. This is no reason for concern.

URINE

A dog's urine is normally clear, colourless to yellow and of a water-like consistency.

If the dog is frequently straining to urinate and passes a little urine often or not at all, or if the urine is reddish brown or blood tinged, call your veterinarian.

If you suspect there is something abnormal with the urine, collect a sample if possible. Try sliding a clean flat dish (disposable) under the dog. Pour the urine sample into a clean screw top jar and keep it in the refrigerator. Take the dog and sample along to the veterinarian as soon as possible.

SPECIFIC DISEASES AND HEALTH PROBLEMS A–Z

ABSCESS

An abscess is a collection of pus circumscribed in a sac enclosed within the tissues of the body.

Causes

Abscesses that can be seen or felt under the skin are caused in many cases by fights with another dog. A tooth penetrates the skin causing damage to underlying tissue. Bacteria are deposited in the tissue at the time of penetration. Foreign bodies such as a splinter of wood or grass seed are another common cause of abscesses in dogs. Sometimes dogs develop internal abscesses on the liver, lungs and elsewhere, following a generalised bacterial infection.

Signs

In the early stages, as the abscess forms, the swelling is diffuse, painful, hard, and may not be noticed. Often you are not aware that your dog has been in a fight unless you see a puncture wound or some blood on the hair. The first sign that you may be aware of is when handling the dog it cries or growls as a reaction to being touched on a painful spot. If you rarely touch the dog, the first sign observed may be a bloody, purulent discharge oozing into the hair and in some cases matting it.

As the abscess matures, it becomes more localised, softer, less painful, and forms a point. At this stage, when pressed by a finger, often it will leave momentarily a pit or indentation. Depending on the size and position of the abscess, the dog may be lethargic, off its food, and/or have a temperature.

Treatment

In the early stages, if a puncture site is obvious, thoroughly cleanse the wound with an iodine based scrub or 3% hydrogen peroxide, removing any dirt, debris or dead tissue. Check the wound to see that no foreign body remains embedded in it. Carefully cut the hair away from the opening.

Take the dog to your veterinarian who will administer antibiotics and recommend that you bathe the dog's wound with hot water that is as hot as you can tolerate with your hand. Hot bathe the area for ten minutes, twice daily, gently squeezing any discharge if present from the puncture hole. Any apparent swelling may disperse and disappear or it may form into a mature abscess, in which case return to your veterinarian.

After examination, the veterinarian will give the dog a general anaesthetic and open the abscess to drain out the pus as well as administering antibiotics. The wound should be kept open as long as possible to provide continuing drainage.

If there is a large pocket after the pus has been drained out, it should be irrigated twice daily by a syringe full of 3% hydrogen peroxide. Drainage can be aided by gently pressing from the outer extremities of the abscess towards the opening. This treatment should continue until the opening is almost closed.

Prevention

If your dog is aggressive and prone to fighting, your vet can give it an injection of medroxy progesterone acetate which helps reduce its aggressiveness for about five months. It has no sedative effect on the dog. Castration of male dogs helps to make them less aggressive.

The afterbirth is normally expelled with the birth of the puppy.

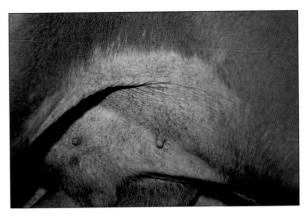

Allergic dermatitis on the abdomen

AFTERBIRTH
(PLACENTAL MEMBRANE)

The afterbirth is normally expelled with the birth of each pup or immediately after. Often the bitch will eat the afterbirth which does not seem to do her any harm, although in some cases it may cause a mild form of temporary gastroenteritis with symptoms of vomiting and diarrhoea.

If the afterbirth is not expelled within eight hours after the last pup is born, contact your veterinarian. If the retained afterbirth is obvious, it is usually removed by manually pulling on it with firm, even tension. If this fails, the use of a drug will be necessary to aid in the separation of the afterbirth from its attachments in the uterus. In this situation antibiotics are often administered to prevent infection of the uterus.

Allergic dermatitis around the lips

ALLERGIC DERMATITIS

Outdoor dogs, being what they are, come in close contact with their environment. Playing, rolling, wandering, investigating and sleeping, they come in contact with numerous types of vegetation. The primary contact points are the muzzle, feet, under the lower abdomen and the hairless area where the forelimb meets the chest.

Cause

Some dogs are allergic to certain types of vegetation at certain times of the year; usually in hot, humid weather when there is a flush growth of vegetation. In most dogs the area under the lower abdomen and in the groin are fairly hairless. Hair, like clothing, protects the skin, so those parts of the skin with less or no hair are more vulnerable. When the skin comes in contact with whatever it is allergic to, it becomes inflamed. This irritates the dog and as a result it bites, scratches, rubs and/or licks the area to get relief. The relief is short lived as the licking, etc., indirectly aggravates the skin which irritates the dog more, and so it continues to bite, scratch, rub and/or lick.

Allergic dermatitis on the toes

Raw, infected, ulcerated, bleeding skin around the eye

126

A vicious circle develops. The dog may rub against or roll on the vegetation to which it is allergic in order to gain relief. This is like pouring petrol onto a fire; it only worsens the problem.

Signs

- The skin at one or all of the primary contact points is inflamed.
- The dog is itchy.
- The dog loses hair.
- The skin may be raw, ulcerated, bleeding and infected.

Treatment

Try to identify what the dog is allergic to and remove it from the environment or keep the dog away from it.

Apply a soothing lotion (calamine) or an anti-inflammatory cream. Use with care, as the application of lotions or creams sometimes attracts the dog to lick the inflamed area.

Rub the cream in thoroughly and divert the dog's attention by feeding it, taking it for a walk, or playing a game with it.

If severe, see your veterinarian who may use antibiotics and cortizone to clear up any infection and to suppress the inflammation, thus stopping self-mutilation. An Elizabethan collar may also be helpful (p. 163).

ANAEMIA

Anaemia is not a disease; it is a symptom of some underlying cause. It is essential to find the causal factor(s) before treatment is initiated.

Anaemia is a decrease in the haemoglobin and/or red blood cells to below the normal level, thus reducing the oxygen carrying capacity of the blood.

Causes

- Haemorrhage—acute or chronic. Acute haemorrhage is

A pale conjunctiva indicating anaemia

due to internal bleeding from a ruptured blood vessel, an abnormality of the blood-clotting mechanism or external bleeding from a wound. Chronic haemorrhage may be due to blood loss associated with a blood-sucking parasite.
- Destruction of red blood cells, which may be due to infection.
- Depression of red cell production which is associated with chronic diseases, e.g. nephritis with uraemia, malignancies, nutritional deficiencies, poisons.

Signs

The colour of the tissue around the eye (conjunctiva), gums and tongue reflects the status of the red blood cells in dogs. The normal colour is pink; white indicates severe anaemia. In many cases the colour of the mucous membranes falls in the range from pink to white. In these cases a full blood count is essential. The purpose of the blood count is to:

- recognise the not so obvious anaemic dog;
- indicate the degree of anaemia;
- diagnose the cause.

Other signs of anaemia are lethargy, laboured breathing, restlessness, loss of appetite, loss of condition and a rough coat.

Treatment

The results of the blood count will determine the type of treatment to be given. The treatment, which will vary according to the cause and severity of the problem, is best left to your veterinarian.

Prevention

Some cases of anaemia can be avoided by good nutrition and a regular worming programme.

ANAL ADENOMA

This is an anal tumour usually seen in male dogs over seven years of age. Occasionally it is seen in neutered females.

Cause

Unknown, although the male sex hormone testosterone is implicated.

Signs

The tumour begins as a small firm round lump. Often as the tumour enlarges, its surface becomes ulcerated and may bleed. It is rarely malignant.

Treatment

Surgical excision of the tumour(s) as well as castration to prevent the tumour(s) recurring.

ANAL BLOCKAGE

This condition occurs most frequently in longhaired Toy breeds.

Cause

The dog passes soft or unformed faeces which stick to the hair immediately around the anus. The partially dried faeces matted in the hair forms a plug blocking the anus.

Signs

The dog attempts to defaecate frequently without success. The faeces matted in the hair produces a foul odour.

Treatment

This is a very unpleasant procedure. Take the dog outside and have somebody hold it while you try to break down the matted faecal mass. This is done by directing water from a hose onto the faecal mass and, at the same time, breaking it up with your hand protected by a glove.

If this procedure is unsuccessful, the faecal mass will have to be very carefully cut away with scissors. Cut only a few hairs at a time, otherwise you may cut the skin.

If you cannot manage the situation, see your veterinarian.

Prevention

Alter the diet to make the dog's faeces firmer. Regularly clip the hair around the anus.

ANAL FURUNCULOSIS

This disease is often referred to as Perianal fistula. It is seen most commonly in German Shepherds, four to eight years of age.

Cause

Unknown, although anal gland infection, chronic diarrhoea and the shape of the dogs anus are implicated.

Signs

- A raw, inflamed, swollen, ulcerated anus.
- Constant licking around the area.
- Pain, especially when passing faeces.
- The anus is often soiled with faeces.

Treatment

Surgical excision of the infected areas and removal of the anal glands.

ANAL GLAND (SAC) BLOCKAGE/INFECTION

There are two small glands either side and just below the anus. They are scent glands that produce a foul-smelling

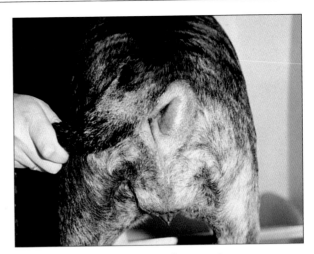

Swollen anal gland on one side

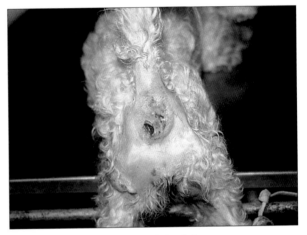

A ruptured anal gland abscess

fluid. The anal glands, as these small scent glands are known, may play a part in the 'communication system between dogs'.

The act of defaecating (passing a motion) also causes the foul-smelling scent or fluid to be discharged from the anal glands. This scent may serve a purpose in the dog's normal behaviour of marking its territory.

Cause

The opening of the anal gland sometimes becomes blocked and results in a build up of the fluid inside. The fluid may become infected or the pressure from it may cause irritation and inflammation.

Signs

Licking around the anus. Scooting along the floor or ground on the anus. Lying down suddenly, jumping up, running a few paces and then lying down again. Swelling of one or both anal glands. An anal gland abscess which is indicated by a red, painful swelling on one side of the anus, which may have ruptured to release a bloody fluid.

Treatment

Consult your veterinarian who will squeeze the discharge from the glands and administer, if necessary, an antibiotic injection to clear up any infection, and an anti-inflammatory injection to alleviate the irritation. If the ducts of the anal glands are blocked repeatedly then surgical removal of the glands is recommended. This operation can be performed readily without any adverse effect on the dog. Prevention can be partially achieved by feeding the dog on a diet whereby its motions are firm. The act of passing a firm motion causes fluid to be expressed regularly from the gland, thus helping to prevent the duct from becoming blocked. If you are so inclined, your veterinarian may show you how to express your dog's anal glands when there are signs of anal irritation.

ARTHRITIS

Arthritis is inflammation of a joint which is made up of bones, cartilage, ligaments and a joint capsule. The joint capsule produces fluid that lubricates the joint. Arthritis, which may be either acute or chronic, is common in dogs.

Causes

Inflammation of the joint is caused by:
• trauma that may be due to a fall, penetration by a foreign body, bite, or blow (e.g. motor vehicle accident);
• infection which may localise in the joint from a general infection or it may enter the joint through a wound;
• poor conformation placing abnormal stress on a joint;
• nutritional deficiencies such as lack of calcium;
• inherited conditions, e.g. hip dysplasia (see p. 155).

Signs

In acute arthritis all the signs of inflammation are evident. The joint is warm, painful to the touch and swollen. The dog limps or holds its affected limb off the ground. Acute arthritis may subside leaving a normal joint, or it may lead to chronic arthritis.

Chronic arthritis is associated with a joint that has been swollen for a long time. Compared with the acute form, the swollen joint is firm or hard, usually not warm to the touch, and not as painful. In many cases movement of the joint is restricted permanently. The dog will limp or hold its affected leg off the ground. If the arthritis involves joints in several limbs, the dog may move slowly and with difficulty and may also find it difficult to lie down and get up. There may be muscle wasting in the affected limb(s).

Treatment

Treatment varies according to the cause. Your veterinarian is best able to diagnose arthritis and pinpoint the cause. In many cases an x-ray needs to be taken. If an infection is present, antibiotics will be administered and hot and cold foments applied. Anti-inflammatory agents such as cortisone can be administered orally, intra-muscular or by direct injection into the joint, and may prove to be very effective.

If the dog is overweight, some reduction in weight may contribute to its improvement.

ASEPTIC NECROSIS OF THE HIP

The blood supply to the femoral head (ball of the hip joint) is impaired causing the head to undergo severe degenerative changes.

Causes

• Hereditary predisposition in Toy breeds.
• Injury to the hip.

Signs

Severe lameness, muscle wasting and restricted movement of the joint.

Treatment

Good results are achieved with surgical removal of the femoral head (ball).

ATRESIA ANI

Some puppies are born with no opening at the site of the anus.

Cause

It is a congenital condition.

Signs

The newborn puppies cannot pass any faeces. They show signs of constipation, abdominal pain and distension, become weak and refuse to suck.

Treatment

Urgent surgical correction.

BABESIOSIS

This disease is transmitted from dog to dog by certain species of ticks. Thus the disease is limited to regions where those ticks are found.

Cause

Babesia is a protozoan or single-cell parasite, microscopic in size. It attacks the red blood cells, destroying them and causing anaemia.

Signs

Anaemia (see p. 127), elevated temperature, jaundice, not eating, lethargy, vomiting and dehydration. The spleen and liver are often enlarged.

Blindness caused by cataracts

Blocked tear duct: tears streaming from inner corner of eye

Treatment

See your veterinarian who can confirm the dog's disease by microscopic examination of the blood. Treatment is effective.

Prevention

Babesiosis can be prevented by tick control (see Tick poisoning, p. 177).

BLINDNESS

Some dogs that are totally blind but live in familiar surroundings know their way around so well that their owners have no idea that they are blind and just regard them as clumsy.

Most blind dogs, providing they do not live in a dangerous environment and are confined to familiar surroundings, can lead a happy life.

BLOCKED TEAR DUCT

Tear ducts are located in the inner corner of the upper and lower eyelids and are connected to the nasal cavity.

Cause

The tear duct may be blocked by pus due to an infection or by being narrow or kinked. Certain breeds of dogs, such as Toy, Miniature Poodles and Maltese Terriers, are prone to blocked tear ducts.

Signs

Tears streaming from the inner corner of the eye. Often both eyes are involved. The hair on the face, either side of the nose, is continually wet leaving a reddish brown stain in light-haired dogs.

Treatment

Take the dog to your veterinarian who will put some fluorescent dye in the eye. If the tear duct is open, the dye will flow from the eye down the duct and appear at the nose within ten minutes.

Be careful to see that the dog does not lick away the dye when it appears at the nose. If the dye is not obvious at the nose, wipe the nose with a white tissue and check for a smear of dye. If there is none, probably the tear duct is blocked.

In these circumstances the veterinarian would give the dog a general anaesthetic and insert a fine cannula into the opening of the tear duct. A syringe containing saline solution would be connected to the cannula and the tear duct flushed out to remove the obstruction. Some tear ducts remain permanently blocked and cannot be cleared by flushing.

BLOOD CLOTTING DISORDER

This refers to a disorder of the clotting mechanism which leads to bleeding externally and/or internally.

Because of the many factors that go to make up the blood clotting mechanism, there are numerous types of blood clotting disorders.

Cause

A number of different breeds have developed genetically inherited blood clotting disorders as indicated in the following table.

Signs

Depending on the type of blood clotting defect, some dogs die at birth or shortly after. Others develop symptoms at various stages in their life and some recover if treated. Some dogs never show any signs of the disease, but carry the gene which is passed onto their progeny.

FACTOR DEFICIENCY IN BREEDS RELATED TO BLOOD CLOTTING DISORDERS	
FACTOR DEFICIENCY	BREEDS POSSIBLY AFFECTED
Factor I or Fibrinogen	St Bernard
Factor II or Prothrombin	Boxer
Factor VII	Beagle, Alaskan Malamute
Factor VIII or Haemophilia A	Brittany Spaniel, Bulldog, Chihuahua, Collie, German Shepherd, Golden Retriever, Greyhound, Irish Setter, Poodle, St Bernard, Samoyed, Beagle, Schnauzer, Sheltie, Weimaraner and Alaskan Malamute
Factor IX or Haemophilia B (Christmas Disease)	Cairn Terrier, Cocker Spaniel, Coon Hound, and St Bernard
Factor X	Cocker Spaniel
Factor XI	Springer Spaniel and Great Pyrenees
Von Willebrands Disease	Dobermann, German Shepherd, Golden Retriever, Miniature Schnauzer and Scottish Terrier

Note: The term 'haemophilia' refers to those disorders associated with a deficiency in Factors VIII or IX.

Dogs with a blood clotting defect may exhibit one or more of the following signs:

• bruising;

• bleeding internally or externally (there may be signs of haemorrhage in the mucous membranes of the gums and conjunctiva);

• bleeding from the umbilical cord in newborn pups;

• pups bleeding from the gums at the time of teething;

• excessive and prolonged haemorrhaging after surgery;

• anaemia, pale mucous membranes.

Treatment

See your veterinarian who can confirm a defect in the blood clotting mechanism by laboratory tests. Treatment will vary according to the type of defect.

Prevention

Avoid inbreeding and do not use dogs with blood clotting defects for breeding.

BLOOD DISEASES AND PROBLEMS

Anaemia (see p. 127)
Babesiosis (see p. 129)
Bleeding (see p. 109)
Blood clotting disorder (see p. 130)
Heartworm (see p. 152)

Haemorrhage of the conjunctiva

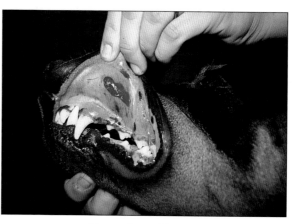

Haemorrhage of the gum

BONE DISEASES AND PROBLEMS

BRUCELLOSIS

This disease is the major cause of infertility in the male and female dog in the US. The particular bacteria causing the disease has not been isolated as a cause of infertility in dogs in Australia.

Cause

The bacteria *Brucella canis*. The most common method of infection is by sexual intercourse. It can also be spread by contact with infected secretions.

Signs

• A non-pregnant infected bitch may show signs of a temperature, swollen painful joints and enlarged lymph nodes. Some infected bitches do not exhibit any signs though they harbour the bacteria in the uterus and vagina.

• Pregnant or breeding bitches show signs of sterility. They may abort during the sixth to eighth week of pregnancy, or give birth to stillborn or weak, sickly puppies that die shortly after birth.

• An infected male dog may show signs of a temperature, swollen painful joints, enlarged lymph nodes and swollen painful testicles. Over a period of time, the testicles become hard, small, and not painful to touch. Sperm production is reduced or non-existent, rendering the dog infertile and a risk to any bitch with which it has intercourse. Some infected male dogs do not exhibit any signs of brucella infection. These dogs are called 'carriers' and usually harbour the bacteria in the prostate gland.

Treatment

Dogs can be positively diagnosed by a blood test done in your veterinarian's laboratory.

Long term treatment with antibiotics is often followed by a relapse, so that dogs which are positive to the blood test should not be used for breeding and should be removed from the breeding establishment and neutered.

Prevention

There is no effective vaccine currently available. Working stud dogs should be tested every three months. The owner of the stud dog should require a veterinary certificate from the owner of the visiting bitch to prove that the bitch has been tested and found to be free of brucellosis before mating.

CALLUSES

Calluses are usually a problem of big, heavy dogs that spend much of their day lying on hard, abrasive surfaces such as concrete or tiles.

The common sites are the elbows in the front legs, the lower thighs and hocks in the hindlegs and the buttocks.

Cause

Calluses form as a result of constant pressure and abrasion from lying on hard surfaces. The callus is nature's way of trying to protect bony prominences, such as the point of the elbow or hock, from being damaged. If you feel the point of the elbow, hock or pelvis you will find there is only skin with no padding of tissue covering the bone to protect it.

Signs

Thick, raised, hairless, dark grey-coloured skin covering the bony prominences. The calluses are very susceptible to infection as they become more raised. Infected calluses ooze serum via small holes or pustules on the surface.

Once the callus is infected, the dog usually licks it constantly.

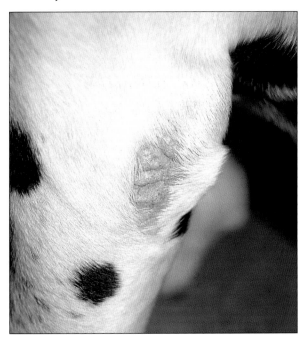

A callus on the elbow

Treatment

Provide a soft surface, such as a trampoline bed or rubber mat for the dog to lie on. If the dog chooses to lie on a hard surface, such as concrete, place the dog in an area where it has no choice but to lie on a soft surface. Applying padded bandages to the affected limb(s) is usually not successful.

Apply a moisturiser to the callus to keep the skin soft and supple and to help prevent it becoming infected. If infected, see your veterinarian who may prescribe antibiotics Infected calluses often do not respond well to conservative treatment and depending on their position may require surgical excision.

CANCER OF THE KIDNEY

If cancer is diagnosed in one kidney and it is a primary cancer which has not spread to other parts of the body, the kidney can be removed surgically. The dog can live a healthy, happy life with one kidney.

CANINE DISTEMPER

Distemper is a worldwide, highly contagious viral disease of dogs. It is sometimes referred to as Hard-pad disease. Other animals affected by the virus are the fox, dingo, wolf, coyote, skunk, mink, ferret and panda.

Spread of the virus need not be by direct contact from dog to dog. The virus can be spread through any discharge from the body: pus from the eyes and nose, urine and faeces or vomit. The distemper virus is similar to the human measles virus. Young puppies are most susceptible. The virus attacks cells of the skin, respiratory tract, intestinal tract and brain.

Pus discharge from both eyes

Cause

The distemper virus Paramyxovirus.

Signs

Signs of the disease vary according to the system affected by the virus. Signs of distemper develop six to nine days after exposure to the virus. Initially, the dog will have a high temperature which may fluctuate up and down every 24 to 48 hours. Lethargy, loss of appetite, vomiting, diarrhoea, watery discharge from the eyes and nose, which later changes to a green pus, coughing, dehydration. Red spots form on the skin which develop into pustules. These symptoms may continue for two to three weeks with the dog appearing to improve and then getting worse.

The nose and pads may become thickened, cracked and dry. Hence the name Hard-pad disease.

Some dogs, two to three weeks after the initial symptoms, show signs of encephalitis, such as twitching, jaw chomping, salivating, head shaking, fitting, blindness and paralysis. Most dogs which develop nervous disorders do not survive.

Treatment

Contact your veterinarian who will administer antibiotics, eye ointment, canine distemper antiserum, depending on the stage of development of the disease, and fluids to counteract dehydration. Good general nursing is recommended: clean the eyes and nose, protect the dog from the environment, and encourage food and fluid intake.

Few dogs survive; those that do may have brown stains on the teeth where the enamel has been eroded, a thickened, crusty nose and pads and/or a twitch which may be associated with other nervous disorders.

Prevention

Vaccination gives good protection against distemper. A vaccination programme (see p. 94) can start as early as six weeks of age. Annual booster vaccinations are recommended to give complete protection. Vaccination of breeding bitches prior to mating will help give the pups good temporary immunity up to at least six weeks of age.

CANINE PARVOVIRUS

This viral disease suddenly appeared worldwide in 1978. The symptoms in the dog are very similar to infectious (feline) enteritis in the cat. It is highly contagious and in many cases fatal, especially in puppies.

It can affect dogs of all ages but has a very high mortality rate in young puppies.

Cause

A virus which attacks both the gastro-intestinal tract and

the heart. It can be transmitted by direct contact or indirectly by contact with vomit, diarrhoea or any contaminated discharges from an infected dog. Contaminated cages and clothing are also sources of infection.

Signs

In puppies, the signs are a sudden onset of vomiting, bloody diarrhoea, dehydration and sometimes death. In adults, the symptoms are similar, although some cases are less acute.

The virus sometimes affects the heart muscle, especially of young puppies. The puppies may die suddenly or show signs of laboured breathing prior to death. Whole litters are involved and any survivors usually die months later from heart failure.

Treatment

See your veterinarian immediately. Antibiotics are of value to control the secondary bacterial infection which usually occurs with a viral infection. Antibiotics have no affect on viruses so the disease itself will run its course.

Your veterinarian will treat the dog according to its symptoms. Drugs to control vomiting and diarrhoea, and fluids given intravenously or subcutaneously to counteract dehydration may be administered. Good nursing is essential.

Prevention

The outcome of this disease is often fatal. Prevention by vaccination is essential (see p. 94).

There are two types of vaccine: killed or modified live virus. The latter acts more quickly to give protection and immunity lasts longer.

Vaccination procedure

Puppies: Vaccination with either killed or modified live vaccine at six to eight weeks, 12 to 14 weeks and 16 to 18 weeks.

Adults: An annual booster vaccination with either killed or modified live vaccine.

Breeding bitches: Vaccination of pregnant bitches using killed vaccine in the last third of pregnancy will produce high levels of antibody in the first milk (colostrum). Providing the puppies suckle soon after birth, they will have a strong temporary immunity. The use of modified live vaccine for pregnant bitches is not recommended.

CATARACT

A cataract is crystallisation of the lens of the eye causing the lens to become cloudy. Light eventually cannot pass through the cloudy lens to the retina at the back of the eye; this results in blindness.

A mature cataract is silvery white.

Causes

Congenital defects, injury, infection, chronic inflammation and diabetes are all known causes of cataracts, which can form in one or both eyes. Cataracts can be an inherited problem.

Signs

An immature cataract is one which partly or wholly clouds the lens but permits some light to penetrate through to the retina so that sight is not completely lost. A mature cataract is dense, silvery white and fills the entire pupil which is usually dilated. Light cannot penetrate the opaque lens so the result is total blindness.

A dog that is totally blind in one eye will often walk into objects on its blind side. If you touch it from the blind side, it may react suddenly in fright.

A dog totally blind in both eyes will walk into objects and be tentative in its movements. If it walks into a corner, it may become confused and unable to find its way out.

A dog partially blind in one or both eyes may balk unnecessarily at objects or it may have difficulty negotiating objects when the light is subdued, as it is at dusk.

Treatment

Generally, dogs with immature cataracts can live a happy life. The development of an immature cataract associated with diabetes can be slowed down with insulin injections.

If the dog is blind because of mature cataracts in both eyes, the dog's sight can be restored by surgical removal of one or both cataracts.

COCCIDIOSIS

This is a parasitic infection of the intestine mainly affecting puppies. Puppies and young dogs are more severely affected than mature dogs. It is found in Australia, Europe and North America.

Cause

Coccidia is a single cell parasite, microscopic in size.

Signs

Symptoms are loss of appetite, dehydration, lethargy, diarrhoea and weight loss. In severe cases there may be blood and mucus in the diarrhoea. Your veterinarian can make a diagnosis on the presenting symptoms and by a microscopic examination of the dog's faeces to look for coccidia oocysts.

Treatment

Consult your veterinarian who will treat the dog with one of the sulphonamides. The disease is self-limiting in many dogs because they develop an immunity. To prevent spread of the disease or re-infection, faeces should be removed daily and contaminated areas should be disinfected with boiling water or an ammonia solution.

COLLAPSED WINDPIPE (TRACHEA)

The trachea is not permanently collapsed. It is held open by rings of cartilage. Under certain conditions, such as stress or excitement, in association with some weakness of some of the cartilaginous rings, the trachea collapses temporarily.

Cause

• It may have some congenital basis as it is more commonly seen in Toy breeds, such as the Toy Poodle, Pomeranian, Yorkshire Terrier and Chihuahua.
• Sometimes the condition follows an infection such as *Parainfluenza*, commonly known as viral tracheitis or kennel cough (see p. 159).

Signs

A coughing spasm often set off by excitement, stress or pressure on the trachea when the dog is being held or is straining on the lead. The cough is harsh, dry and honking. The dog's tongue may turn blue during a coughing episode.

Treatment

Because there are numerous causes of coughing, see your veterinarian who will make a diagnosis. Treatment will vary from the restriction of the dog's exercise and excitement to the use of sedation and bronchodilators and, in some cases, surgery.

COLLIE EYE ANOMALY

The incidence of this disease is high in the Scotch Collie, and it occurs to a lesser extent in the Shetland Sheepdog.
The retina and optic nerve are affected.

Cause

Genetically inherited defect.

Signs

Usually evident at six to 16 weeks of age. May be difficult to detect in pups mildly affected, whereas severely affected pups may be blind in one or both eyes.

Treatment

There is no treatment.

Prevention

Have all Scotch Collie and Shetland Sheepdog puppies, between six to 16 weeks of age, examined by a specialist veterinary opthamologist. Those puppies and the parents of those puppies with the disease should not be used for breeding.

COLLIE NOSE

Collies and related breeds, with a long nose covered with unpigmented skin and exposed to lengthy periods of intense sunlight, develop a chronic solar dermatitis.

Cause

Lack of pigmentation of the skin of the nose which is an inherited characteristic.

Signs

In the early stages, the exposed skin on the nose appears red and inflamed. Further exposure leads to crusty, flaky, itchy skin with hairloss. Ulcers may develop and, if they persist, are probably cancerous. The eyelids and lips may become affected.

Treatment

During the summer months, keep the dog out of the sun between 10 am and 4 pm.
Zinc cream applied to the affected areas offers protection from the sun, as well as softening the skin and healing any ulcerated areas.
Sunscreen agents applied in the early stages can prevent this condition from developing. Tattooing the unpigmented nose to provide artificial pigment is also an effective preventive measure.

CONJUNCTIVITIS

The conjunctiva is the membrane lining the inside of the eyelids, seen when you pull the upper or lower eyelid away from the eyeball. Conjunctivitis is inflammation of the conjunctiva.

Causes

• Foreign bodies, e.g. grass seeds;

The conjunctival membrane is red and swollen.

A sign of conjunctivitis is a yellow pus discharge.

- injury (fight wounds);
- infection, both bacterial and viral;
- allergies;
- chronic irritation of a dog's white eyelids by the sun and chemicals, e.g. insecticidal shampoos, rinses and sprays.

Signs

The conjunctival membrane is very red and swollen. It produces a discharge varying from copious amounts of clear, watery fluid that runs down the cheek to thick, yellow pus that lies in the corner of the eyelids, sometimes matting them together.

If one eye is involved it usually indicates an injury or foreign body; if both eyes are involved the cause is often a viral infection or allergy.

Treatment

Make an appointment to see your veterinarian. In the meantime, bathe the eye with water as hot as your hand can tolerate, for ten minutes four times a day. While bathing the eye, wipe away any discharge adhering to the lashes or lids. Keep the dog out of the wind and direct

sunlight. If you can see a foreign body in the conjunctiva, remove it provided that it can be done readily. If not, leave the eye alone, as you may increase the irritation and even damage the eyeball. Leave it for the veterinarian to extract.

There are numerous eye ointments, all of which have a specific purpose. They should not be used indiscriminately for conjunctivitis, as some can worsen certain conditions. If there is ulceration of the cornea (see p. 146) and it is incorrectly treated, the result may be a permanently damaged eye or even blindness.

CONSTIPATION

This is relatively common in dogs. Often the owner is not aware the dog is constipated until it is noticed that the dog is sick and showing signs of straining. By this time the dog is usually severely constipated and needs veterinary attention quickly.

Causes

- Eating bones or ingesting prey, e.g. a bird.
- Pelvic deformity due to secondary hyperparathyroidism (see p. 169) or a fracture following a motor vehicle accident.
- Damage to nerves supplying the bowel or recurring bouts of constipation causing the large intestine to lose its muscle tone and become permanently stretched.

Signs

The dog strains vigorously producing a small amount of hard faeces, fluid faeces which may be mistaken for diarrhoea, or nothing at all. Once the dog strains vigorously, it is usually severely constipated. In these cases it may refuse food, be lethargic and vomit because of the absorption of toxins from the constipated mass in the bowel.

Treatment

Simple cases can be treated with 5–15 ml (1–3 teaspoons) of paraffin oil in the food or administered orally in conjunction with coloxyl (a faecal softener, one to two tablets daily for two to three days).

More advanced cases may be treated with coloxyl containing danthron. The coloxyl softens the faeces while the danthron stimulates the bowel to contract and expel the faeces.

If it is an advanced case of constipation, see your veterinarian. Generally, when you recognise your dog is constipated it is most often an advanced case. Your veterinarian may treat the dog conservatively with drugs or he may anaesthetise the dog and remove the faeces by giving it an enema.

In some cases the faecal mass is so hard and large that surgery has to be performed for its removal.

Prevention

This will vary according to the cause. In dogs that are prone to repeated bouts of constipation it is important to observe how often the dog defaecates and the volume and consistency of the faeces.

Milk, canned dog food and liver have a laxative effect. Paraffin oil (5–15 ml) given two to three times a week is helpful. Bran mixed into the food may be beneficial. Careful use of coloxyl tablets, with or without danthron, twice weekly can also help to prevent constipation.

COUGHING DISEASES AND PROBLEMS

Canine parainfluenza (see p. 133)
Choking (see p. 110)
Collapsed windpipe (see p. 135)
Heart disease (see p. 151)
Heartworm (see p. 152)
Kennel cough (see p. 159)
Pneumonia (see p. 171)
Snorting and snuffling (see p. 177)
Tonsillitis (see p. 178)
Viral tracheitis (see p. 159)

CYST(S) BETWEEN THE TOES

This problem is known professionally as Interdigital Cyst(s). Usually only one cyst occurs between the toes, but it is not uncommon to see several. They are seen most commonly in Bulldogs, Bull Terriers and Pugs.

Cause

Unknown.

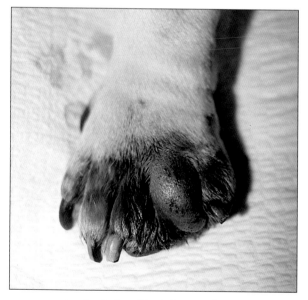

A red, raised swelling in between the toes

Signs

A red, raised swelling in between the toes, usually of the front feet. Discharge from the swelling is through one or more openings. Constant licking often causes dermatitis of the toes.

Treatment

See your veterinarian. Antibiotics will bring about an improvement but the cyst(s) usually recur(s). Complete surgical excision of the cyst(s) is the most successful approach.

CYSTITIS

Cystitis is inflammation of the bladder.

Causes

• Injury

• Calculi (stones) in the bladder.

• Tumour involving the mucous membrane lining the bladder.

• Infection—In females, infection is usually due to bacterial contamination of the vulva during the act of defaecating. The bacteria find their way up the urethra to the bladder.

Signs

• Urinating frequently.

• Passing small amount of urine in places where the dog normally would not urinate.

• Frequent licking around the genital area.

• The urine may be clear, tinged slightly with blood (pink), or practically all blood.

• The urine may have a more pungent odour than usual.

• The dog may strain frequently, leading the owner into thinking that it is constipated.

Treatment

See your veterinarian who will collect a urine sample from the dog and test it before commencing treatment which usually involves antibiotics and urine acidifiers if the urine is alkaline. In an acid urine, crystals tend to dissolve and bacterial infections clear up more readily.

Increase your dog's fluid intake by having clean water readily available. Add water to canned food and milk, although not too much, as you may make it unpalatable. Add a small amount of salt to the food to increase the thirst but take care not to make the food unpalatable. Take the dog off dry food or reduce it to less than 20 per cent of the daily intake. If the dog lives mainly inside the home, encourage it to go out frequently, or give it free access to the garden. The dog's urine should be checked about a week after the antibiotic treatment is finished as some cases of cystitis are persistent.

If cystitis is still present, the urine can be swabbed and cultured to identify the infection and determine the best antibiotic to use. An x-ray will help to determine if the cystitis is due to stones (calculi) or a tumour.

DANDRUFF

Causes

• It may be the after-effect of inflamed skin caused by an allergy, e.g. fleas or vegetation. Once the inflammation subsides, the superficial skin cells die and flake off.

• Deficiency of saturated and unsaturated fatty acids in the diet.

• Washing the dog in a shampoo that is too harsh or not rinsing the dog thoroughly after shampooing.

• Mange, which is caused by a mite (see p. 164).

Signs

Dry white skin flakes on the surface of the skin and in the hair especially along the back, around the neck and head.

Treatment

• Wash the dog in 0.5 per cent Malathion (maldison) solution to get rid of any fleas or mites.

• Add a saturated and unsaturated fatty acid supplement to the diet.

• Use a special medicated shampoo for dry skin and make sure you rinse it off thoroughly.

DEAFNESS

Deafness in dogs may be easily overlooked. If testing your dog for deafness, make sure that it is not responding to visual stimulation or to vibrations felt through its body or that it is just ignoring you.

Causes

• Congenital deafness associated with such breeds as Dalmatians, Bull Terriers and Sealyhams.

• Infections

• Deterioration of the hearing apparatus, more evident in the ageing dog.

• Administration of certain drugs such as the antibiotic Streptomycin.

• Ear canals blocked with wax.

Signs

It does not appear to hear such noises as:

• a dog barking;

• a car approaching;

• a loud whistle;

• a tapping on an empty tin with a spoon;

• the sound of its name.

Treatment

Syringing the ears under a general anaesthetic can restore hearing to those dogs with blocked ears. The use of antibiotics and anti-inflammatory agents can cure inflamed, infected ears.

Deafness from birth or associated with old age cannot be treated.

DIABETES MELLITUS

There are two types of diabetes: *Diabetes mellitus*, which is commonly known as sugar diabetes, and *Diabetes insipidus*, which is known as water diabetes. Water diabetes is rarely seen by the small animal veterinarian. Sugar diabetes is caused by decreased insulin production in the body. This in turn allows the sugar level in the body to rise and the well-recognised signs of sugar diabetes to appear.

Cause

The pancreas contains cells called islets of langerhans which produce insulin. If the pancreas is diseased (pancreatitis) and the islets of langerhans are involved, the production of insulin is either reduced or stopped. There are other causes of diabetes which are not well understood.

Signs

• Thirst, drinking and urinating excessively.

• Ravenous appetite and weight loss.

• Bowel motions are often of a putty colour and consistency.

• Appetite may decrease as the disease progresses.

• Dog may become depressed.

Treatment

See your veterinarian who can confirm the diagnosis by doing a blood sugar test and a urine test. The blood sample should be taken from the dog approximately 12 hours after it eats.

Treatment involves hospitalisation to stabilise the dog's blood sugar level by administration of insulin injections. This may take four to seven days, then your veterinarian will show you how to inject the insulin, which has to be done daily. The injections are relatively painless and easy to give. The diet need not be changed, but the times when the dog is fed after the insulin injection are important. Your veterinarian will supply you with insulin, needles, syringes and sticks for testing the sugar level in the urine. Regular monitoring of the dog's blood sugar by your veterinarian is important.

Diabetic dogs can enjoy a happy, healthy life for years providing they have their daily insulin injection.

DIAPHRAGMATIC HERNIA

Cause

A fall, blow to the body, or a motor vehicle accident. The diaphragm tears allowing some or almost all of the abdominal contents (liver, stomach, spleen and intestines) to pass into the chest. The abdominal organs when in the chest cavity, compress the lungs and thus adversely affect the dog's breathing.

Signs

The extent of the effect on the dog's breathing will depend on the amount of abdominal content that has passed into the dog's chest cavity. Occasionally the abdominal content does not always pass immediately into the chest cavity following the accident. Months later it may do so, causing the dog's breathing to become distressed.

The dog maintains a sitting position, refuses to lie down and may refuse to eat or drink. Its breathing is rapid and shallow.

Treatment

Surgical repair by your veterinarian.

DIARRHOEA

Diarrhoea in dogs is characterised by increased frequency of defaecation. The faeces (motion) is of a porridge or fluid-like consistency, often with a very offensive odour.

Causes

• Diet
—milk
—change of diet
—excessive eating
• Parasites
• Infection
—bacterial
—viral
• Other causes
—pancreatitis
—poisons

Diet

Milk: Some dogs develop diarrhoea when fed milk, even in small quantities. Diarrhoea is often observed in young puppies after weaning.

Change of diet: Dogs do not need variety in their diet like humans do. If you observe your dog's bowel motions to be normal on a nutritious type of diet, do not change it.

Excessive eating: Some dogs do not know when to stop eating, and if you continue to provide food they will continue to eat it. Often, eating in excess of their normal diet or drinking an excessive amount of milk will cause diarrhoea.

Parasites

Parasites not only include round, hook, whip and tape worms, but also protozoan infections such as coccidia, giardia and toxoplasma (see pp. 134,150,179).

Infection

Bacterial: There are a number of different bacterial infections, such as salmonella, that can affect the intestine causing diarrhoea.

Viral: The most common and most dangerous viral infection causing diarrhoea is the Parvovirus (see p. 133).

Other causes

Pancreatitis: This is not uncommon in the dog. The inflamed or infected pancreas does not produce sufficient enzymes for proper digestion of the food, particularly fat.

Poisons: (See p. 112.)

Signs

The signs will vary according to the cause and severity of the diarrhoea. The dog often appears well and may want to eat normally. The bowel motion may be porridge- or fluid-like, with a very offensive odour. The colour may vary from green, yellow, grey to black, with or without the presence of blood. The dog will defaecate more frequently and in areas such as inside the house or apartment where it would not normally do so. The dog may strain and have an inflamed anus with faeces matted in the hair around the anus, tail and hind limbs. Dehydration occurs as a result of severe or ongoing diarrhoea.

Treatment

If the dog is bright and alert, do not feed it for 24 hours. Provide water only, making sure it is always available. If the dog has not passed a motion or the motion appears firmer, offer a small amount of boiled chicken or lean grilled meat, but only a quarter of what it would eat normally in a day.

Large volumes of food aggravate an already inflamed or infected intestine, so keep the volume of food down. As fat or dairy products aggravate diarrhoea, they should be excluded from the dog's diet until the dog has fully recovered.

As the bowel motion improves, increase the volume of chicken or grilled meat. Once the motions have been normal for three to four days, slowly reintroduce the dog's normal diet.

If the diarrhoea persists for more than 24 hours, take your dog to the veterinarian. On the other hand, if you notice your dog has diarrhoea in association with some other symptom, such as blood in the motion, lethargy, vomiting, loss of appetite or straining, see your veterinarian as soon as convenient. If possible, also take along a sample of the dog's bowel motion for examination by your veterinarian.

DIETARY ALLERGY

The two common types of food allergies seen are those affecting the skin and the gastro-intestinal tract.

Cause

The dog's immune system is hypersensitised to a certain type of food or foods. When the dog eats the food its immune system overreacts.

Signs

Skin:
• itching
• swelling of the face or small lumps all over the body
• the hair over the lumps may be erect.

Gastro-intestinal tract:
• vomiting
• diarrhoea.

Treatment

The treatment is simple: prevent the dog having access to food to which it is allergic. It may be difficult to determine if the dog really does have a food allergy and to exactly what food it is allergic. This may be done by placing the dog on a diet of chicken or lamb and boiled rice and water for a three week period. If at the end of the three weeks there is no reaction, add one new item of food every two days, starting with the common foods that cause allergies, e.g. milk and beef.

Dietary allergies are not common in dogs.

DISTICHIASIS
(INGROWN EYELASHES)

On the inner border of the eyelid is a second row of short eyelashes.

Cause

This condition is inherited in a wide cross-section of dogs.

Signs

Due to the short eyelashes rubbing on the cornea, the eye becomes inflamed and watery, and the dog squints.

Treatment

See your veterinarian. If there are only a few eyelashes, they may be plucked out, but usually they grow back.

If there are numerous eyelashes, they are best removed surgically under a general anaesthetic. If the eyelashes are not removed, they will lead to constant irritation and possible permanent damage to the cornea, resulting in impaired vision.

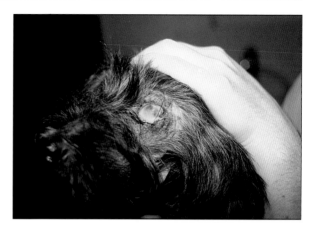

Dry eye: eye covered with tacky, thick yellow pus.

DRY EYE

This term is used to describe a decrease in or lack of tear production, usually in one eye but it may be in both. It is a disease of older dogs and seen more often in Poodles than other breeds.

Cause

The lachrymal (tear) glands fail to produce tears as a result of an infection or the ducts (openings) of the glands are blocked.

Signs

The healthy eye has a shiny, moist, glistening surface. The surface of the dry eye is dull, often ulcerated and covered in tacky, thick yellow pus. The dog will have an associated conjunctivitis (see pp. 135,195). Over a period of time the surface (cornea) of the eye becomes infiltrated with black pigment.

Treatment

See your veterinarian who can confirm the diagnosis by measuring the dog's tear production. An eye ointment or eye drops containing antibiotics and anti-inflammatory drugs will be administered to control infection and inflammation.

It is very important to keep the eye surface and eyelids free of pus by bathing, and to instil artificial tears hourly for an indefinite period. If conservative treatment is impractical or unsuccessful, one of the salivary ducts can be transplanted to the inside of the corner of the eye. The saliva washes over the eye keeping it permanently moist.

EAR DISEASES AND PROBLEMS

Deafness (see p. 138)
Ear haematoma (see p. 141)
Ear infection (see p. 141)
Ear mites (see p. 142)
Middle ear infection (see p. 166)

The whole ear flap is swollen.

EAR HAEMATOMA

Ear haematoma is a circumscribed swelling of the ear flap containing blood.

Cause

Rupture of a blood vessel in the ear flap caused by a bite, blow, infection or ear mites. The ear mites cause the dog to scratch the ear or shake it vigorously to the point where a blood vessel in the ear flap is ruptured.

Signs

Swelling of ear flap. The swelling can vary in size involving the whole or a part of the flap. Swollen ear in early stages is soft to the touch but usually not painful.

Soft swelling if tapped gives the impression of tapping a fluid-filled cavity.

Treatment

In the early formation of a haematoma, an ice pack will help to stop the internal bleeding and will reduce the swelling. If a blood-filled cavity has formed, take the dog to your veterinarian who will give it a general anaesthetic in order to drain the blood from the ear and to stitch a splint to the back of the ear flap. This procedure will stop the drained cavity refilling with blood and will aid the ear to heal in its original shape.

If the haematoma is not opened and drained, the blood is converted into a hard fibrous swelling over a number of weeks. The ear contracts and is distorted in shape; it is often referred to as a cauliflower ear.

The initiating cause, such as an infection or ear mites, is treated at the same time.

EAR INFECTION

This condition is technically known as otitis externa and is often referred to as canker. It is an infection associated with inflammation of the external ear canal.

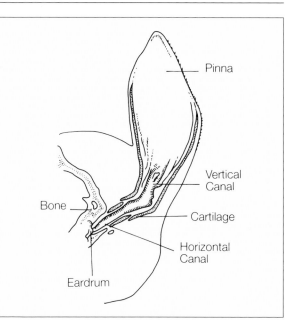

The Ear Canal

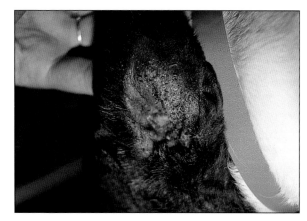

The skin is inflamed inside the ear.

Causes

All dogs have a right-angled bend in the ear canal. The glands in the wall of the canal secrete wax which lies in the canal and does not drain readily because of the bend. Consequently, the warm, waxy environment provides a breeding ground for bacteria, fungii and yeasts. The membrane lining the ear canal becomes inflamed, producing more wax.

Signs

• shaking the head

• scratching of one or both ears

• skin inflamed behind the ear with hair missing

• odour from the ear

• discharge from ear canal, brown and waxy to creamy pus which may be blood tinged and matted in the hair around the opening to the ear canal

141

- skin inflamed inside the ear
- holding the head to the side of the affected ear
- drooping of the affected ear.

Treatment

Look inside the ear. Remove any foreign bodies, e.g. a grass seed. If you are unable to remove the foreign body or there is evidence of pus or a heavy, waxy discharge, take the dog to your veterinarian who, on examination, will prescribe a particular ear drop to administer which may be anti-inflammatory, anti-bacterial or anti-fungal, or a combination of all three. If the discharge is thick and dry an ear drop with an oil base to soften the wax will be prescribed; if the discharge is moist to wet, an ear drop with an alcohol base to dry the secretion will be prescribed.

If the infection is persistent, a swab may be taken and a culture done to identify the type of infection so that the most effective antibiotic for treatment can be prescribed.

When the ear is badly infected, a general anaesthetic is often necessary to enable the veterinarian to clean the ear in order to see more clearly the cause and site of the problem. The right treatment can then be prescribed and administered to the crucial area.

Some chronic infections require a surgical procedure known as an ear resection. In this procedure the vertical section of the ear canal is excised, thus providing permanent drainage.

EAR MITES

Ear mites are found in dogs of all ages but their presence is more common in puppies. Sometimes signs of their presence are not obvious to the untrained eye and the problem goes undetected for a long time.

Cause

The mite, *Otodectes cynotis*, living in the ear canal can be seen with the naked eye. It is very small, white in colour and sensitive to light causing it to move away from any light rays that might penetrate the ear canal.

Signs

- scratching one or both ears
- skin around or behind the ear may be abraded from scratching
- excessive scratching may rupture a blood vessel in the ear and cause a haematoma to form (see p. 141)
- continual shaking of the head
- heavy dark wax in the ear and down the ear canal can be seen on close inspection
- presence of minute mites which can be seen by looking quickly down the ear canal with the aid of a pencil torch.

Treatment

Apply an oil-based ear drop containing an insecticidal agent to the ear canal; four drops into both ears twice daily for seven days. After three days, when the wax has softened, clean both ears thoroughly once daily before applying the drops.

Treat all dogs and cats in the household even if you are aware of only one animal showing signs of ear mites.

If difficulty is encountered in clearing up the problem, then all dogs and cats in the household should be washed in a diluted Malathion (maldison) solution, i.e. 15 ml (3 teaspoons) of Malathion to 1 litre (¼ gallon) of water, as the mites not only live in the ear canal but can also live on the body.

ECTROPION

The eyelids turn out, exposing the conjunctiva, the pink mucous membrane lining the eyelid. It is common in Basset Hounds, Blood Hounds, Cocker Spaniels and St Bernards.

Cause

The condition in most cases is an inherited characteristic found in certain breeds. The socket is too large for the eyeball, or the lower eyelids are too long and tend to sag. Ectropion may also be caused by injury to the eyelid.

Signs

It usually occurs in the lower eyelids of both eyes. The conjunctiva when exposed becomes irritated by wind, dust, flies etc. If continually irritated, the inflamed conjunctiva becomes infected, leading to discharge from the eyes.

Treatment

See your veterinarian who can correct the defect by surgery.

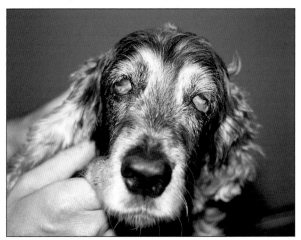

Ectropion: lower eyelids turning out, exposing the conjunctiva.

An elderly dog will need special care.

ELDERLY DOG

It is difficult to set an average age for the life span of dogs in general as there are such variations in age from breed to breed and dog to dog. In practice, the larger the dog, the shorter the life span, e.g the life span of a Great Dane is eight to ten years, a Labrador Retriever 11 to 13 years and a Miniature Poodle 14 to 16 years.

SIGNS OF OLD AGE

The signs vary with individual dogs and may develop so slowly that they go unnoticed until they are advanced and obvious. The common signs are:

• Reduced sense of sight and hearing. Your dog does not respond to your call and/or it bumps into objects and appears disorientated.

• Reduced appetite which may be due to reduced sense of smell and consequently taste.

• Weight loss, which may be due to eating less as well as loss of muscle mass due to reduced exercise. Old dogs spend much of the day lying around.

• Coat loses colour and appears dull, unkempt and dirty.

• Bad breath due to plaque, tartar and gingivitis (see pp. 92, 150).

• Constipation (see p. 136).

• Urinary incontinence (bed wetting, see p. 179).

• Diarrhoea (see p. 139).

• Susceptibility to certain diseases (see Arthritis, p. 129; Cancer, p. 133; Diabetes, p. 138); Heart disease, p. 151; Nephritis (Kidney disease), p. 159; Worms, p. 95).

CARE OF THE ELDERLY DOG

• **Proper nutrition:** As dogs get older, their ability to digest and absorb nutrients is reduced. Feed your dog smaller meals of high quality food more frequently.

The diet should contain a greater amount of vitamins, zinc, essential fatty acids and fibre. Add a specially formulated dog vitamin and mineral supplement to the diet. Do not use a human vitamin–mineral supplement; a dog's requirements differ.

There are available highly palatable prescription diets with reduced amounts of high quantity protein, phosphorus, sodium, magnesium and calories.

Excessive amounts of protein, phosphorus and sodium may worsen kidney and heart diseases.

Elderly dogs exercise less thereby needing fewer calories because they expend less energy. If obesity or a tendency to put on weight is a problem, a diet containing fewer calories is recommended. However, if your dog is too thin, consult your veterinarian as the problem may be more involved than a simple dietary one.

• **Medication:** Your veterinarian may recommend the use of anabolic steroids to prevent wasting, geriatric tablets to counteract the ageing process, and anti-inflammatory agents to improve mobility.

• **Grooming:** Regular grooming helps the dog to look and feel better, and prevents skin problems associated with a matted dirty coat.

• **Exercise:** Exercise is important to maintain muscle tone and joint flexibility. It also stimulates the dog to urinate and defaecate which assists in preventing cystitis (see p. 137) and constipation (see p. 136). You can encourage exercise by putting the dog outside regularly or by taking it for a walk.

• **Sleeping area:** Provide an area for sleeping which is warm and draught free in winter and provides shade and protection from the elements in summer.

• **Worming:** Worm the dog every three months (see p. 95). Continue giving daily or monthly heartworm preventative treatment.

• **Veterinary checkups:** Take your dog to your veterinarian regularly for a checkup and its annual vaccination (see p. 94), particularly against distemper (p. 133), hepatitis (p. 153), parvovirus (p. 133) and parainfluenza (p. 133).

The risk of disease increases with age, so careful observation of any alteration in your dog's daily habits and regular examinations by your veterinarian will aid in the early diagnosis of a possible life threatening disease. An early diagnosis may enable the disease to be treated successfully. If the disease cannot be treated, a decision on euthanasia (putting to sleep) can prevent unnecessary and prolonged suffering.

EUTHANASIA (PUTTING TO SLEEP)

There comes a time when you feel a decision about putting your old dog to sleep should be made or at least should be discussed with your veterinarian.

Some people are reluctant to approach their veterinarian on this matter. Rest assured that your veterinarian is there to assist and advise you and that he or she has discussed the same problem with clients many times before. Do not hesitate to discuss the matter with your veterinarian. Just because the dog is old is not a sufficient reason in itself to justify euthanasia. But if the dog is old, its quality of life is unacceptable, and there is no hope of improvement, then a decision about euthanasia should be made.

Over the years you become emotionally involved with your dog and understandably your emotions sometimes cloud your reasoning. Some people will not or cannot make the decision to put their old dog to sleep because the thought of it hurts them too much to arrive at that final decision. In not making the decision they are unnecessarily putting their old dog through further dis-

comfort and pain. When your veterinarian advises you to put your dog to sleep he or she is thinking of what is the kindest thing to do for the dog and of shielding you from the stress of watching your dog go through worsening pain or discomfort from which it is not going to recover. Once the decision to euthanase your dog has been made, you may wish to be with your dog when your veterinarian puts it to sleep. It is a painless and peaceful procedure. A concentrated anaesthetic is injected into a vein and the dog goes peacefully to sleep within seconds.

Following euthanasia, you may wish to bury your dog at home, have your veterinarian take care of the burial or have the dog buried or cremated at a pet cemetery. The decision is a personal one.

After the death of a dog, the owner usually suffers a sense of loss and grief. Some allow time to heal their hurt, but others take a more positive step; they acquire a new puppy and a new caring, loving relationship begins. In that sense, life is renewed.

ENTROPION

Entropion is turning in of the eyelid which causes the hairs to rub on the surface of the eyeball (cornea), thus irritating it. Some breeds, such as the Chow Chow, are more subject to entropion than others.

Cause

Some puppies are born with this condition, often with both eyes affected. Chronic conjunctivitis and laceration of the eyelids can be the cause of entropion in adult dogs.

Signs

Weeping of the affected eye with a wet patch below it, partial closure of the eyelids of the affected eye, rubbing of the eye to alleviate constant irritation.

Treatment

Contact your veterinarian as this condition can be corrected successfully by surgery.

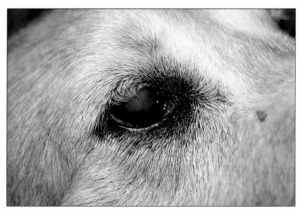

The eyelashes are rubbing the surface of the eyeball.

In young puppies the affected lid may be corrected by turning out the lid six or more times a day and by applying an eye ointment.

EPILEPSY—CONVULSIONS SEIZURES—FITS

(See First aid, p. 111.) There are two types of epileptic fits: Grand Mal, where the dog slumps or falls to the ground, and Petite Mal, where the dog remains on its feet.

Causes

• Trauma, e.g. a blow to the head causing temporary or permanent brain damage.

• Infection—viral or bacterial; may cause meningitis (inflammation of membrane covering surface of brain) and/or encephalitis (inflammation of the brain). Distemper (see p. 133) is an example of a viral infection which causes encephalitis.

• Poisoning (see p. 112)—snail and slug poisons (Metaldehyde and Organo Phosphate Carbamate); insecticidal rinses (Lindane, Gammexane, Chlordane, Dieldrin, Aldrin).

• Milk Fever (see Eclampsia, p. 190)—low blood calcium level (hypocalcaemia).

• Brain tumours

• Congenital Idiopathic Epilepsy—Idiopathic means an unknown cause.

• Low blood sugar level (hypoglycaemia).

• Worms—puppies with a heavy worm infestation in the intestine.

• External stimulation, e.g. loud music, over-excitement, hot weather, loud noises.

Signs

The signs will vary according to the cause. A dog with congenital epilepsy may initially show such signs as apprehension, dilated pupils, restlessness, followed by facial twitching, champing of the jaw, foaming at the mouth, head shaking, collapse, lying on its side rigid with its head back, paddling with its legs, and may be urinating and defaecating. This phase usually lasts from one to three minutes. The dog may recover quickly or remain confused, disorientated and wobbly for hours.

Treatment

Usually the dog is lying on its side unconscious, paddling with its legs, champing its jaw, frothing at the mouth and twitching. People are concerned that the dog will swallow its tongue. Do not try to take hold of the dog's tongue as you may be badly bitten by the unconscious dog champing its jaws.

Observe the dog but do not touch it. Touching the dog while fitting may aggravate and prolong the fit. Usually the fit lasts for about three minutes and then the dog recovers although it may seem a little disorientated temporarily. Once it has recovered, see your veterinarian.

If the dog continues fitting beyond five minutes, you need to take the dog to your veterinarian immediately. If there is a break in between fits, pick the dog up by the scruff of the neck with one hand whilst supporting the dog's body with the other hand, and place it gently into the car. Continue to hold the dog securely while another person drives the car. If the dog is impossible to handle phone your veterinarian.

The treatment administered by your veterinarian will vary according to the cause. There are different types of drugs known as central nervous system depressants used in the treatment of congenital epilepsy. The purpose of these drugs is to control the epileptic fits without depressing the dog or affecting its quality of life.

EPULIS (GUM TUMOUR)

Epulis is excessive gum tissue development around the pre-molar teeth as found in some Boxers. It is non-cancerous. Other tumours found in the mouth are usually malignant.

Cause

Unknown. Proliferation of gum tissue in Boxers is probably hereditary.

Signs

In Boxers, when their mouth is open, a growth made up of gum tissue is evident. The growth is usually about 1 cm (2 in) in diameter.

Treatment

See your veterinarian who will surgically remove the growth using electro-cautery to control haemorrhage.

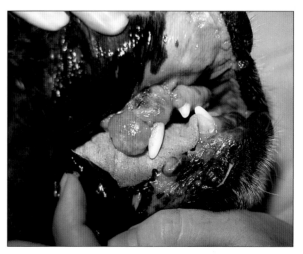

Excessive gum development around the pre-molar tooth

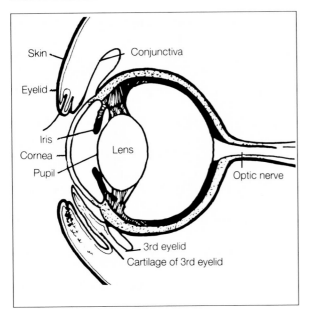

The Eye

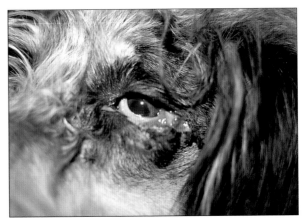

A lacerated eyelid

An ulcer lighlighted by green dye

EYE DISEASES AND PROBLEMS

EYE INJURIES

Any injury to the eyeball or eyelids should be regarded as serious, and veterinary attention should be sought quickly. Damage to the eyeball may lead to permanent blindness and any break in an eyelid may lead to a loss of tears and a dry eye.

EYE ULCERS

As the cornea or surface of the eye is exposed, it is more subject to injury than are other parts of the eye. In many cases injury is followed by ulceration.

Causes

• Injury;
• foreign body;
• dry eye (lack of tear production);
• eyelids do not close completely;
• infection;
• entropion, i.e. turning in of the eyelid with eyelashes rubbing on the surface of the cornea;
• hair from facial folds rubbing on the surface of the cornea as seen in the Pekingese.

Signs

The obvious one is the sight of tears streaming down the cheek, the eyelids partially or completely closed. The appearance of the cornea, i.e. the surface of the affected eye, can vary from clear to a dull, hazy appearance in a small area, to the whole surface of the eye being opaque and bluish-white in colour. Often the ulcer can only be seen by the veterinary surgeon using special techniques for examining the eye. Scar formation following corneal ulceration is common. Its effect on vision depends on the size, thickness and position of the scar.

Treatment

Early veterinary treatment will help minimise scar formation and maintain proper vision. You can help by cleaning and bathing the eye, using a clean wad of cotton wool soaked in hot water as hot as your hand can just tolerate.

If a foreign body is present and can be readily removed, do so, otherwise leave it for the veterinarian to extract.

Place the dog in a shaded area or darkened room as corneal ulcers are very sensitive to direct sunlight. Wind, dust and flies aggravate the problem.

Some shallow ulcers respond well to eye ointment, whereas those that do not respond or are deep and extensive, respond well to the third eyelid being pulled across the surface of the eye (cornea) and stitched to the inside of the upper eyelid. Thus the ulcer is covered by the third eyelid which is left in place for two to four weeks.

EYELID TUMOURS

These tumours are usually observed in the early stages because they are so obvious on the eyelid.

Cause

Unknown.

Signs

They are usually a single, dark coloured lump on the rim of the upper or lower eyelid. If the tumour rubs on the surface of the eye (cornea), it will cause the eye to weep and may damage the cornea.

Treatment

Surgical removal of the tumour is usually very successful as most of them are benign. Early removal of the tumour while it is relatively small, minimises damage to the cornea and surgical trauma to the eyelid.

FATTY TUMOUR (LIPOMA)

The word tumour means lump. A lipoma is a benign fatty tumour, i.e. a lump made up of fat surrounded by a capsule. They do not spread, and are not life threatening.

Cause

Unknown. They occur more frequently in older fat dogs of both sexes and in dogs that genetically have a greater ratio of fat to muscle, e.g. Labradors, Golden Retrievers.

Signs

The lump or lumps can vary in size from 1 cm (½ in) to 30 cm (12 in) in diameter. They are usually mobile and are located under the skin although some may be embedded in the muscle tissue.

They are firm, round, smooth and not painful to the touch. They are a blemish and tend not to cause any trouble. If they grow to a large size, they can impair the dog's movement or impinge on other structures in the area. They rarely change to a liposarcoma which is an aggressive malignant fatty tumour.

Treatment

If small, watch to see if they are developing and if so they should be surgically removed.

FLATULENCE

To pass wind from the anus is a normal bodily function of the dog as a result of gas being produced during the digestion of food in the stomach and intestine. Frequently passing large volumes of foul smelling gas (wind) is considered abnormal.

Causes

• Eating rapidly and gulping air with the food.

• Eating excessive amounts of grass or vegetables such as cauliflower and cabbage.

• Intestinal irritation due to change of diet, infection or worms.

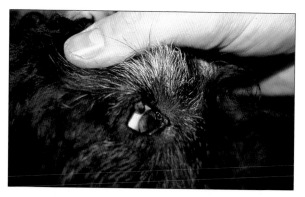

A tumour on the rim of the eyelid

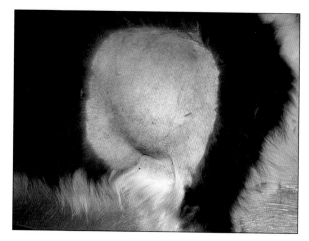

A large, fatty tumour under the skin

Treatment

- Feed three or four small meals a day.
- Change the diet. Try different brands of canned and dry food. If you prepare the dog's food, cut down on the amount of vegetables in the diet and check the quality of the meat that is included.
- Worm the dog.
- Have your veterinarian check the dog for some abnormality of the stomach or intestine. A drug to slow down peristalsis, i.e. intestinal movement, may be prescribed.
- Try giving the dog charcoal tablets obtained from your local pharmacy.

FLEA ALLERGY

This is one of the most common skin conditions in the dog, especially in warm climates. Fleas also play a part in the tapeworm lifecycle (see Worms, p. 95) and in large numbers can cause severe anaemia.

Cause

The flea is a blood sucker and bites the dog for that purpose. This causes a local allergic reaction which irritates the dog. The dog bites or scratches the irritated area to get temporary relief. At the same time this aggra-

vates the inflamed skin which irritates the dog more and so the dog bites and scratches more. Thus a vicious circle develops and the skin problem gets progressively worse.

Signs

The skin is red, inflamed and irritated to the point where there may be small crusty scabs due to the dog scratching.

Hairloss along the back towards the base of the tail if evident can vary from thinning to baldness.

The skin may be broken in areas due to scratching and licking. After years, it becomes thickened, scaly and infiltrated with black pigment (melanin).

Brush the hair back along the dog's back and around the base of its tail. Look carefully and you will probably see fleas and flea dirt or excreta which is really waste from digested blood. The excreta is seen as small black specks lying in the coat and on the skin.

Treatment

If the dog is continually scratching and biting, take it to your veterinarian who may give an injection of cortisone to stop the irritation, to allow the skin to repair itself and return to normal, and for the hair to grow back.

To help clear up the existing condition and prevent it recurring you must get rid of all the fleas. Treatment involves the infested dog, other cats and dogs in the household, and their environment.

Different types of treatment are:

1. Insecticidal rinse: There are many different types, most of which are very effective and last for about one week on the dog. Shampoo the dog first or at least wet the coat before applying the rinse. Otherwise, when you dilute the rinse with water as directed and pour it on the dog, most of the rinse will run off because the dog's coat is partially waterproof.

Read carefully the directions on the label particularly in regard to dilution and age for use. It is important for the person washing the dog to have minimal body contact with the rinse, undiluted or diluted. The rinse has an odour to which the dog might object. The task of rinsing may then become a difficult one.

You can allow the dog to drip dry or it may allow you to use a hair dryer. Dogs that lick themselves after washing should be towel dried to prevent ingestion of excessive amounts of the chemical in the rinse.

Most dog insecticidal rinses are poisonous to cats.

2. Insecticidal shampoo: (containing Pyrethrins and Piperonyl Butoxide) These do not have the pungent odour of the insecticidal rinse. They can be used on puppies as well as on mature dogs. The shampoo kills fleas at the time of the wash but it does not have any longlasting, residual effect. The shampoo must be rinsed off thoroughly. It can be used in conjunction with flea collars and sprays. If you start to bathe the puppies when they are

SIGNS OF FLEA ALLERGY

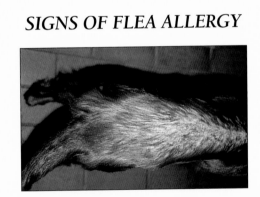

Red, inflamed and irritated skin.

Thickened skin, scaly and infiltrated with black pigment.

weaned from the mother they usually become accustomed to being washed.

Shampoos have a good cleansing effect on the skin and coat, but they do not have a longlasting effect against fleas.

3. Insecticidal tablet or liquid: It is administered twice weekly via the mouth or food. It is fairly effective but should not be given in conjunction with any other flea treatment.

4. Insecticidal sprays (containing Pyrethrins and Piperonyl Butoxide) The pressurised can type gives a hissing noise as the spray is released and may frighten the dog.

The pump action type is reasonably easy and quick to apply. Brush the hair back to expose the skin and spray with a fine mist holding the bottle about 15 cm (6 in) from the dog. Wipe any excess off the hair with a towel, because if the dog licks the spray on the coat it may salivate profusely. It is not toxic. It will kill the fleas at the time of spraying and can be used on both the bitch and her puppies and their environment but it does not have a longlasting effect.

5. Flea collars: There are numerous brands of flea collars that vary in their effectiveness and period of action. If the collar gets wet, the insecticidal product can be leached out of the collar rendering it ineffective.

Some dogs are allergic to flea collars, developing a severe inflammatory skin reaction underneath the collar. When you put on a collar check the skin underneath it for about a week. If there is no reaction, there is no need for further checking; if there is a reaction, take off the collar and seek veterinarian advice.

The collar is reasonably effective and easy to apply, but it does not control fleas in the dog's environment.

6. Flea powders: There are numerous types of flea powders which vary in effectiveness and length of action. Some can be used on young puppies over four weeks of age and can also be sprinkled on their bedding. They are not as effective as other products in treating adult dogs, although they may be used in conjunction with flea collars.

When applying the powder, brush it well into the coat and then wipe the excess powder off the surface with a damp cloth.

7. Fleas in the dog's environment: The flea egg and flea larvae live in debris shed from the dog (hair, skin, etc.), onto bedding, carpets, door mats and the dog's favourite sleeping places. Where possible, vacuum these areas, burning the contents of the vacuum cleaner, and use insecticidal sprays (Pyrethrins and Piperonyl Butoxide) twice weekly on the areas where the dog lies.

There is a relatively new product containing Methoprene and Pyrethrins available in a pressurised can.

Follow the directions on the can. The contents of the can are released in a mist which spreads throughout the house. The product claims that the flea eggs and larvae and even adult fleas in the house are eliminated for a period of up to nine months.

(See Flea infestation of puppies and bitch, p. 198.)

FLY STRIKE

This problem is seasonal and more common in longhaired dogs. Some dogs, such as German Shepherds, are prone to fly strike of the ears.

Cause

Blowflies are attracted to open wounds and more so if the hair around the infected wound is matted with pus. Hair matted with faeces around the anus is a prime target for fly strike. The blowfly lays eggs in the matted hair and the eggs develop into maggots which invade the skin, anus and vagina causing severe tissue damage.

Signs

Often the dog is lethargic and off its food. On close inspection you will see maggots wriggling in the wound or around and even in the anus and sometimes in the vagina. Dried blood and scabs on the ears may be seen.

Treatment

If extensive, contact your veterinarian. In some cases of fly strike, where there is extensive tissue damage, toxins are produced which poison the dog and may prove fatal. Your veterinarian may need to anaesthetise the dog and cut away any dead tissue, as well as administer antibiotics.

Prevention

In spring and summer, longhaired dogs should be checked regularly around the anal area.

The hair around the anus and vagina should be cut short to prevent contamination with faeces. Dogs that are

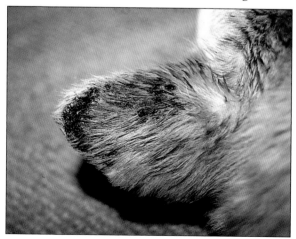

Fly strike of the ears

prone to develop matts in their coat should be brushed and combed regularly. A weekly insecticidal rinse is also helpful. Regularly apply fly-repellant ointment to the affected parts of the ears, and if necessary keep the dog in a fly-proof area during those hours of the day when flies are most prevalent.

GIARDIASIS

This disease can be overlooked, and in some cases is diagnosed by your veterinarian due to the dog's lack of response to conventional treatment for diarrhoea.

Cause

Giardia canis is a single-cell parasite, microscopic in size. Most dogs are infected by drinking contaminated water, being in contact with, or eating, dog faeces (see Coprophagia, p. 74).

Signs

Diarrhoea which has come on suddenly or persists for a lengthy period of time. The diarrhoea may contain blood and mucus.

Treatment

The cause can only be identified in the pathology laboratory. Take a fresh sample of the dog's faeces in a sealed container to your veterinarian. Metronidiazole (Flagyl) is highly effective in treating giardiasis.

GINGIVITIS

Causes

• Bacterial infections.

• Irritant substances licked from a contaminated coat.

• Plaque and tartar on the teeth.

Signs

• Red inflamed gum along the tooth–gum margin, which is usually in the region of the pre-molar and molar teeth, especially of the upper jaw.

• There may be evidence of bad breath and saliva drooling from the mouth. The saliva may be blood tinged.

• The dog shows interest in food but is reluctant to eat, or tentatively eats the food.

• The teeth may be clean or covered in varying amounts of plaque and tartar.

• The gums often bleed if touched.

Treatment

See your veterinarian. If necessary, the dog will be given a general anaesthetic and its teeth will be cleaned with an ultrasonic descaler. Any loose or unhealthy teeth will be extracted.

Anti-inflammatory agents to reduce the redness and pain, and antibiotics to clear up any infection may be administered.

Encourage the dog to eat by feeding it soft food (canned) with plenty of flavour and odour. Gingivitis often recurs; extraction of the pre-molar and molar teeth in severe chronic cases will often give a permanent cure.

Prevention

A regular six monthly check up by your veterinarian and ultrasonic descaling, if necessary, will help to prevent gingivitis.

GLAUCOMA

Is a swelling of the eye due to increased pressure from the fluid within the eyeball.

Causes

In some breeds of dogs, e.g. Beagle, American and English Cocker Spaniel, it is an inherited condition. Other causes are injury or disease.

Signs

The affected eye is larger than the other eye and may be inflamed and have a cloudy surface, often with a dilated pupil.

Once the eyeball is noticeably larger than the other, glaucoma is advanced.

Glaucoma is usually a painful condition which may not be obvious in the dog.

Treatment

Early diagnosis is important to prevent blindness and the eye becoming grossly enlarged. The services of a veterinary opthamologist with special equipment are necessary to detect glaucoma in the early stages.

The condition can be controlled by constant treatment for the rest of the dog's life.

Glaucoma: eye swollen and inflamed with a cloudy surface

If the eye is grossly enlarged, painful, and does not respond to treatment, surgical removal of the eye will give the dog permanent relief from pain.

When the eye is removed, the eyelids are stitched together and remain permanently closed. It is not aesthetically unpleasant to look at.

HARDERIAN GLAND INFECTION
(CHERRY EYE)

The Harderian gland is located on the inside of the nictitating membrane (third eyelid). The function of the healthy gland, which is not visible, is to produce tears.

Cause

Infection.

Signs

A round, bright red, fleshy swelling appears from behind the third eyelid in the corner of the eye.

Treatment

Sometimes with antibiotic treatment the swollen gland will return to normal size and disappear behind the third eyelid. In cases that do not respond to antibiotics, the Harderian gland should be removed surgically. Care is taken not to damage the third eyelid.

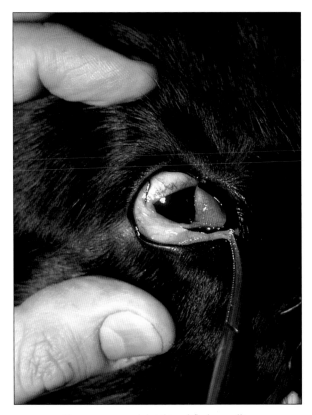

Cherry eye: round, bright red fleshy swelling in the corner of the eye.

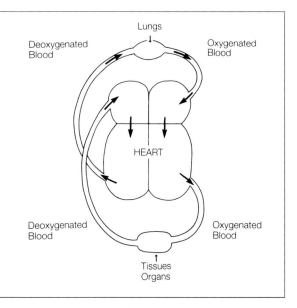

The Heart

HEART DISEASE

The heart is a four-chambered, muscular pump, made up of special muscle fibres. The heart's pumping action is controlled by electrical impulses released from a small node situated in the heart muscle, but this automatic control is overridden by other factors when a dog is excited or disturbed.

The function of the heart is simply to circulate blood to the numerous tissues and organs throughout the body. Basically, cells are replenished with oxygen and their waste products are removed. The oxygenated blood goes to the tissues and organs, where it exchanges its oxygen for carbon dioxide and other waste products. It is then said to be deoxygenated blood, and travels back to the heart and is again pumped to the lungs, where the waste products are removed and the blood is reoxygenated.

Dogs, like humans, have a relatively high incidence of heart disease.

Causes

The dog may be born with a heart defect. Viruses and bacteria may also damage the heart muscle and valves. The causes of certain heart conditions, such as heart muscle wasting (cardiomyopathy), have not yet been finally determined.

Signs

The signs of a heart problem include:
• laboured, rapid breathing and rapid heart rate following moderate exercise;
• fatigue and poor exercise tolerance or general lethargy and reluctance to exercise or play;
• coughing associated with movement, exercise or excite-

ment, or a persistent, intermittent cough together with drinking excess water and swelling of the abdomen; (The above signs are not specific indicators of heart disease but you should be suspicious if your dog exhibits them.)

• Heart murmur, detected with a stethoscope, is associated with incomplete closure of the heart valves. When the heart muscle contracts on a supposedly closed chamber, some blood leaks through the partially closed valves, thereby reducing the cardiac output, the oxygenation of the tissues and exercise tolerance.

Other heart conditions may be detected by your veterinarian using an electrocardiogram, enabling the evaluation of abnormalities in the heart. X-rays indicate heart size, shape and position of the heart in the chest.

Treatment

Treatment by your veterinarian will vary according to the type of heart disease diagnosed and its associated symptoms. The aim of any treatment is to improve heart function and to reduce fluid retention.

Good general nursing, such as protecting your dog from stress caused by excitement, over-exertion, excessive hot or cold temperatures and humidity, is helpful.

Make sure clean water is always readily available. Check with your local water authority as to what the level of sodium is in your water supply. If the level of sodium is above 150 ppm, use distilled water.

Your veterinarian can supply prescription diets that have a greatly reduced salt content. Reduction of salt content (sodium) in the diet helps to decrease fluid retention thereby improving blood circulation and organ function including the function of the heart. Avoid feeding the dog those canned and dried foods that have a relatively high salt content to enhance their palatability.

If the prescription diets are unavailable, you can prepare your own salt-reduced diet of rice plus lamb or beef or chicken.

HEARTWORM

This disease—rare in cats—is very common in dogs in most countries with tropical or subtropical regions, such as the US, southern Europe, Australia and India.

Cause

A worm called *Dirofilaria immitis* which lives in the right ventricle of the heart and the pulmonary artery. The

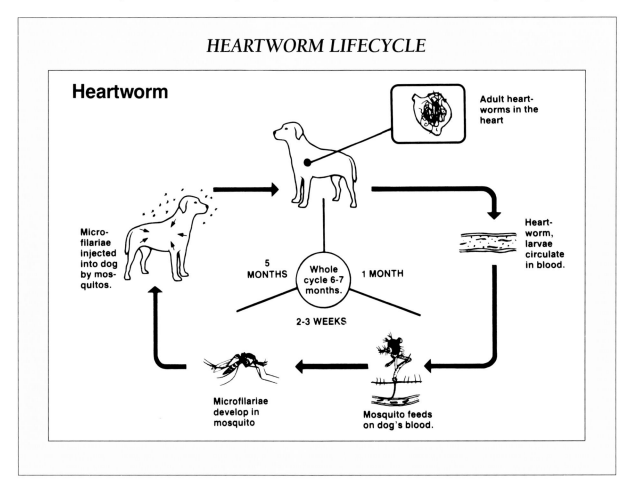

HEARTWORM LIFECYCLE

pulmonary artery is the major blood vessel leading from the heart to the lungs. The worms can vary from 10 centimetres to 25 centimetres in length.

The female worm produces microfilaria (larvae) which are released into the bloodstream. Certain species of mosquito ingest microfilaria when sucking blood from an infected dog. The same mosquito when biting another dog releases microfilaria into its tissues or bloodstream. Over a period of six months or more, the microfilaria find their way to the heart and pulmonary artery and live there as mature adults. Heartworm is not transferred directly from dog to dog, cat to cat or dog to cat. A dog or cat can only become infected by being bitten by a certain species of mosquito carrying the microfilaria.

Signs

Signs vary with the number of heartworms in the right side of the heart and pulmonary artery. In many cases there are no signs of the disease. Signs may include lethargy, chronic cough, anaemia, laboured breathing, swollen abdomen and drinking excess water.

The heartworm may float free in the blood stream and block an important blood vessel, acting like an embolism or clot to cause death.

Treatment

Your veterinarian can diagnose heartworm by a blood test. X-rays of advanced cases usually show enlargement of the pulmonary arteries and right side of the heart.

Treatment involves intravenous injections of an arsenical compound to kill the adult worm, followed a month later by another type of drug to kill the microfilaria. This method of treatment is usually very successful.

Prevention

When puppies are six weeks of age, they should be started on a heartworm preventative treatment programme if they live in a heartworm area.

A blood test for heartworm cannot detect the disease in puppies under six months of age. If you live in a heartworm area, you are advised to have your growing puppies blood tested for heartworm when over six months of age. Even puppies that have been on a heartworm preventative treatment programme should be tested as they may have caught the disease before going on the programme.

Adult dogs, too, if living in a heartworm area, should have a blood test before being placed on a preventative treatment programme. At present, there are two methods of prevention: Diethyl carbamazine (D.E.C.), which comes in a tablet or liquid form and is given daily, and Ivermectin, which is in tablet form only but is given monthly. Ivermectin is the more efficient and effective form of prevention.

If you intend travelling through a heartworm area, start preventative treatment two weeks before travelling and continue for eight weeks after leaving the area.

HEPATITIS

The liver plays an important role in digestion, and in the production of proteins, fats, sugars, vitamins, and in detoxifying poisons and waste products.

Hepatitis is inflammation or damage to the liver. The liver has tremendous powers of recovery and unless the damage is overwhelming, the liver cells can regenerate and restore the liver back to normal function. Hepatitis in dogs is not contagious to humans .

Causes

Trauma due to a motor vehicle accident or some other injury. Viral or bacterial infections. Poisons ingested or absorbed through the skin in sufficient quantity will damage the liver. Poor blood circulation to the liver due to heart disease. Primary and secondary cancer of the liver.

Signs

Not eating, vomiting, abdominal pain, diarrhoea, lethargy, urine dark in colour, and jaundice (yellow discoloration of the conjunctiva and gums).

Treatment

Consult your veterinarian who can diagnose the disease, and often its cause, by examination, urine tests, blood tests, x-ray and in some cases by an exploratory laparotomy, i.e. opening up the abdomen to examine the liver in detail. The treatment administered to the dog by your veterinarian will vary according to the cause and symptoms.

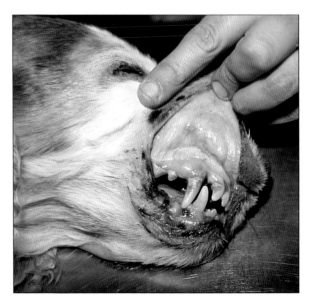

Jaundice: yellow discolouration of the gums

You can assist in the recovery of your dog:
- Provide clean, fresh water.
- Feed four or more small meals per day.
- Make sure the food is fat free, e.g. lean meat, chicken or fish.
- Give NO milk or dairy products.
- Give a vitamin–mineral supplement high in the vitamin B group.
- Provide protection from the environment (heat and cold).
- Do not allow the dog to overexert itself.

Prevention

There is a very affective vaccine available against viral hepatitis (see Vaccination programme, p. 94).

HERNIATED DISC (SLIPPED DISC)

The dog's spine is made up of a number of vertebrae (bones), each separated by a disc. These discs act as shock absorbers and allow movement between the vertebrae, giving the spine its flexibility. Each disc is made up of a tough outer cartilage with a gelatinous centre. If the disc herniates it ruptures releasing its gelatinous fluid which creates pressure on the spinal cord. In most cases, the rupture of a disc is due to wear and tear or abnormal pressure exerted by the vertebrae during some form of vigorous activity.

The spinal cord, which is made up of nerve fibres, runs through the spinal canal. Pressure from the gelatinous fluid causes the spinal cord formed by the vertebrae to become inflamed and swell. Subsequent damage to the cord may be partial or complete, temporary or permanent.

The common sites of disc problems are in the back, particularly in the region of the last three thoracic and first two lumbar vertebrae. Fewer problems occur in the neck.

This dog is paralysed in the hind legs.

Causes

Conformation: Dogs with short legs and long bodies, such as the Dachshund, Corgi and Pekingese, are prone to disc problems in the back. Excessive movement and stress are placed on their back because of their shape or conformation.

All these breeds, because of their conformation, can herniate a disc in the normal daily routine of running, jumping, twisting and turning when in play.
Beagles are prone to disc problems in the neck and back.

Injury: Severe trauma such as caused by a motor vehicle accident.

Signs

The signs may be sudden and acute, or gradual and progressive.

Back: arched back, refuses to move, crying, weak in the hindlegs, ataxia (unco-ordinated movement of the hindlimbs), trembling with pain, unable to stand, and paralysis of the hindlimbs.

Neck: Head tucked in, little or no head and neck movement, does not want to put its head down to eat or drlnk and cries in pain when touched around the head or neck.

Treatment

See your veterinarian who will make a diagnosis based on the type of breed, examination and x-rays which may include a myelogram, a technique that involves injecting a dye into the spinal canal to highlight the herniated disc.

Conservative treatment involves pain relievers, cage rest, anti-inflammatory agents to alleviate swelling and inflammation of the spinal cord, and tranquillisers to keep the dog quiet and reduce muscle spasm. It is not recommended to alleviate pain completely as that may induce the dog to become active too quickly thereby aggravating the problem. Cases that are deteriorating whilst on conservative treatment may respond very well to surgery.

Those dogs that are completely paralysed in the hindlimbs and have no pain sensation are referred to as paraplegics. Euthanasia is usually recommended for the paraplegic dog because of the problems associated with nursing, and its poor quality of life.

HERPES VIRUS

This is a viral disease affecting young puppies up to three weeks of age.

Cause

The herpes virus thrives at a temperature of 36.5°C or 98°F which is the norm for puppies up to three weeks of age. The bitch may have the virus but is unaffected by it because of her higher body temperature. The puppies may acquire the infection from their mother.

Signs

The puppies stop suckling, cry continually, are restless, show signs of abdominal pain and distension, may develop diarrhoea, suffer from hypothermia, and may die within 24 hours.

Treatment

There is no specific treatment. Elevate the temperature of the puppies to 38°C or 101°F and see your veterinarian.

HIP DYSPLASIA

Hip dysplasia is a malformation of the hip joint. Approximately 90 per cent of dysplastic dogs are affected in both hips. The hip joint is a ball and socket joint with the ball fitting perfectly into the socket. In some dogs the acetabulum or socket is too shallow and/or the head of the femur, i.e. the ball, is too flat or irregular in shape. This results in a poorly formed joint subject to wear and tear on the joint surfaces and the development of arthritis. The ligament and capsule around the joint become slack and the muscles of the hindquarter waste.

Causes

Hip dysplasia is an inherited condition which may be influenced by diet, exercise and growth rate in the first six to 12 months of the dog's life. Compared with the smaller breeds, the incidence of the disease is higher in the heavier, larger breeds and its signs are more pronounced.

The incidence of hip dysplasia in some breeds of dogs examined in Denmark, Finland and Sweden is given below:

St Bernard	82 per cent
Golden Retriever	60 per cent
Rottweiler	56 per cent
Labrador Retriever	55 per cent
Boxer	45 per cent
German Shepherd	44 per cent
Chow Chow	38 per cent
Poodle (Standard)	26 per cent

Signs

The signs may develop in some dogs as young as three to four months of age. In others, the signs may not develop until the dog is one to three years old.

X–RAYS SHOWING HIP DYSPLASIA

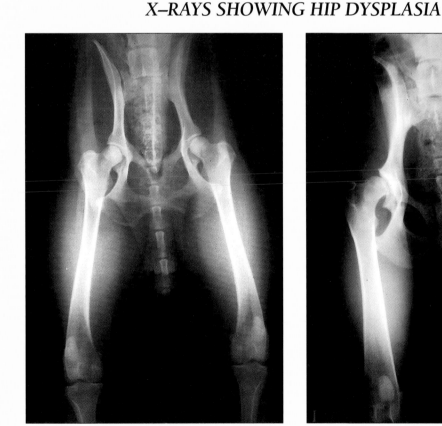

X-ray of normal hips

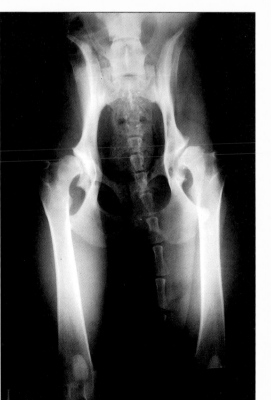

X-ray of grade 4 hip dysplasia

155

The incidence if hip dysplasia is higher in the larger breeds, such as the Rottweiler.

The signs of hip dysplasia may take one or more of the following forms:

• awkward movement in the initial stage;
• dog's activity restricted;
• difficulty in getting up after lying down;
• when trying to jump up, the dog finds it difficult;
• may show fluctuating lameness from one hindleg to the other;
• may walk with a rolling gait in the hindquarters.

Severe cases may be determined by x-ray as early as three months of age. The normal practice is to x-ray dogs when they are 12 months old to determine if they are dysplastic.

Your veterinarian will assess whether or not your dog is dysplastic based on the signs shown by the dog, the degree of laxity in the joint as determined by manipulation, and the changes in the joint as revealed by x-rays. Radiographically, the dog's degree of hip dysplasia is graded from one to four. Grade one are those cases with minimal change and grade four cases virtually have dislocated hips with varying degrees of osteoarthritis, related usually to the age and breed of the dog.

Treatment

Treatment will vary according to the symptoms. Hip dysplasia leads to inflammation of the bones, cartilage and soft tissue which go to make up the hip joint. Inflammation causes pain and lameness. Conservative treatment with drugs will help to alleviate pain and improve mobility. As the condition advances, some cases fail to respond to drug therapy and become severely handicapped. Surgical treatment of these cases has produced some excellent results.

Prevention

Veterinary associations in many countries have formed committees whose role is to give an independent and objective opinion on x-rays for hip dysplasia submitted by veterinarians. Dogs found to be free of the disease are issued with a certificate. Hip dysplasia can be progressively eliminated by using dogs and bitches for breeding that have been given such a certificate. Keep in mind that even if both parents have been certified free of hip dysplasia, it does not guarantee that their puppies will be free of it, although the chance of the puppies having the disease will be lessened considerably.

When a dog is certified hip dysplasia free, it should be identified with a tattoo in the ear or by some alternative means so that it can be positively identified (see Identification, p. 44). In the US, the Orthopedic Foundation for Animals (OFA) is the hip dysplasia certification body.

HOT SPOT

(ACUTE MOIST DERMATITIS)

More commonly found in the longhaired, thick-coated breeds, e.g. Golden Retriever and German Shepherd, but it may be seen in any breed and is not uncommon in the Labrador Retriever.

Cause

An initial irritation of the skin may be caused by a slight abrasion, parasites (fleas), vegetation, etc. The irritation stimulates the dog to lick, bite or scratch the area, causing further damage to the skin. The damaged skin is invaded by bacteria which set up an infection causing further inflammation and irritation. The infected skin oozes serum into the surrounding area, matting the hair. The infection then spreads rapidly through the moist, matted hair.

Signs

A somewhat circular area of hairless, moist, red, infected, ulcerated skin surrounded by matted wet hair. Sometimes an unpleasant odour is associated with the infection.

It is more common in hot, humid weather and the signs may develop rapidly within six to 12 hours.

Treatment

See your veterinarian who may need to sedate the dog to clip the hair well away from the infected area. This assists in drying up the infection as well as preventing its spread.

The administration of antibiotic and anti-inflammatory injections, tablets and lotion will ensure a rapid and complete cure.

If the dog continues to lick and bite the infected area, an Elizabethan collar (see p. 163) around the neck will stop such self-mutilation, allowing the area to dry out and heal.

HYPOTHYROIDISM AND HYPERTHYROIDISM

The thyroid gland secretes a hormone which influences the rate of the body's metabolism.

Hypothyroidism is a term used to describe a dog's illness brought about by a decrease in or complete lack of production of the thyroid hormone.

Hyperthyroidism is an illness that results from an over-production of the thyroid hormone.

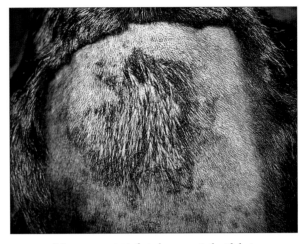

A hot spot: moist infected pus, matted with hair

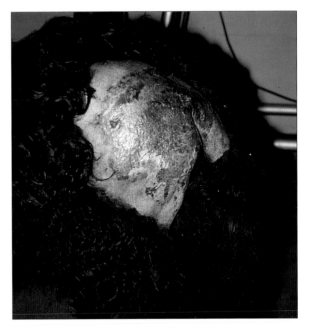

Hair clipped well away from the hot spot

HYPOTHYROIDISM

Cause

Unknown.

Signs

• Sleeping for longer periods throughout the day.

• Decreased exercise tolerance.

• Tendency to put on weight.

• Seeks warmth because of low body temperature.

• Harsh, brittle, dry coat; increased hair loss under neck, under and along the sides of the abdomen and along the back of the hindlegs.

• Infertility in both males and females.

• The skin may become darker in colour.

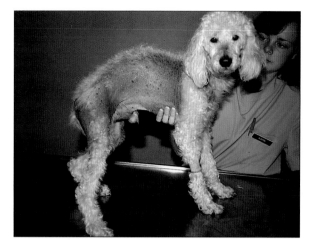

Hair loss along the side of the dog's body

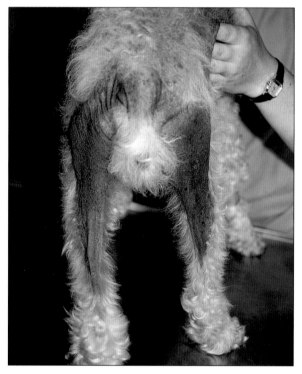

Hair loss on the hind legs

Treatment

See your veterinarian who can positively diagnose the condition by a blood test. Hypothyroidism is readily treated with thyroid hormone administered in the form of a tablet.

HYPERTHYROIDISM

Cause

Tumour of the thyroid gland.

Signs

• Enlargement of the thyroid gland in the neck.

• Increased thirst and appetite.
• Weight loss.
• Restlessness.
• Poor exercise tolerance.

Treatment

Consult your veterinarian who can positively diagnose the condition by a blood test. The treatment may be drugs or radioactive iodine which destroys overactive thyroid tissue, or surgical removal of the tumour.

HYSTERIA

Some forms of external stimulation, e.g. thunder storm, readily excite some breeds to the point where they become hysterical, which may be defined as uncontrollable excitement.

Cause

Some breeds, e.g. Dachshunds, Toy Poodles, West Highland White Terriers, Beagles, Australian Silky Terriers and Yorkshire Terriers, are prone to becoming excited or anxious due to some kinds of external stimulation. They hyperventilate, removing too much carbon dioxide from the blood, which produces hysterical behaviour.

Signs

Whining, yapping, rapid panting, running around, barking, howling, jerking, muscle twitching. The dog does not respond to the owner's attempts to calm it and if the hysterical behaviour is prolonged, the dog may collapse.

Treatment

If possible, remove the source of stimulation. Encourage the dog to breathe with its nose just inside an open plastic bag for a few minutes to increase the carbon dioxide level of the blood. Be careful not to put the dog's head fully into the plastic bag thereby aggravating its hysterical state and perhaps causing it to suffocate.

See your veterinarian who may provide you with tranquillisers to give to the dog prior to exposure to stressful situations which produce hysteria.

INFECTIOUS VIRAL DISEASES AND PROBLEMS

Canine distemper (see p. 133)
Canine parainfluenza virus (Kennel cough) (see p. 133)
Canine parvovirus (see p. 133)
Herpes virus (see p. 154)
Infectious canine hepatitis (see p. 153)
Rabies (see p. 172)

KENNEL COUGH

This highly contagious disease is also known as viral tracheitis It is commonly called kennel cough because most dogs become infected in boarding kennels, dog pounds, animal shelters or in places where numbers of dogs congregate, e.g. dog shows and obedience training classes.

Cause

Kennel cough is primarily caused by the canine *Parainfluenza* virus often associated with a secondary bacterial infection (*Bordatella bronchiseptica*). The infection is spread by infected mucus or airborne droplets from a coughing dog.

Signs

The dog will cough as if something is caught in the throat; sometimes coughing in a spasm to the point of retching and bringing up a white frothy foam. Dogs with kennel cough are usually bright and continue to eat. Dogs with a foreign body lodged in the back of the throat often refuse food or vomit it up almost immediately after eating. Your veterinarian, by examination and x-ray if required, can differentiate between kennel cough and a foreign body. There may be watery discharge from the eyes and nose. The cough usually lasts for approximately ten days but may persist for six to eight weeks. Some dogs with a persistent, harsh cough end up with a collapsed trachea. Most dogs recover completely from the disease although it may be fatal in dogs which have a heart condition or some other respiratory disease.

Treatment

Rest and good general nursing. See your veterinarian who may prescribe antibiotics, antihistamines, and a cough suppressant.

Prevention

In kennels, avoid overcrowding and isolate any dogs with a cough.

Vaccination of puppies with *Parainfluenza* and *Bordatella bronchiseptica* vaccines at 12–14 weeks and 16–18 weeks of age. Adults should have an annual booster vaccination.

KERATITIS (BLUE EYE)

This is inflammation of the cornea, i.e. the clear surface of the eyeball.

Causes

• Infection.

• Irritation due to eyelashes rubbing on the cornea (see Entropion, p. 144).

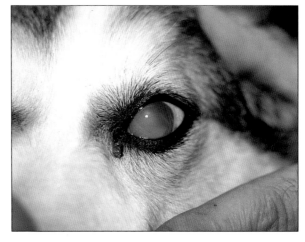

Keratitis: surface of the cornea develops a bluish colour.

• Hair from facial fold rubbing on the cornea (common in Pekingese).

• Vaccination with live hepatitis vaccine.

• Trauma from a foreign body embedded in the conjunctiva or trapped behind the third eyelid.

Signs

The normally clear surface of the eyeball becomes hazy, cloudy or develops a bluish colour. It may involve a small area of the cornea or the whole surface. There may or may not be discharge from the eye.

Treatment

See your veterinarian as keratitis indicates some relatively serious problem with the cornea. The treatment will vary according to the cause which is best determined by your veterinarian.

KIDNEY DISEASES

The dog has two kidneys which filter waste products from the bloodstream. If the kidneys are not functioning properly, the waste products accumulate in the blood and have a toxic or poisoning effect on the dog. Waste products build up in the blood may eventually be fatal.

If up to 75 per cent of each kidney is damaged, the dog can still function and enjoy a good quality lifestyle.

Kidney disease or Nephritis can be divided into two main groups: acute and chronic.

ACUTE KIDNEY DISEASE

This form occurs more frequently in younger dogs (2–6 years of age) and is characterised by sudden onset with obvious symptoms.

Causes

• Infection, both bacterial and viral.

• Trauma, e.g. motor vehicle accident, leading to:
    (a) direct damage to the kidneys;
    (b) shock, which results in reduced blood flow causing both damage to the kidneys and decreased filtration of the blood.

• Other diseases may cause damage to the kidneys by reducing blood flow or by causing debris to accumulate in the blood, thus blocking the filtration system within the kidneys.

• Poisons, such as ethylene glycol (antifreeze), arsenic (insecticide and herbicide), thallium (rat poison) and a poisonous snake bite, which may damage the internal structure of the kidneys.

• Certain antibiotics, e.g. neomycin and gentamycin, can cause kidney damage.

Signs

• Not eating (but may show interest in food by hovering over the food bowl).

• Drinking may be increased or decreased depending on how toxic the dog is.

• Vomiting.

• Lethargy.

• Dehydration. In cases that are fairly severely dehydrated the skin loses its elasticity. When the skin is pinched behind the neck, rather than snapping back into place, it remains in a pinched fold.

• Urinating more frequently if the dog is drinking more.

• Coat looks harsh and rough.

Treatment

Contact your veterinarian. Nephritis can be readily diagnosed by blood tests for urea and creatinine. Your veterinarian will treat your dog according to the causes and symptoms. The treatment may involve:

• antibiotics;

• anti-vomiting drugs;

• fluid and electrolyte therapy given intravenously, subcutaneously (i.e. under the skin), or orally if the dog is not vomiting. It is more difficult to give the same volume orally than it is by the other routes.

During the period when the dog is not eating or drinking at home, it should be hospitalised for fluid therapy. Otherwise it will dehydrate and exacerbate the problem because of reduced blood circulation through the kidneys and concentration of toxins (waste products) in the bloodstream.

Regular blood tests for urea and creatinine can help the veterinarian assess the dog's progress. It is a sign that recovery is taking place when the dog starts to eat and drink.

Once your dog goes home it is important that it

should be given a balanced diet to reduce stress on the damaged kidneys. A balanced diet containing a reduced amount of high quality protein, sodium and phosphorus will help to reduce the quantity of waste products produced and the work load on the kidneys. Try to avoid giving your dog meat, eggs, cheese or bones. In addition, provide your dog with fresh, clean water and good nursing. Avoid exposing it to extremes of temperature.

Your veterinarian can provide you with a prescription diet that has been formulated by veterinary nutritionists for dogs with kidney disease. The diet is highly palatable and readily accepted by most dogs.

CHRONIC KIDNEY DISEASE

This disease can take months or years before symptoms are obvious enough to make the owner aware that the dog is seriously ill. The signs or symptoms are more subtle than acute kidney disease and unless you are alert to the signs they may go unnoticed for some time.

Causes

• Infection: bacterial and viral.

• Other diseases, e.g. diabetes.

• Cardiac disease.

• Other unknown causes.

Signs

As the disease progresses slowly over months or years the signs correspondingly may also develop slowly or the dog may compensate and the signs may be hidden up to the point where the dog can no longer compensate and the signs appear suddenly. The signs may be:

• drinking excessively

• urinating excessively

• weight loss

• lethargy

• poor appetite

• coat rough and harsh due to dehydration

• occasional vomiting

• bad breath

• anaemia

Treatment

Contact your veterinarian who can confirm chronic kidney disease by a thorough clinical examination and pathology tests. Often one or both kidneys on palpation are hard, irregular in shape, and larger or smaller than normal. A urine sample may indicate the presence of blood, a high level of protein and a low specific gravity which indicates the urine is very dilute. A blood test which shows that the urea and creatinine levels are elevated indicates the extent of the damage to the kidneys and the dog's chances of recovery.

After treatment has been administered for a number of days, a second test is useful to determine if the levels have moved up or down.

Treatment which will vary according to the symptoms and causes may include:
• antibiotics to clear up any bacterial infection;
• anabolic steriods to aid in repair of damaged kidney tissue, to prevent weight loss and to stimulate weight gain;
• a vitamin supplement (many chronic kidney disease cases are anaemic due to waste products in the blood affecting red blood cell production from the bone marrow).

Your veterinarian can provide you with a prescription diet containing a reduced amount of protein, sodium and phosphorus. The prescription diet will reduce the workload on the kidneys while supplying the nutritional requirements of the dog.

Most dogs with nephritis have a poor appetite so gradually introduce the new diet over a 14 day period. Start by mixing a small amount of the prescription diet with your pet's normal food and gradually increase the new prescription diet, at the same time decreasing the old diet until the changeover is complete. Try to avoid giving meat, eggs, cheese or bones to your dog. With proper dietary management, progressive chronic nephritis may be stopped or slowed down.

If your dog is not eating or drinking, it will dehydrate which will make the disease worse. Your veterinarian will hospitalise your dog and give it fluids intravenously or under the skin to help flush the waste products out of the blood. This often gives the kidneys the opportunity to improve their function and makes the dog feel better thereby stimulating it to eat and drink.

Chronic kidney disease sometimes gets progressively worse. Human patients rely on dialysis machines to survive while waiting for a kidney transplant. This treatment is not feasible for the dog. If your dog, after intensive treatment with fluid therapy in hospital, will not eat or drink and its urea and creatinine levels are still abnormally high, consider having your dog put to sleep.

LEPTOSPIROSIS

This is a disease which affects not only the dog, but also humans, cattle, sheep, rats and wild animals. The disease can be transferred from the dog or other species to humans. Rats are the main source of infection.

Cause

Leptospirosis is caused by a bacteria which is passed out in the urine of infected animals, sometimes for months after they have recovered from the disease. The bacteria can live in a moist environment for lengthy periods.

Dogs become infected by eating food or drinking water contaminated by rat urine or by eating an infected rat. Another method of infection is contamination of mucous membranes or an open wound with urine from an infected animal.

Signs

A number of dogs that contract leptospirosis show no obvious signs of the disease. The incubation period is five to 15 days. The initial symptoms are loss of appetite, lethargy, high temperature, vomiting and diarrhoea followed by abdominal pain, and walking with an arched back and stiff gait. Often the kidneys and liver are involved leading to jaundice, a sign of which is the yellowing of the mucous membranes, easily recognised around the eyes and gums. The mucous membrane of the mouth and tongue may become ulcerated.

Treatment

Consult your veterinarian who can make a definite diagnosis by clinical examination and blood tests.

Dogs showing signs of the disease should be hospitalised for treatment, and to minimise the risk of spreading the disease to other animals and humans.

Treatment involves antibiotics, drugs to control vomiting and diarrhoea, and fluids administered intravenously to counteract dehydration. Care should be taken to see that there is no direct skin contact in handling vomit, faeces and urine from infected dogs.

Prevention

Vaccination at 12 to 14 weeks and again at 16 to 18 weeks, followed by an annual booster. In high risk areas a booster every six months is recommended. Do not allow your dog access to garbage, dog urine or pools of stagnant water. Exterminate the rat population in the local area.

LICE

Lice are not a common problem in dogs.

Cause

Those dogs most often affected are debilitated, with a dirty, matted coat.

Signs

They are found on the head and along the back of the dog. Lice have a brown head and a greyish body and are found on the skin surface, not on the hair.

The dog is itchy and scratches itself, causing red, inflamed skin to shed dry flakes into the matted hair. Eggs are attached to the hair shaft and can be seen in good light.

Treatment

Clip any matted hair away and then shampoo to clean the

coat before giving a 0.5 per cent Malathion (maldison) rinse. Repeat three times at seven day intervals.

Worming and nutritious feeding of the dog are also recommended.

LICK SORE (GRANULOMA)

Lick sores usually occur more often in shorthaired, large dogs. They are to be seen on the lower parts of the fore and hind limbs. The site of the sore may be due to the fact that the lower part of the limbs are more accessible to the dog's tongue.

Cause

A lick sore may begin as an abrasion or it may be due to the dog being bored, anxious or insecure. In some cases, the cause is unknown. The dog licks a part of the lower limb causing redness of the skin and hair loss. The inflamed skin irritates the dog causing further licking. The licking gives temporary relief but indirectly aggravates the problem and a vicious circle develops.

Signs

• Initially, a circular area of red skin, sparsely covered in hair, appears.

• Constant licking causes complete hair loss.

• The skin becomes thickened and raised.

• The surface of the skin eventually ulcerates, often with a border of thickened, grey coloured skin.

Treatment

Once the sore is thickened, discoloured and ulcerated, it is difficult to treat effectively.

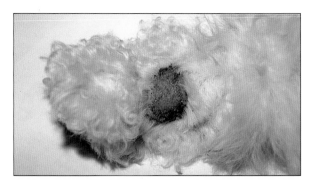

Lick sore: circular area of thickened, raised, ulcerated tissue

There are numerous known methods of treatment that achieve varying degrees of success according to the size and depth of the sore.

In the early stages, prevent the dog from licking the sore by using an Elizabethan collar (see p. 163) or by applying a medical preparation to the sore which is abhorrent to the dog's taste.

Such a mixture is made up of menthol, camphor, eucalyptus and turpentine oil. Bandaging usually has limited success.

If the response to such treatment is poor, see your veterinarian who may treat the sore with cortisone, cobra venom or surgical excision.

Once the sores have cleared up and the hair has regrown, prevent the problem recurring by eliminating the predisposing cause.

This can be done by being more conscious of the dog's need for health care, spending more time with it and providing it with a companion.

The use of a sedative may be beneficial in some cases.

Lick sores occur more often in shorthaired large dogs, such as Labradors.

ELIZABETHAN COLLAR

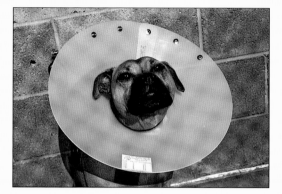

A commercial Elizabethan collar

A home-made Elizabethan collar

A dog's vision is limited when it is wearing an Elizabethan collar.

An Elizabethan collar is used to prevent a dog biting itself, pulling out its stitches, chewing a plaster cast or tearing off a bandage.

Your veterinarian can supply you with a commercially designed and manufactured collar or you can make one at home for your dog.

1. Select a bucket of a suitable size, i.e. one that when the bottom is cut out, the dog's head can just pass through and when it is in place the rim will protrude about 5 cm (2 in) beyond the dog's muzzle. (If the dog's muzzle protrudes beyond the rim of the bucket, the dog will still be able to interfere with its wound, stitches, plaster cast or bandage.) It is advisable to use a bucket that is made of soft plastic; if it is brittle, it will split and break up when knocked about.

2. Cut a hole in the bottom of the bucket and then punch approximately six to 10 small holes evenly spaced around and close to the edge.

3. Thread and tie string or nylon cord through each hole to make small loops so that the dog's collar can be just threaded through them.

4. Put the dog's head through the hole in the bottom of the bucket and tighten the collar firmly so that it anchors the bucket to the neck.

Whilst wearing the Elizabethan collar, the dog should be confined for its own safety.

The dog can sleep comfortably when wearing the collar but you will need to take the collar off to allow the dog to eat. The alternative is to leave the collar on and hold the food or water bowl up to the dog's mouth while it is eating or drinking.

LYMPHOSARCOMA

This is the most common form of leukaemia seen in dogs.

Cause

Unknown.

Signs

Generalised enlargement of all the lymph nodes. The enlarged lymph nodes are not painful to touch.

Weight loss, lethargy, anaemia.

Treatment

See your veterinarian who can make a definite diagnosis by doing a biopsy on one of the lymph nodes.

This disease is ultimately fatal. Chemotherapy can reverse the symptoms within 24 hours and with continued treatment can give the dog good quality of life for up to 16 months.

MAMMARY (BREAST) CYSTS

Cause

Blockage of a duct within the mammary gland.

Signs

A dark-coloured, fluid-filled cyst in the mammary gland.

Treatment

Surgical removal of the cyst or complete excision of the mammary gland.

MAMMARY TUMOUR

Cause

Usually occurs in older female dogs that have not been neutered. The tumours are usually malignant.

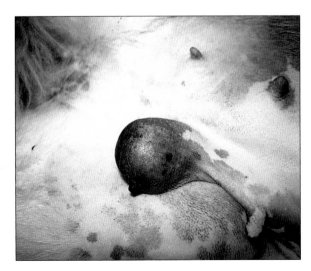

An advanced mammary tumour

Signs

In the early stages, a small hard lump, approximately 0.5 cm (0.2 in) in diameter, can be felt in the mammary gland. At a later stage, the tumour may be the size of a walnut and the skin over the surface of the tumour may be inflamed, smooth, shiny and, or ulcerated.

Treatment

Before resorting to surgery, your veterinarian will x-ray the chest to make sure there are no secondary tumours in the lungs. If the x-rays of the lungs are clear, the tumour is surgically excised. If the tumour is of such a size that it involves a large portion of the mammary gland, then the whole of the gland will be removed. Histopathology on the lump will determine if it is benign or malignant

MANGE

When people see a dog with hairloss and crusty, infected, thickened skin, they often refer to the dog as being mangy. There are numerous causes of this type of skin condition. Mange is a specific disease caused by a mite. There are two common types of mange, namely demodectic and sarcoptic mange, which affect the dog.

DEMODECTIC MANGE

This form of mange is seen more frequently. In many cases the signs are hairloss associated with little or no irritation.

Cause

A mite called *Demodex canis* which can only be seen under the microscope. Many dogs that have a good healthy skin and coat carry demodex mites in the hair follicles.

It is thought that pups pick up the mange mites from their mother when suckling.

The disease is more prevalent in young shorthaired dogs, e.g. Dobermanns.

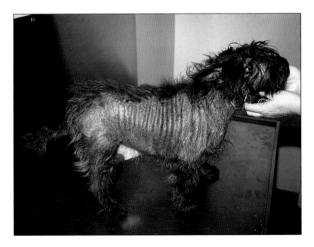

Severe sarcoptic mange

Demodectic mange: hair loss around the eye

Demodectic mange: localised area on the face

The difference between those dogs that have the mites and are healthy and those that develop the disease is due to some deficiency of the immune system.

Signs

The early signs are thinning of the hair, sometimes evident only when viewed from a certain angle.

The common sites of the disease are around the eyes, forehead, under the neck, the front legs and the outside of the hindlegs.

As the disease develops, the hairloss becomes more evident and the skin becomes dry, scaly, discoloured and thickened.

The disease may remain localised or spread over most of the body. This generalised type of the disease is associated with dermatitis, pustules and infection of the skin. This form of the disease is itchy which causes the dog to scratch and further aggravate the condition.

Treatment

See your veterinarian who will scrape the skin and examine the scraping under the microscope. A skin biopsy is sometimes used to diagnose the disease.

There are numerous methods of treatment: insecticidal rinses (e.g. Amitraz, which in most cases gives a very good response), oral insecticides (e.g. Cythioate), and injections (e.g. Avermectin).

The dog's general health care should include:
• a good nutrition programme including a balanced vitamin–mineral supplement;
• an adequate worming schedule;
• a twice weekly wash with benzyl peroxide shampoo;
• alleviation of any stress that may be caused by such conditions as overcrowded and/or unclean housing.

SARCOPTIC MANGE

This disease is contagious to humans and other animals. In humans it is known as Scabies and the usual signs are itchiness and red spots on the skin.

Cause

A mite called *Sarcoptes scabii* can affect dogs of all ages. It is more commonly seen in country dogs because of their contact with foxes and wombats, many of which carry the disease.

Signs

The common sites are the ears and elbows but some dogs are affected all over the body. The dog is very itchy, and hairloss is caused mainly by scratching.

The skin is very red, often covered with heavy white flakes. Dogs with a generalised infection, develop a thickened, wrinkled skin which is very greasy to touch.

Treatment

See your veterinarian who will confirm the diagnosis by taking a skin scraping from the affected areas.

Wash the dog once a week in benzyl peroxide shampoo and follow it with one of the insecticidal rinses such as 1 per cent Malathion (maldison) or diazinon for at least a month.

Pay attention to good nutrition, regular bathing, and a clean, uncrowded environment.

MEGAOESOPHAGUS (ACHALASIA)

This is a problem not uncommon in puppies. At the point where the oesophagus opens into the stomach there may be a constriction or spasm of the muscles which impairs the passage of food into the stomach. Over a period of time the lower oesophagus becomes permanently distended acting as a reservoir for food, further aggravating the distension.

Cause

A congenital condition; cause unknown.

Signs

• Puppy regurgitates food, usually straight after eating.

• Puppies show signs of the problem when they start to eat solid food.

• Weight loss or lack of weight gain and poor development in puppies.

• Pneumonia may develop due to inhalation of vomited food.

Treatment

• See your veterinarian who will confirm the condition by a series of x-rays including a barium swallow.

• Feed the puppy from an elevated position so that its head is up.

• Add water to the food to make it into a paste.

• Feed four small meals a day. If the puppy does not respond to this method of management, surgery may be indicated.

MIDDLE EAR INFECTION

The middle and inner ear structures are important for hearing and balance.

Cause

It is usually caused by a bacterial infection associated with inflammation of the middle and inner ear. There are several routes to the middle ear that the infection can take. It can pass along the external ear canal and through a ruptured ear drum, along the eustachian tube from the throat or via the bloodstream as a generalised acute infection localising in the middle ear.

Signs

There may or may not be discharge from the ear. The head is tilted towards the affected side. There may be sideways movement (flickering) of the eyes. Usually the dog will have a drunken sway when it moves and it will tend to circle in one direction, sometimes falling over on its side.

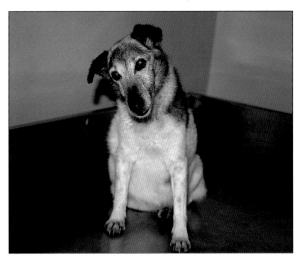

Middle ear infection: the dog's head is tilted towards the affected ear.

Treatment

Take the dog to your veterinarian who will treat the condition according to the cause. The treatment may involve antibiotics, anti-inflammatory agents, surgical drainage, and hospitalisation until the dog regains its balance. Response to treatment is sometimes slow. Some cases are left with a permanent head tilt, a tendency to wobble, and deafness.

MOUTH DISEASES AND PROBLEMS

Broken teeth (see p. 92)
Choking (see p. 110)
Displacement of teeth (see p. 91)
Epulis (see p. 145)
Erosion and discolouration of dental enamel (see p. 92)
Fish hook in lip (see p. 110)
Gingivitis (see p. 150)
Malocclusion (see p. 92)
Overshot jaw (see p. 92)
Plaque and tartar (see p. 92)
Root tooth abscess (see p. 175)
Supernumerary teeth (see p. 92)
Swollen jaw (see p. 177)
Undershot jaw (see p. 92)

OBESITY

A dog's weight varies according to diet, exercise and type of breed. An obese dog is one that is obviously fat. Obesity is more common in older dogs.

Cause

The primary cause of obesity is the dog overeating.

Secondary causes are lack of exercise, desexing, and advancing age. The dog's genetic makeup will also have an influence on its weight, e.g. a Whippet is a dog of slender build whereas a Labrador is heavier. As the dog puts on weight, it tends to exercise less, setting up a vicious circle.

Signs

An obese dog looks overweight. It may have a large abdomen that hangs down and protrudes outwards. You can feel the fat deposited under the skin especially over the ribs and around the abdomen.

Obesity predisposes your dog to arthritis, joint and ligament problems, back problems, heart disease, breathing difficulties, diabetes, heat stress and constipation.

Treatment

Consult with your veterinarian to confirm that your dog is obese and that its obesity is not due to a medical problem.

GUIDE TO NORMAL WEIGHTS OF BREEDS

BREED	DOG KILOS	DOG POUNDS	BITCH KILOS	BITCH POUNDS	BREED	DOG KILOS	DOG POUNDS	BITCH KILOS	BITCH POUNDS
Afghan Hound	27–32	59–70	23–30	51–66	Greyhound	30–32	66–70	27–30	59–66
Airedale Terrier	20–23	44–51	20–23	44–51	Labrador Retriever	27	59	25	55
Australian Kelpie	20.5–25	45–55	18–27	40–59	Maltese	2–4	4–9	2–4	4–9
Australian Silky Terrier	3.5–4.5	8–10	3.5–4.5	8–10	Newfoundland	63.5–68	140–150	50–54.5	100–120
Basenji	11	24	10	22	Old English Sheepdog	27–41	59–90	23–27	51–59
Basset Hound	18–27	40–59	16–23	35–50	Pekingese	3.5	8	3.5–5.5	8–12
Beagle	13–16	29–35	11–13	24–29	Pomeranian	2	4	2–2.5	4–5
Border Collie	19–24	42–53	18–22	40–48	Poodle (Standard)	29–33.5	64–74	29–33.5	65–74
Boxer	30	66	28	62	Poodle (Miniature)	5–7	11–15	5–7	11–15
British Bulldog	25	55	23	51	Poodle (Toy)	3.5–5.5	8–12	3.5–5.5	8–12
Bull Terrier	18–23	40–51	18–23	40 -50	Retriever (Golden)	30–32	66–70	25–27	55–59
Bull Terrier (Staffordshire)	13–17	29–37	11–13	24–26	Rottweiler	45.5–54.5	100–120	36–41	79–90
Cavalier King Charles (Spaniel)	4.5–8	10–18	4.5–8	10–12	Samoyed	20.5–25	45–55	16–20.5	35–45
Chihuahua	1–3	2–7	1–3	2–7	Setter (English)	27–30	59–66	25–28	55–62
Collie	20.5–29.5	45–65	18–25	40–50	Setter (Irish)	27–30	59–66	25–27	55–59
Dachshund (Long Hair)	8	18	8	18	Spaniel (Cocker)	11–13	24–29	11–13	24–29
Dachshund (Smooth Hair)	11	24.2	10	22	Spaniel (American Cocker)	11–13	24–29	11–13	24–29
Dachshund (Wire Hair)	9–10	20–22	8–9	18–20	Spaniel (Springer –English)	23	51	23	51
Dalmatian	27	59	25	55	Weimaraner	25–30	55–66	20–25	44–55
Dobermann	34–41	75–90	29.5–36	65–79	Welsh Corgi (Cardigan)	10–12	22–26	9–11	20–24
Fox Terrier	7–8	15–18	7–8	15–18	Welsh Corgi (Pembroke)	9–11	20–24	8–10	18–22
German Shepherd	34–38.5	75–85	27–32	59–70	West Highland White Terrier	8–9	18–20	7–8	15–18
German Short Haired Pointer	25–32	55–70	20–27	44–59	Whippet	10–13	22–29	8–11	18–24
Great Dane	54.5	120	45.5	100	Yorkshire Terrier	3	7	3	7

Weight loss is achieved by reducing calorie intake and increasing exercise. You can record your dog's weight by holding your dog and standing on a set of bathroom scales. Record the combined weight of yourself and the dog. Subtract your weight from the combined weight to find the dog's weight.

The amount of weight loss that you should aim for in your dog is 250 g (½ lb) per week (small dog), 500 g (1 lb) per week (medium sized dog) and 750 g (1 ½ lb) per week (large dog). Reduce your dog's calorie intake by reducing the volume of food gradually and by feeding it three or four small meals a day.

You can obtain from your veterinarian a prescription diet that is high in fibre, low in fat and calories, and which completely covers your dog's nutritional requirements. The advantage of this type of diet is that the dog can eat the same volume of food and lose weight. The prescription diet is highly palatable and useful, not only for achieving weight loss but also preventing weight gain.

Do not feed your dog snacks or other foods in between meals and make sure the whole family is aware of the dog's weight reduction programme. Encourage your dog to exercise. If it is an indoor dog, put it outside for a number of hours every day.

Weigh your dog weekly and record the weight gain or loss.

NERVOUS SYSTEM DISEASES AND PROBLEMS

Convulsions (see pp. 111,145)
Eclampsia (see p. 190)
Fits (see pp. 111,145)
Herniated disc (see p. 154)
Milk fever (see p. 190)
Radial nerve paralysis (see p. 174)
Seizures (see p. 145)
Slipped disc (see p. 154)
Tick poisoning (see p. 177)
Wobbler syndrome (see p. 181)

OSTEOCHONDRITIS DISSECANS

This is a disease of young, fast-growing, large breeds. An area of cartilage lining the surface of the joints, particularly in the shoulder, elbow and hock, dries out and degenerates, leaving an ulcerated cartilage surface.

Cause

• Trauma: Injury or damage caused by repeated over-vigorous activity during the dog's growth phase.
• Hereditary: The dog may inherit faulty conformation, e.g. very straight hindlegs in some Rottweilers. Poor

Obesity is caused by overeating and lack of exercise.

conformation can produce abnormal strain on joints predisposing or causing osteochondrosis. The condition may be inherited so that dogs with good conformation develop the disease.

• Over-supplementation: There is some evidence in the UK that puppies with a pre-disposition which are fed excessive supplements of vitamins and minerals are more likely to develop OCD than those which are not.

Signs

A low grade intermittent lameness which progresses to become persistent and severe. Usually in one forelimb or one hindlimb, or may be bilateral, i.e. in both forelimbs or both hindlimbs. The affected joint(s) may be swollen. Most often seen in dogs six to 14 months of age.

Treatment

See your veterinarian who can diagnose osteochondrosis by examination, manipulation of the joints and x-ray.

Enforced rest by confining the dog is always helpful.

Depending on the degree of degenerative change in the joint surface, your veterinarian may administer by injection a drug which stimulates repair of damaged cartilage surfaces. If the response to this method of treatment is poor or the degeneration of the joint surface is severe, surgery will be necessary to curette the ulcerated and fragmented cartilage.

Response to surgery varies according to the severity of the disease and the dog's conformation.

OSTEOPOROSIS

(Nutritional Secondary Hyperparathyroidism)

The ratio of calcium to phosphorus is important for good bone formation and skeletal development in the dog. The optimum calcium to phosphorus ratio is 1.2–1.4 calcium to 1.0 phosphorus. Calcium absorption into the system can be diminished by a low vitamin D content. A deficiency of calcium or a low calcium–high phosphorus ratio stimulates the parathyroid gland causing osteoporosis.

Cause

Dogs on meat only diets, develop the disease. Meat is very high in phosphorus and very low in calcium and does not contain enough iron, magnesium, copper, sodium or iodine. Meat diets have a calcium to phosphorus ratio of approximately 1:20.

Signs

Dogs, particularly those in the growth phase, that are on high meat diets have such problems as poorly formed bones, bowed legs, flat faces, an overall stunted appearance, lameness, joint pain and deformed spinal column and pelvis. The bones generally are very susceptible to fracture.

Treatment

The dog's diet should be changed to one based on a complete and balanced canned and/or dry food. Add calcium to the diet daily for about a month in the form of calcium carbonate at the rate of 1 teaspoon of powder per 5 kg (10 lb) of body weight. It is most important that the calcium supplement does not contain any phosphorus, such as calcium phosphate, because it will not rectify the imbalance in the calcium–phosphorus ratio.

PANCREATITIS

The pancreas is a gland attached to the small intestine just as it leaves the stomach. The pancreas produces enzymes essential for digestion of food and insulin for sugar metabolism. There are two forms of pancreatitis, acute and chronic; the latter may be the aftermath of the acute form.

ACUTE PANCREATITIS

Causes

• Eating meals containing large amounts of fat.
• Infection.
• Other unknown causes.

Signs

• Most dogs affected are middle aged and overweight.
• Sudden, severe abdominal pain.
• Vomiting.
• The signs will vary according to the degree of damage to the pancreas. In some cases, the enzymes produced by the pancreas digest the pancreas itself, causing death.

Treatment

See your veterinarian who will diagnose the disease by examination and specific blood tests.

Treatment will vary according to the signs and may include intravenous fluids, antibiotics, analgesics to relieve pain, and anti-emetics to stop vomiting.

Once the dog shows signs of recovery, three or four small, low fat meals a day are suggested, e.g. steamed chicken and boiled rice.

CHRONIC PANCREATITIS

A dog with chronic pancreatitis may develop *Diabetes mellitus* (see p. 138) or an inability to digest food properly due to the deficiency of pancreatic enzymes.

Cause

The result of one or more attacks of acute pancreatitis.

Signs

• Faeces are of a putty colour and consistency.
• Weight loss to the point of looking pathetically thin.
• Susceptible to bouts of diarrhoea often brought on by minor changes in the diet.

Treatment

Contact your veterinarian who will dispense an enzyme supplement to compensate for the damaged pancreas not functioning properly.

Control the dog's diet by giving it three or four small meals a day, low in fat and high in carbohydrate.

PARONYCHIA
(INFECTED NAIL BED)

This is an infection under the nail bed or quick.

Cause

When the dog runs around outside, dirt or some foreign body sometimes becomes wedged between the nail and the quick, causing an irritation and ultimately an infection.

Signs

The nail bed or quick is red, swollen and painful to touch. The dog usually licks the sore toe constantly and often is lame on that leg. The hair around the nail bed and on the toe may become sparse due to the dog licking it continuously. There may be a dark, cheese-like discharge from under the nail bed.

Treatment

If the infection is obvious, see your veterinarian. Other-

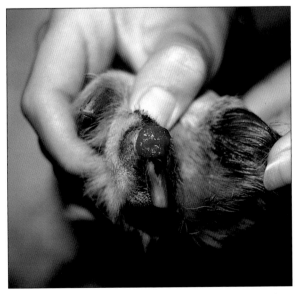

This sore has developed from a chronically infected nail bed.

wise, gently scrub the base of the nail with a nail brush using warm water and soap and chlorhexidine or betadine. Use a downward action in order to work out any dirt, grit or foreign material. Apply an antiseptic cream or lotion to the inflamed area. If the dog continues to lick the toe, put an Elizabethan collar (see p. 163) on the dog to prevent it from aggravating the condition further.

PATELLA LUXATION
(SLIPPING KNEECAP)

This condition is seen more commonly in the Toy breeds and is an inherited defect. Some of the breeds affected are the Maltese Terrier, Toy Poodle, Chihuahua and Pomeranian.

Cause

The patella (kneecap) sits in a groove, called the patella groove. The groove may be shallow, or the ridge on one side or the other of the groove may be flat allowing the kneecap to slip out of place.

In some dogs with bowed hindlegs, the ligaments and tendons attached to the kneecap pull the kneecap out of its groove. This problem often occurs in both hindlegs.

Signs

The dog may be walking along and suddenly holds its hindleg high up off the ground because its kneecap has slipped out. Usually the kneecap slips back into place of its own accord. When this happens, the dog will put the leg down to the ground and walk normally.

Treatment

If the kneecap does not slip back into place of its own accord, you can help it to do so by flexing and extending the affected leg and massaging the stiff (knee) joint. Surgery can be performed to anchor the patella permanently in the patella groove.

PENIS AND PREPUCE (SHEATH) INFECTIONS (BALANOPOSTHITIS)

The male dog's genitalia are designed anatomically so that the penis is completely enclosed by the prepuce (sheath), except when the dog urinates or is sexually aroused.

The penis in the prepuce, which provides a moist, warm environment, is in an ideal situation for the growth and proliferation of bacteria. A small amount of creamy discharge at the openlng of the prepuce is normal.

Causes

Infection; injury; foreign body; tumour.

Signs

• Pus dripping from the prepuce may be blood stained.
• An unpleasant odour is associated with the discharge.
• If the penis is exposed, it appears inflamed and may bleed when touched.

Treatment

Put an antibacterial solution, e.g. chlorhexidine, into a bucket of warm water.

Have somebody hold the dog on its side while you gently but firmly pull the prepuce back to expose the penis.

Wash the penis, removing any pus or discharge, and rinse the penis thoroughly with clean, warm water.

Smear a mild antiseptic cream inside the prepuce and around the penis.

You can apply the ointment by putting the nozzle of the tube just inside the opening of the prepuce and squeezing the tube. Remove the nozzle and pinch the opening of the prepuce to keep it closed. With your other hand, massage the outside of the prepuce to spread the ointment evenly inside the prepuce and over the penis. If the penis and/or prepuce appear heavily infected, see your veterinarian who, depending on the cause, will administer antibiotics and give you an antibiotic ointment to apply.

PENIS PROTRUDING FROM PREPUCE (SHEATH) (PARAPHIMOSIS)

The penis is unable to retract back into the sheath.

Causes

• In some cases, following mating, the penis is swollen and cannot retract into the sheath because the constriction of the sheath's rim will not allow it to do so.
• Some dogs have long hair around the opening of the sheath. When the penis is extended, the hair sticks to it and as the penis retracts, the hair pulls the rim of the sheath inwards, thus creating a constriction that prevents the penis retracting any further.

Signs

An engorged, discoloured, protruding penis.

Treatment

Carefully remove any long hairs that may be causing an obstruction.

Lubricate the penis and the sheath opening with paraffin oil or another suitable lubricant. Gently push the penis in, with the fingers of one hand as you pull the sheath out over the penis with the other hand. If unsuccessful, seek the help of your veterinarian.

PERINEAL HERNIA

Cause

Chronic constipation or an enlarged prostate gland stimulates the dog to strain when urinating or defecating, causing the hernia.

Signs

A swelling to be seen on one or both sides of the anus.

Treatment

Surgical repair of the hernia in conjunction with castration to reduce the size of the prostate gland and prevent the dog from straining.

PNEUMONIA

This is an infection and/or inflammation of the lung tissue.

Causes

There are numerous causes of pneumonia, i.e. viruses, bacteria, parasites, or inhalation of foreign material. There are many predisposing causes, e.g travelling, overcrowding and malnutrition, all of which lower the dog's resistance to infection.

Signs

The signs will vary with the suddenness of onset and the volume of lung tissue involved. Generally, the dog will be off its food and lethargic. Breathing is rapid and shallow. Often a cough, nasal discharge and a high temperature are associated with pneumonia. The breath may have a foul odour and if you place your ear to the chest, moisture may be detected as the dog breathes in and out. The dog will sit in one place, not wanting to move or lie down.

Treatment

Consult your veterinary surgeon immediately. Keep in mind that good nursing is an essential part of any treatment. Keep the dog in a well-ventilated, draught-free area. Keep its temperature as even as possible, but not too high. Fresh water and nutritious, palatable food should be available to encourage eating and drinking. Electrolytes in the water are important as they help to prevent dehydration.

POLYPS

A polyp is a growth originating in the mucous membrane lining of the nose, vagina or rectum. It is round in shape and attached to the mucous membrane by a pedicle or stem.

Polyps protruding from vagina

Cause

Unknown. A polyp may be a pre-cancerous growth.

Signs

Nasal polyps may be indicated by bleeding from one nostril and/or noisy breathing due to impairment of air flow through the nostril.

Vaginal or rectal polyps may be seen protruding from the vaginal or anal orifice and are sometimes associated with bleeding.

Treatment

If accessible, polyps are readily removed by surgically cutting the stem at its point of attachment to the mucous membrane.

PROGRESSIVE RETINAL ATROPHY
(PRA)

The retina is a highly specialised layer of nerve cells lining the back of the eye. Light stimulates the cells of the retina which send signals to the brain via the optic nerve.

The retina of dogs with progressive retinal atrophy degenerates to the point where they go blind.

Cause

It is an inherited defect reported in many breeds, e.g. Border Collie, Dachshund, Golden Retriever, Labrador Retriever, Poodle, Shetland Sheepdog and Welsh Corgi.

Signs

As the condition develops, the dog appears clumsy, bumps into objects, stumbles and appears confused, especially at night or in poor light. Eventually the condition leads to total blindness.

Treatment

There is none.

Prevention

Do not use for breeding those dogs with progressive retinal atrophy (PRA), or their relatives. Your veterinarian or veterinary opthamologist can detect PRA by examining the retina. In some dogs it is not evident until five years of age.

PROSTATE GLAND ENLARGEMENT

More than 50 per cent of male dogs, older than five years, have an enlarged prostate gland.

Causes

Cancer; infection; cysts; inflammation.

Signs

Straining to urinate, dribbling urine from the penis, squatting to urinate, blood in the urine. Straining to defaecate, constipation. Constant straining may cause a perineal hernia (a hernia on one or both sides of the anus).

Treatment

Treatment will vary according to the cause: antibiotics; female hormone therapy; castration; or removal of the prostate gland.

Constipation can be treated by altering the diet, administering parrafin oil and/or an enema (see p. 136).

PUPPY DISEASES AND PROBLEMS

Achalasia (see p. 165)
Atresia ani (see p. 129)
Cleft palate (see p. 195)
Coccidiosis (see p. 134)
Diarrhoea (see pp. 84,139,195)
Displacement of teeth (see p. 91)
Fading puppy syndrome (see p. 195)
Hare lip (see p. 196)
Herpes virus (see p. 154)
Hypothermia (see pp. 112,196)
Megaoesophagus (see p. 165)
Navel infection (see p. 196)
Orphan puppies (see p. 193)
Supernumerary teeth (see p. 92)
Umbilical hernia (see p. 196)

RABIES

(See Vaccination programme, p. 94.) This is a highly contagious viral disease of warm blooded animals and almost always fatal. It is a disease of major significance because it is transmissible to humans. Rabies is widespread throughout the world although Australia, United Kingdom, Ireland, Japan, Hawaii, Netherlands, Norway, Sweden and New Zealand are free of the disease.

Cause

The virus is transmitted by the bite of an infected animal. It is found in heavy concentration in the saliva of the infected animal. Dogs that contract rabies usually develop what is called the furious form, a sign of which is the tendency to attack and bite. The virus can be spread if a fresh wound is contaminated by infected saliva.

The period of time from being bitten to the symptoms showing can vary from weeks to months.

There are three phases of the disease. The first phase is characterised by a change in personality and a tendency to hide in dark places. This phase may be easily overlooked.

The second phase, the furious stage, develops two days after the first signs of the disease. This phase can last up to four days. The dog may suddenly attack, biting its victim viciously.

The third phase is the dumb stage which develops over 48 hours. Paralysis starts in the hindquarters and progresses forward along the body until the dog is completely paralysed. This is followed by death.

Treatment

If you suspect your dog has been bitten by a rabid animal, wash the wound thoroughly with soap and water and take your dog to your veterinarian immediately. Give the veterinarian information about the type of rabies vaccine your dog has had and when. This information will determine how the dog will be treated, providing it shows no symptoms of the disease.

Once the dog has developed signs of rabies, treatment is useless and the only course open to the veterinarian is to euthanase it.

The World Health Organisation recommends that unvaccinated dogs known to have been bitten by a rabid animal should be euthanased immediately because of the risk to humans and other animals.

If you suspect your dog shows signs of rabies, do not approach it. If it is in an enclosed space, lock it in and immediately contact your veterinarian.

Prevention

Every dog should be vaccinated in countries which are known to have rabies. This is in the interest of the dog, other animals, the owner and other people.

There are both killed and modified live virus vaccines to combat this disease. The vaccine is not available in countries that do not have the disease.

Vaccination procedure

Puppies: First vaccination at three months of age.
Adult dogs: Booster vaccination annually.

Every puppy should be vaccinated against rabies at three months of age in those countries known to have the disease.

RADIAL NERVE PARALYSIS

This condition is not uncommon in dogs hit in the shoulder region by a motor vehicle. The radial nerve runs along the inside of the shoulder joint, supplying the forelimb.

Cause

The radial nerve may be either stretched, bruised, crushed or cut at the time of injury. Fracture of the humerus is sometimes related to radial nerve damage.

Depending on the severity of damage to the nerve, the dog may have temporary or permanent paralysis in the affected forelimb.

Signs

• The forelimb hangs limply with the leg bent at the carpus (wrist) and the upper surfaces of the toes drag along the ground. If the nerve is temporarily damaged, recovery usually takes place within three weeks, otherwise there is a strong possibility that the paralysis is permanent.
• The upper surface of the toes dragging along the ground may be worn away so deeply that the bones are exposed.
• Severe wasting of the muscle of the affected forelimb also occurs.
• Sometimes there is referred pain causing the dog to bite its foot.

Treatment

See your veterinarian who may treat the dog with anti-inflammatory drugs to reduce swelling and inflammation. Bandage the toes or attach a leather boot to protect them.

If there are no signs of recovery after three weeks, consider amputation. The useless limb often hinders the dog's ability to get around, the tops of the toes wear, allowing a serious infection to develop, and the dog may suffer from referred pain. Dogs with three legs can get around quite well.

RECTAL PROLAPSE

The mucous membrane lining the rectum protrudes through the anus.

Cause

Usually this problem results from persistent diarrhoea and is more often seen in puppies than in mature dogs.

Signs

A red, sausage-shaped, swollen mass, usually about 5 cm (2 in) long, protrudes from the anus. The dog may strain and attempt to lick the prolapsed rectum.

Treatment

See your veterinarian immediately. The dog will be anaesthetised, and the veterinarian will reduce the swelling of the prolapsed rectum, push it to its correct position and put a purse-string suture in the anus which will keep the rectum in place for three to four days. Antibiotics will be administered. Sometimes the problem requires more extensive surgery.

RINGWORM

Ringworm is a highly contagious skin disease caused by a fungus. It is not caused by a parasite or worm. The disease is more common in young dogs and puppies. It is contagious to humans (especially young children) as well as to other dogs and cats.

Cause

The fungus (*Microsporum canis* or *Microsporum gypseum*) is spread either by direct or indirect contact . The fungus lives on hair, so the disease can be caught from loose hair shed by an infected dog . It can be spread by man, for example, by using infected grooming equipment.

Signs

The ringworms may be anywhere on the body but the common sites are the head and forelimbs.

The lesions appear as a circular area of hairloss varying in diameter from ½ cm to 2 ½ cm (1 in). There may be one or more lesions which may or may not have a definite border. It takes approximately two weeks from the time of contact for hairless patches to appear.

The skin in the bald patch has a dry, grey, scaly appearance.

Treatment

Wash the dog in a 0.3 per cent halamid (chloramine)solution twice weekly for three weeks to kill the fungus on the skin. Your veterinarian will prescribe

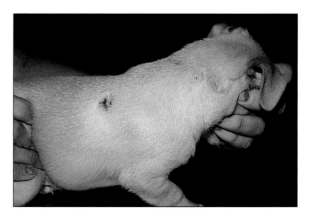

Circular areas of hair loss indicating ringworm lesions

Griseofulvin tablets to be given for three weeks. Isolate the dog for three weeks. Vacuum areas where the dog lives, to pick up any loose infected hair. Soak grooming equipment in a 0.3 per cent halamid (chloramine) solution. Hair regrowth may take a month or more after successful treatment. Once a dog has had ringworm it usually develops immunity.

Your veterinarian will make an initial diagnosis on the appearance of the lesions and on any history of a family member having ringworm. The veterinarian can confirm that it is a ringworm by shining an ultraviolet lamp (Wood's lamp) over the suspicious area of skin in a darkened room. If it is ringworm, the lesion will glow a fluorescent green colour. A skin scraping with some hair can be sent to the laboratory for culture.

ROOT TOOTH ABSCESS

The most common root tooth abscess in the dog involves the fourth upper molar tooth. This tooth is called the Carnassial tooth and has a three-pronged root which enters into the Maxillary sinus.

Cause

Decay of the Carnassial tooth.

Signs

Swelling of the cheek below the eye. Swelling may fluctuate up and down and finally remain swollen. The eye on the side of the swelling may be partially closed and weep. The swelling on the cheek may erupt, discharging pus.

Treatment

See your veterinarian who will anaesthetise your dog, extract the Carnassial tooth, and administer antibiotics.

RUPTURED CRUCIATE LIGAMENT

The dog's stifle (knee) joint is stablised by numerous ligaments, two of which are the anterior and posterior cruciate ligaments. The anterior cruciate ligament is the most commonly ruptured ligament in the stifle (knee) joint. It is seen in all breeds but more commonly in the shortlegged robust dogs, e.g. Corgi and Beagle.

Causes

• Most commonly caused by the dog running quickly and making a sudden change of direction as in chasing a ball.

• Injury, such as caused by a motor vehicle accident.

Signs

The dog will hold the affected hindleg off the ground. There is not much sign of obvious pain associated with a ruptured anterior cruciate ligament. The lameness does not improve with time.

Treatment

Consult your veterinarian who can diagnose this condition by manipulation of the affected stifle (knee) joint.

The ligament will not repair itself and, if not treated, the unstable joint will become arthritic in time.

The ruptured ligament is replaced surgically with a new ligament fashioned from the dog's own tissues. This technique for the repair of ruptured anterior cruciate ligaments is very successful.

SALIVARY CYST

There are several salivary glands situated in both sides of the neck below the ear and under the lower jaw.

Ducts run from the glands and open into the mouth where the saliva is released.

Salivary cyst: swelling in the neck

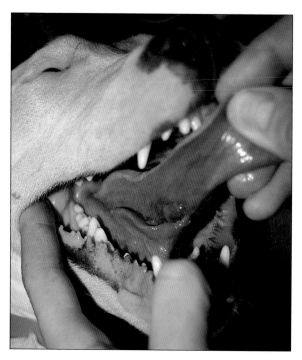

Ranula: soft, fluid-filled swelling under the tongue

Cause

Infection or formation of a calculi (stone) which blocks the duct. The saliva produced by the gland builds up behind the obstruction causing that part of the duct and associated gland to swell.

Signs

• Swelling in the neck, at the base of the lower jaw on one side.
• The size of the swelling may fluctuate up and down and may increase in size immediately after eating.
• There may be a soft fluid-filled swelling under the tongue on one side. This is called a Ranula.

Treatment

See your veterinarian, who may administer antibiotics and drain the swelling. If this is unsuccessful, surgical removal of the affected salivary gland is necessary. Removal of the gland will not affect the production of saliva as there is a set of such glands on both sides of the neck.

SKIN DISEASES AND PROBLEMS

Abscess (see p. 125)
Acute moist dermatitis (see p. 157)
Allergic dermatitis (see p. 126)
Calluses (see p. 132)
Collie nose (see p. 135)
Cyst(s) between toes (see p. 137)
Dandruff (see p. 138)
Demodectic mange (see p. 164)
Dietary allergy (see p. 140)
Flea allergy (see p. 148)
Fly strike (see p. 149)
Hot spot (see p. 157)
Hypothyroidism(see p. 157)
Infected nail bed (see p. 170)
Lice (see p. 161)
Lick sore (see p. 162)
Mange (see p. 164)
Paronychia (see p. 170)
Ringworm (see p. 174)
Sarcoptic mange (see p. 165)
Skin fold infection (see p. 176)

SKIN FOLD INFECTION

Cause

Skin folds in particular areas are prone to infection because they provide a moist, warm environment which is ideal for the growth of bacteria.

Moist skin folds are more prominent in some breeds than in others.

Signs

Lip fold dermatitis: This is common in Cocker Spaniels. The most common indicator is a repulsive, foul odour coming from or around the dog's mouth. The fold is in the lip on either side of the lower jaw.

Facial fold dermatitis: This is common in those dogs with a brachycephalic (pushed in) face, e.g. Pekingese, Bulldog, Boxer and Pug. The fold is moist, inflamed, infected and may have an odour.

Vulval fold dermatitis: This is common in overweight female dogs, although it may also be related to inherited conformation. The author has seen a number of German Shepherd bitches with vulval fold dermatitis.

The dog constantly licks the vulva and the fold on either side is often ulcerated. There may be an odour associated with the dermatitis.

Tail fold dermatitis: This is seen in overweight dogs with folds just above the base of the tail. It is common in those breeds with a corkscrew tail such as Pugs, Bulldogs and Boston Terriers.

The folds are inflamed, infected, and may have an odour.

Treatment

Keep the folds clean, dry and free of hair. Paint the area with tincture of iodine, e.g. Betadine, to kill any bacteria and dry out moist skin.

Cosmetic surgery to eliminate the lip, facial, and vulval folds offers a permanent cure. Tail folds are more difficult to deal with surgically and may have to be treated conservatively.

SNEEZING

The common causes of sneezing in dogs are allergies, foreign bodies, infections and tumours. Dogs investigate their environment by sniffing. In this process they inhale into the nasal cavity numerous irritants, such as house dust, pollens, foreign bodies, which cause infections.

ALLERGIC SNEEZING

Cause

House dust, pollens or some other irritant.

Signs

Frequent sneezing or a spasm occurs when the dog sneezes rapidly in succession a dozen times and then may not sneeze again for hours. There is usually no discharge from the nose but in some cases there may be a fine spray of clear fluid. The eyes are usually clear but they may be slightly watery. The dog is otherwise healthy.

Treatment

Try to identify what the dog is allergic to in the house or garden. If the sneezing persists, see your veterinarian who may prescribe antihistamines.

FOREIGN BODY

Cause

Either inhalation of a foreign body up the nostril or ingestion of a foreign body, e.g. a blade of grass, which passes over the top of the soft palate and into the back of the nose.

Signs

The sneezing is continuous, vigorous and may involve sneezing rapidly in succession a dozen times or more followed by a rest period. There may be bleeding from the affected nostril.

Treatment

In most cases, the dog will need to be anaesthetised by your veterinarian to identify the position of the foreign body and remove it. If the foreign body is protruding from the nose, remove it yourself.

INFECTION

Cause

It may be a primary infection; or it may be a secondary infection associated with a nasal tumour, an infected root of a tooth or disease of the turbinate bones in the nasal cavity.

Signs

• Frequent, irregular bouts of sneezing,
• Thick pus discharge from one or both nostrils. The discharge may be blood tinged.
• The nostrils if partially blocked, cause noisy, snuffling breathing.
• The condition may appear to clear up only to erupt again.

Treatment

See your veterinarian who may administer antibiotics and anti-histamines. If the sneezing and pus discharge recur, a swab may be taken from the nasal pus to identify the infection and determine the best antibiotic to use.

A thorough examination and x-ray may help to determine the specific cause and hence the line of treatment to follow.

SNORTING AND SNUFFLING

This is usually a temporary condition, but may be an established habit in some dogs.

Causes

• Long soft palate flopping over the opening of the windpipe.
• Dust or other irritants at the back of the nose, often accumulated from the dog's natural act of sniffing.
• Other unknown causes.

Signs

• Loud snorting, snuffling, choking noise.
• The head is often held down with the neck flexed.
• It lasts about 30 seconds and then the dog appears perfectly normal.
• It occurs infrequently, at random, without any warning.

Treatment

None. See your veterinarian who will examine the dog to make sure that there is no throat, nasal or tonsil infection.

SWOLLEN JAW

The correct term is mandibular osteopathy, i.e. the deposition of excessive bone in the lower jaw. It is usually seen in young dogs. The excessive bone deposit adversely affects the joint that controls lower jaw movement. The West Highland White, Scotch and Cairn Terriers are subject to this disease.

Cause

Unknown.

Signs

Painful swelling of the lower jaw.

The dog cries with pain when the jaw is opened or at the time of eating. Weight loss or lack of weight gain in young dogs is due to them not wanting to eat because of the pain.

Treatment

Consult your veterinarian who can confirm the diagnosis by examination and x-rays. If treatment with anti-inflammatory agents is instigated before excess bone is deposited, the results are usually successful.

TICK POISONING

Tick poisoning occurs in various parts of the world. Ticks are active in late spring and early summer.

There are various species of the tick, one being *Ixodes holocyclus*, which causes tick poisoning in dogs and cats on the east coast of Australia.

The adult female tick will vary in colour from grey to blue to brown. It is oval in shape and, depending on how engorged it is with blood, will vary in size from 2 mm (⅛ in) to 8 mm (⅓ in).

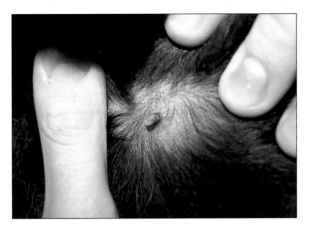

A tick attached to the dog's skin

It is only the female tick which attaches itself to the host dog or cat, poisons it and eventually causes paralysis. The male tick does not attach itself to a host.

The primary hosts for *Ixodes holocyclus* are native animals, such as possums and bandicoots, although dogs, cats, humans or any warm blooded animal are suitable host substitutes.

The female tick lays 2000 to 3000 eggs which hatch into larvae in about 50 days. The larvae attach themselves to a passing host and suck blood from the host for five days and then drop off. The nymph, after a period of 20 to 40 days, attaches itself to a second host and sucks blood from it for approximately five days and then drops off. Over a three to 10 week period the nymph develops into an adult tick. The adult tick attaches itself to a third host and sucks blood for six to 20 days. An adult female tick attached to a dog will poison it within four to six days.

Signs

The early signs are a change in the dog's voice to a croaky, husky bark. If the tick is around the face there may be paralysis of the eyelids or lip on the side of the face to which the tick is attached. The pupils are dilated, the tongue may poke out of the mouth, and the dog may vomit.

The hindlimbs become wobbly and the paralysis progresses to the chest muscles often causing a grunting, distressed type of breathing. The dog becomes paralysed in both the front and hindlimbs. The cause of death is paralysis of the respiratory muscles, i.e. the dog actually dies from asphyxiation.

Treatment

If you find a tick on your dog, remove it immediately. Do not put methylated spirits, turpentine or other such preparations on the tick because as the tick dies slowly it will inject more poison into the dog. Do not grab the body of the tick and try to pull it off as it may break. Furthermore, in squeezing the body of the tick you may stimulate it to inject more poison into the dog before you can remove it.

To remove a tick, first direct another person to hold the dog firmly, but not tightly, around the neck. If the dog is held too tightly you may restrict its breathing further and cause it to struggle violently, thus making it more difficult to remove the tick.

Hold the hair away from the tick so that you can see where the head of the tick is attached to the dog's skin. With a pair of tweezers grasp the tick at its point of attachment to the skin and pluck it out. Examine the tick to see if you have removed all of it. If you have left part or all of the head in the skin, do not worry. It will not continue to poison the dog but it will act like a foreign body such as a splinter and may cause swelling and inflammation of the skin around it. Dab some antiseptic on the site after removal.

Even if tere is no sign of poisoning, observe the dog closely as the poison already in the dog's system may take up to 48 hours to take effect after the tick is removed.

Search the dog thoroughly as it may have more than one tick.

If your dog is showing any signs of tick poisoning no matter how mild, take it to your veterinarian who will hospitalise the dog, administer anti-tick serum by injection and treat the dog according to its symptoms. It is important for the dog to be kept cool as heat will aggravate the dog's breathing difficulty.

Prevention

• Keep your dog out of the bush as much as possible, especially in late spring and early summer.

• Go over the dog in a methodical way every day looking and feeling for a tick by rolling the skin between your fingers. Concentrate your search in the head and neck area, as 80 per cent of ticks are found there; the other 20 per cent could be found anywhere on the body. It usually takes four to six days for a tick to poison the dog, so if you go over it every day you have four chances of finding it before the dog shows evident signs of poisoning.

• Rinse the dog once a week in an insecticidal solution.

• Longhaired dogs may be clipped short in spring as ticks do not attach themselves as readily to short hair as they do to long hair. Also, clipping the hair short makes it easier to find the ticks.

TONSILLITIS

Many people are surprised to hear that dogs have tonsils. They are located on either side of the throat or pharynx. As dogs cannot complain of a sore throat, some cases of tonsillitis are not diagnosed. Tonsillitis usually occurs in young dogs. There are two forms of tonsillitis: acute and chronic.

Cause

Infection is the common cause for both acute and chronic tonsillitis. Dogs licking, sniffing and eating off the ground are prone to ingest or inhale an infection.

ACUTE TONSILLITIS
Signs

Examination of the throat reveals enlarged, inflamed tonsils, sometimes covered with flecks of pus. The dog may also be:

* off its food;
* running a temperature;
* vomiting (but not always);
* lethargic;
* salivating due to not wanting to swallow.

Treatment

See your veterinarian who will administer an injection of antibiotics followed by a course of antibiotic tablets or liquid, depending on the severity of the tonsillitis and which medicine the owner finds easier to administer.

Soft food, such as canned food, will encourage the dog to eat.

CHRONIC TONSILLITIS

The infected tonsils fail to respond to antibiotics or the infection recurs shortly after the course of antibiotics is finished.

Treatment

The discharge from the tonsils can be swabbed and cultured to identify the bacteria and to determine a suitable antibiotic for the infection. Following this, if the tonsillitis persists, a tonsillectomy (surgical removal of the tonsils) is recommended.

TOXOPLASMOSIS

Toxoplasmosis is primarily a disease of cats, and is found in the UK, US, Australia and Europe. This disease is a health risk to humans.

Cause

* *Toxoplasma gondii*, a single cell parasite, microscopic in size.
* Dogs may become infected by eating other animals whose tissues contain toxoplasma cysts, e.g. birds, rodents, or raw meats, in particular pork or lamb.
* Unborn puppies can acquire the infection in the uterus from their infected mother.
* Dogs may ingest oocysts from eating cat faeces. This is not a common occurrence.

Signs

The majority of infected dogs show no signs of the disease. Dogs that develop symptoms usually fall into two categories:

* Infected young dogs, which often develop an acute form, showing such signs as a high temperature, rapid laboured respiration, hepatitis, diarrhoea and, in some cases, death.
* Infected older dogs, which usually develop the chronic form, showing such signs as weight loss, diarrhoea, pale gums, wobbliness and blindness.

Treatment

Consult your veterinarian who can make a definite diagnosis based on symptoms and pathology tests on the dog's blood and faeces. The dog can be treated with antibiotics. Those dogs that recover, whether treated or not, eventually develop immunity.

Prevention

* Do not feed dogs raw meat. Feed canned or dry food. If feeding fresh meat, cook it thoroughly. Deep-freezing meat reduces the risk of toxoplasmosis.
* Try to prevent your dog from hunting.
* Control vermin in your immediate environment.

URINARY INCONTINENCE

This problem is relatively common in older desexed female dogs. Incontinence occurs when urine dribbles or leaks from the bladder and the dog is unaware of it happening.

Causes

* Spinal injuries or disease.
* Hormonal imbalance.
* The aftermath of prolonged cystitis.
* Ectopic ureter—a rare condition where the ureter empties into the vagina rather than into the bladder.

Sign

Dribbling urine.

Treatment

Consult your veterinarian. A female sex hormone tablet will be prescribed which will improve the tone of the sphincter muscle around the neck of the bladder, giving the dog good bladder control.

URINARY SYSTEM
DISEASES AND PROBLEMS

Balanoposthitis (see p. 170)
Bladder stones (see p. 137)

179

VOMITING

Do not confuse vomiting with regurgitation of food or gagging. Regurgitation of food usually takes place with little or no warning signs. The dog does not appear distressed, and the regurgitated food appears to be undigested. Gagging is usually stimulated by a collection of mucus or foreign material (e.g. grass) in the back of the throat. The dog often makes a loud noise as it attempts to expel the cause of the irritation from the throat.

Unlike humans, a dog may vomit occasionally without anything being wrong with it. Vomiting four to five times over 12 to 24 hours is abnormal, especially if associated with some other symptom (such as lethargy, not eating and diarrhoea), and you should seek veterinary advice.

A dog will eat grass to alleviate an irritation in the stomach.

Causes

- Foreign material
- Infection
- Travel sickness
- Worms (see also p. 95)
- Overeating and sensitivity to food (see also pp. 140,166)
- Constipation (see p. 136)
- Megaoesophagus (Achalasia), see p. 165

Signs

Vomiting is characterised by restlessness, salivation, swallowing, contraction of the abdominal muscles and extension of the head and neck, finally followed by expulsion of food, fluid or foreign material, which is often accompanied by a retching noise.

Treatment

• Foreign material

Grass: A dog will eat grass to alleviate an irritation of the stomach. The grass stimulates vomiting which cleans out the source of irritation.

Occasional eating of grass and vomiting is acceptable, provided the dog otherwise is eating well and is not losing weight. If the dog is eating grass and vomiting frequently, but is not eating well and is losing weight, have your dog examined by your veterinarian.

Obstructions: The most common obstruction is a bone in the stomach or intestine. Usually, the dog is lethargic, refuses to eat, vomits frequently and shows signs of abdominal pain and dehydration. Take the dog to your veterinarian for treatment.

• Infection

The signs may be similar to an obstruction, depending on type, location and seriousness of the infection. If your dog is showing signs of lethargy, refusing to eat, and dehydration, in conjunction with vomiting, see your veterinarian who will treat the dog according to the causes and symptoms.

• Travel sickness

Travel sickness is relatively common, especially in young dogs. Do not give your dog anything to eat or drink for 12 hours prior to travelling. If vomiting persists, see your veterinarian who will prescribe a sedative in combination with an antivomiting drug, depending on the severity of the motion sickness.

• Worms

A heavy infestation of roundworms in the upper small intestine, especially in young dogs, may cause vomiting. Occasionally, roundworms will be obvious in the vomit.

• Overeating and sensitivity to food

Usually, dogs that vomit following overeating or sensitivity to food are in good condition and are generally healthy.

Some dogs gulp their food as if it were their last meal for some time. This causes distension of the stomach and may stimulate the dog to regurgitate or vomit the food.

You cannot instruct the dog to eat slowly or to eat less. To prevent this problem arising, feed the dog three or four small meals per day, thereby decreasing the amount of food the dog ingests at any one time.

Some dogs may be sensitive to additives in the food, especially the commercial preparations. Others may be sensitive to the temperature of the food, e.g. cold from the refrigerator. Make sure the food is served at room temperature.

Try a number of different brands and types of food and observe the response.

VOMITING DISEASES AND PROBLEMS

Constipation (see p. 136)
Foreign material (see this page)
Grass eating (see this page)
Infection (see this page)
Megaoesophagus (see p.165)
Obstruction (see this page and p.110)
Overeating (see this page and p. 166)
Sensitivity to food (see this page and p. 140)
Travel sickness (see this page)
Vomiting (see p. 180)
Worms (see p. 95)

WOBBLER SYNDROME

This disease is characterised by poor co-ordination and weakness, particularly in the hindquarters. More commonly seen in the large breeds, especially the Great Dane.

Cause

It is agreed that narrowing of the canal formed by the vertebrae (bones) in the neck causes damage to the spinal cord, which in turn is responsible for the wobbles condition. It is not certain what causes narrowing of the canal.

The disease may be inherited.

Signs

Poor co-ordination, wobbling, weakness, clumsiness and difficulty in getting up and down. The condition may remain static or progress from slight wobbling to exaggerated, drunken movements.

Treatment

If you suspect your dog is a wobbler, contact your veterinarian who will conduct detailed tests and take x-rays in order to diagnose the problem.

Some cases are suitable for surgery, whereas euthanasia should be considered for those dogs severely affected.

BREEDING

Bitch: *Reproductive cycle and stages—Mating and problems—Artificial insemination*
Pregnancy diagnosis—False pregnancy—Management of bitch during pregnancy
Abortion—Birth and labour—Post-natal care

Puppies: *Care of newborn puppy—Diseases and problems—Weaning—Worming*
Puppy care and your veterinarian

Birth control: *Desexing bitch and dog (stud)—Alternatives to desexing*

Infertility: *Bitch—Stud*

Professional breeders are usually interested in one particular breed and aim to produce dogs that conform to the breed standard. Some professional dog breeders, in order to breed a dog with a certain physical appearance, disregard its temperament and physical soundness. Line breeding and inbreeding to develop certain physical characteristics may lead to genetic defects appearing in certain breeds. In some breeds, these genetic defects are responsible for a lifetime of discomfort, pain and/or restricted movement, such that the dog may require surgery and, in some cases, euthanasia. The majority of professional breeders are well-informed, responsible people. They check the line (pedigree) of their dog and have it checked by a veterinarian for any genetic defects, e.g. hip dysplasia, before embarking on a breeding programme.

Sometimes, owners of a household pet that is a bitch want to breed from it. Some owners maintain that allowing their bitch to have a litter of pups makes for a happier and more contented dog. *There is no medical or psychological evidence to support this notion.* Other owners express the opinion that they would like to breed from their bitch to involve their children in practical sex education and give them the pleasure of assisting with rearing the puppies. In some cases, rearing the puppies is an involved and time consuming task, often left to the parents. Furthermore, the birth of puppies often takes place at night, and consequently goes unnoticed.

There are careless owners who have no intention of breeding, but do not have their bitch spayed and do not keep it securely isolated when in oestrus. An unwanted pregnancy often results.

In many countries there are too many puppies and not enough homes to accommodate them. This fact is

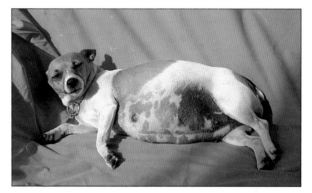

A heavily pregnant bitch

borne out by the number of animal welfare shelters and stray dogs in existence.

Before breeding, make sure that you have homes for the puppies, especially if they are a mixed breed.

REPRODUCTIVE CYCLE OF THE BITCH

The bitch's ability to reproduce usually begins from seven to 12 months of age, but may be as early as six months and as late as 24 months. Small breeds usually come on heat earlier than large breeds.

The bitch is not a seasonal breeder and on an average comes on heat every six months, but may vary between five and 11 months. Some dogs, e.g. the Dingo and Basenji, come on heat only once a year.

The bitch may come on heat throughout her life. She is most fertile up to five years of age, after which the conception rate and litter size decrease. After seven years of age, the interval between heat cycles increases.

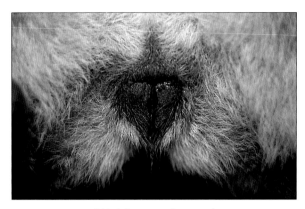

A bitch in season (stage one)

STAGES IN THE REPRODUCTIVE CYCLE

Stage one (Pro-oestrus): This stage usually lasts nine days. The vulva is swollen and firm. There is bloody discharge from the vagina. The bitch secretes pheromones which are hormones that sexually attract the male dog through his sense of smell. During this phase, the bitch resists any sexual advances and will not allow the male dog to mount her.

Stage two (Oestrus): This stage usually lasts nine days. The vulva is softer and not as swollen. The bloody discharge may continue or change to a straw-coloured fluid. During this phase the bitch will stand still, allowing the male to investigate her. She will elevate her tail and move it to one side. This is called flagging which makes penetration of the vagina by the male much easier.

It is only during this stage that ovulation and pregnancy can occur. If the bitch is successfully mated, pregnancy follows, otherwise she progresses to the third stage.

Stage three (Dioestrus): This stage lasts for approximately 65 days. It is characterised by the bitch rejecting the dog. The swelling of the vulva subsides, vaginal discharge ceases and the bitch is no longer attractive to male dogs. During this stage some bitches develop a pseudo-pregnancy often referred to as false or phantom pregnancy (see p. 186).

Stage four (Anoestrus): The fourth stage lasts for approximately four months and is characterised by sexual inactivity.

MATING

AGE AND PLACE OF MATING

The ideal age for the first mating of a bitch and a stud dog is about 20 months. By this time they have reached full physical maturity and the possibility of birth difficulties (dystocia) in the bitch will be minimised.

The area should be in a quiet location so that neither the male dog nor the bitch is distracted prior to, or during, mating. The bitch should be taken to the male dog (stud), because he feels secure in his own territory and will be able to give his full attention to serving the bitch.

SIGNS OF READINESS TO MATE

Readiness to mate can be determined by:
• the bitch's response to the male's advances (When she shows she is receptive, such as by standing still and flagging, she should be mated. If you have ready access to the male dog, mate the bitch every second day from the time she will accept the male until the time she rejects him.)
• the vulva (It will be softer and less swollen.)
• the vaginal discharge (It will have changed from a bloody colour to a straw-colour. This change does not always occur.)
• the stage of the bitch's oestrus (heat) cycle (This can be determined from a smear taken from the vagina and the vaginal cells and examined under the microscope by your veterinarian.)
• the time of ovulation (This can also be determined by the level of the hormone progesterone in a blood sample taken from the bitch.)

PRECAUTIONS PRIOR TO MATING

• Avoid the stress of a long journey as it may dampen the bitch's interest or cause her to go off heat.
• Make sure she is wormed and up to date with her vaccinations.
• If possible, place the bitch in a pen alongside the stud dog, to allow them to become accustomed to each other. Once she is showing obvious interest in the stud dog, i.e. standing still with her tail elevated and to one side, let him in with her.
• If suitable pens are unavailable, the dogs should be introduced to each other while on leads. Once it is obvious the female is receptive to the male, release them into an area from which they cannot escape.
• In some countries (e.g the US), the bitch and stud should be tested for Brucellosis before mating.

THE MATING

The stud dog will smell and lick the bitch around the vulva and when ready she will adopt the mating position of standing still with tail elevated and to one side. The stud dog will mount her from behind and grip onto her with his forelegs about the flank region. With rapid, pelvic thrusting movements the dog's penis is introduced into the vagina. Ejaculation usually occurs within 20 to 30 seconds. Muscles around the opening of the vagina contract to clasp around the grossly swollen gland at the base of the stud's penis. The male dog is unable to withdraw his penis and is 'tied' with the bitch sometimes for up to 40 minutes or more.

Shortly after ejaculation he will dismount and turn around, still 'tied' but facing the opposite direction to the bitch. It looks very uncomfortable, but remember that this is a natural stage in the mating and no harm will come to the dog or bitch. Do nothing except to keep them confined in the quiet mating area. Later on, they will separate naturally. It is thought that the reason for assuming this back to back position at the conclusion of the mating goes back to the times when dogs in this vulnerable situation had to guard against attack by predators.

Throughout the duration of the 'tie', the male intermittently ejaculates seminal fluid containing only a few spermatozoa.

MATING PROBLEMS

THE MALE

If the dog is a shy, nervous type of dog, it is easily put off. Select a quiet area for the mating, preferably with an experienced, relaxed bitch. Two assistants are often helpful, one to restrain and position the bitch while the other encourages and positions the male.

The dog may be uninterested because it knows the bitch is not ready, or because of lack of libido, inexperi-ence, overuse, or it dislikes the bitch. If you suspect it is lack of libido, consult your veterinarian. An inexperienced dog should be left alone in a quiet place with a mature, experienced, placid bitch that is in the second stage of her heat (oestrus) cycle.

Male dogs should be 20 months of age before starting full stud duties. A mating with one bitch, two to three times every two weeks is about the ideal frequency to maintain the male dog's libido and fertility.

Some dogs are selective about the bitch they serve and vice versa. They may reject one bitch because of colour, size, age, odour or some other factor that is not obvious to the handler and five minutes later, they may accept and vigorously serve another bitch.

THE FEMALE

The most common problem is that the owner has organised the bitch to be mated when she is in the first stage of her oestrus cycle instead of in the second phase, which is when she is ready to allow the male to have sexual intercourse with her.

Shy, nervous, inexperienced bitches should be handled with patience, encouragement and mild restraint. Over aggressive male dogs may aggravate the situation. If the mating is unsuccessful, consult your veterinarian who will examine your dog and may recommend a mild sedative.

Golden Retriever puppies suckling from their mother.

ARTIFICIAL INSEMINATION

Artificial insemination or artificial breeding refers to the technique whereby semen is collected from the male dog and is inseminated into a bitch that is on heat and about to ovulate.

Artificial insemination is indicated when the male is physically unable to mount and/or penetrate the bitch. On the other hand, the bitch may not stand to be served by the male or she may have some vaginal abnormality such as a stricture which prevents penetration by the male's penis.

For artificial insemination procedures to be carried out correctly and given a chance of being successful, the services of a veterinarian should be sought. The veterinary surgeon would collect and evaluate the semen from the stud dog, evaluate the bitch's heat cycle, assess the bitch's health and suitability, and carry out the insemination procedure.

PREGNANCY
PREGNANCY DIAGNOSIS

Because of the short gestation period (63 days), it is important to know as soon as possible if the bitch is pregnant so that proper management during the pregnancy and preparation for the whelping (birth) can be initiated. There are three methods of pregnancy diagnosis.

• **Abdominal palpation:** Twenty eight days after the first mating, your veterinarian can palpate the abdomen and confirm the bitch is pregnant by feeling discrete golfball-like swellings developing in the uterus. The veterinarian can estimate the number of foetuses developing in the uterus. This procedure is quick, inexpensive, and is not harmful to the bitch or to the developing puppies, if done carefully. After 35 days, it is more difficult to determine pregnancy by this method due to a more generalised swelling of the uterus.

• **Ultrasound:** Developing foetuses and foetal heart beat can be detected by ultrasound examination when the bitch is about 28 days pregnant.

• **X-ray:** At approximately six weeks of age the skeletal outline of the puppies can be detected by x-ray. Prior to this, the puppies' bones are not calcified enough to show up. This procedure can determine the approximate size of the foetuses.

SIGNS OF PREGNANCY

• At five weeks, the bitch's nipples will become enlarged and the abdomen increases in size.
• At seven weeks, mammary glands (breasts) enlarge.
• At eight weeks, the mammary gland may secrete watery milk two to three days prior to the birth of the puppies.

FALSE PREGNANCY

Sometimes referred to as pseudopregnancy or phantom pregnancy. If the bitch is not mated or for one reason or another does not become pregnant following mating, she may show signs of pregnancy. There may be enlargement of the nipples, mammary glands and abdomen. Rarely is there any milk production. Psychological changes associated with pregnancy may also be seen. After approximately 45 days the condition regresses spontaneously. If the bitch is particularly uncomfortable, consult your veterinarian who can alleviate the symptoms with treatment.

MISMATING

Unless a bitch in heat is strictly confined in a dog-proof area, a male dog or a number of male dogs will mate with her. A bitch in heat will often actively seek out a male dog. A bitch in heat is not selective and will mate with any male dog that is available.

It is possible for a bitch to give birth to a litter of puppies sired by different fathers.

If your bitch is mated by a male dog and you wish to stop the pregnancy, consult your veterinarian who can give the bitch a hormone injection within 72 hours of being mated and it will stop the pregnancy developing. The injection will intensify and prolong the heat cycle, so the bitch has to be kept strictly confined, otherwise she may be mated again and could become pregnant.

MANAGEMENT OF THE BITCH DURING PREGNANCY

The average gestation period for the bitch is 63 days but it can vary from 58 to 71 days. During the gestation period, pay particular attention to the following:

Nutrition: The volume of food during the first six weeks of pregnancy need not be markedly increased. For good foetal development, it is important that there is no nutritional deficiency. A well-balanced diet, which can be provided by commercial rations (canned, semi-moist and dry food), is perfectly adequate.

Overfeeding can lead to a fat lazy bitch, which could cause problems at the time of birth (dystocia).

If the bitch is on a high meat diet, a calcium supplement is important but it should not contain any phosphates.

Calcium carbonate, lactate or gluconate are quite satisfactory. A balanced vitamin–mineral supplement should be included in the diet.

In the last three weeks of pregnancy there is an increase in the bitch's food intake until she is eating double by the eighth to ninth week. Three or four small meals a day will assist her digestion as the growing foetuses take up a lot of room in the abdomen, restricting the normal expansion of her stomach for her food intake.

Exercise: This will vary according to the breed, the stage of pregnancy and the size of the bitch's abdomen. Exercise should be encouraged to help in maintaining good muscle tone which is desirable for a smooth birth. Overweight, lazy bitches are more likely to have difficult, complicated births. Normal exercise routines should be maintained until the last week of pregnancy, then tapered off. Those bitches that develop a grossly swollen abdomen, due to the fact that they are carrying a large litter, should have limited exercise of a light nature.

Worming: Worm the bitch ten days before mating and ten days before whelping. She should be wormed against roundworm, hookworm, whipworm and tapeworm. The worm preparation should contain Praziquantel, Febantel and Pyrantel Embonate. This preparation is not detrimental to the bitch, nor to the developing foetuses.

Vaccination: Live vaccine should not be given to pregnant bitches. Breeding bitches that are vaccinated annually with modified live vaccine, but not during the gestation period, will give a strong temporary immunity to the puppies via the bitch's colostrum (first milk).

Housing: In the last ten days of pregnancy, provide a whelping box. This can be easily constructed with sides of such a height as to allow the bitch easy access in and out but preventing the puppies from crawling, rolling or falling out. The base should be of material that can be readily cleaned. Cover the base with newspaper or other material that can be shredded by the bitch to make a nest. Soiled paper can easily be discarded. The area of the whelping box should be large enough to allow the bitch to stretch out and suckle the puppies in comfort.

Place the box in a quiet location where the bitch feels warm, comfortable and secure. Provide water and food in close proximity to the box.

ABORTION

Abortion refers to the abnormal expulsion of a foetus, dead or alive, after the first three weeks of pregnancy until the full term. Abortion is not common in the bitch. Abortion cannot be substantiated in the first three weeks of pregnancy for several reasons. It is difficult to diagnose that the bitch is pregnant. If the developing embryo dies, generally it is absorbed by the bitch rather than being expelled. Even if it were expelled,, it possibly would not be noticed because of its small size and gelatinous nature, or the bitch may eat the foetuses.

If your bitch aborts, follow these procedures:

• Move other bitches in the area where the abortion occurred to an isolated area.

• Take the foetus, foetal membrane and bitch to your veterinarian who will take a cervical swab from the bitch for laboratory examination and perform a post-mortem

on the aborted foetus. A tissue sample may also be taken.

• Isolate the bitch that has aborted in an area that can be disinfected readily at a later date. Keep the bitch isolated until the laboratory test results are known, generally in about two weeks.

• Disinfect the general area where the abortion has taken place with chlorhexidine or a similar preparation.

• Wash your hands thoroughly before handling other dogs, particularly pregnant bitches.

The three most common types of abortion are bacterial, hormonal and viral.

Bacterial abortion: (See Brucellosis, p. 132.) Bacteria are easier to identify than viruses and do not spread as readily. The identification procedure is to swab the cervix of the bitch and the aborted foetus and then culture the swabs.

Some bacterial abortions can be prevented by having your bitch swabbed prior to mating to determine if she has an infection, what type of infection it is, and the best antibiotic to be used for treatment which should be given prior to mating and during pregnancy.

Hormonal abortion: Bitches that have a history of aborting which is unrelated to infection or other known causes are suspected of having a hormonal imbalance. Hormonal abortions usually occur around the seventh week of pregnancy.

The progesterone levels of pregnant bitches can be assessed and may be used as a guide for treatment. Progesterone injections given by your veterinarian every seven days, commencing on the 35th day of pregnancy, and ceasing seven days before the full term, should help to prevent abortion due to a progesterone deficiency.

Hypothyroidism may be linked with abortion. There is a blood test that assesses the activity of the thyroid gland and if the gland is not functioning properly, treatment is available.

Viral abortion: Viruses are not a common cause of abortion in the bitch. Canine herpes virus is a respiratory disease of young puppies and can cause abortion in the latter stages of pregnancy. Other viruses, such as Distemper, Hepatitis and Parvovirus, may cause spontaneous abortion in the pregnant bitch.

THE BIRTH

How many puppies will there be? What sex will they be? Will they be normal? You will perhaps ponder these sorts of questions until the birth is over. In many cases, the pups will prove to be healthy and just what you wanted. Witnessing the birth of the first litter of pups, you may be disturbed by the bitch's vigorous straining or by the sight of the afterbirth—keep in mind that these situations are facets of the natural, normal process of birth.

PRECAUTIONS

Keep the bitch confined so that she cannot disappear and have her pups in some obscure, inaccessible place.

Have the necessary equipment available: scissors, thread, tincture of iodine, disinfectant, cotton wool and a clean bucket for hot water. In case you need to contact your veterinarian, keep the phone number nearby.

SIGNS OF LABOUR

• Some bitches will appear restless, getting in and out of the whelping box frequently.

• The bitch begins to make a nest from bedding in the box.

• Milk may be readily expressed from the nipples.

• A temperature drop from 38.5°C to 37.5°C, approximately 24 hours prior to birth.

• Loses interest in eating food.

• Grooms herself vigorously especially around the vulva.

• Sixty three days from the time of mating is the normal period to expect the bitch to go into labour The actual duration of pregnancy may vary from 58 to 71 days.

• There may be a white mucous discharge from the vagina.

NORMAL LABOUR

It should be kept in mind at all times that the bitch is an individual and may not follow precisely the normal labour pattern outlined below. Observe the bitch's labour from a vantage point which does not disturb her. If disturbed, the bitch can inhibit the first stage of labour.

Stage one: This stage usually lasts 12 to 24 hours and in the older experienced bitch may go unnoticed. The bitch appears restless, getting in and out of the whelping box, panting, occasionally whimpering, trembling, lying down, looking at her flank, licking her vulva and sometimes vomiting. During this stage, there are mild contractions of the uterus and the cervix dilates, but no visible or obvious contractions are observed. Some bitches want you to be with them during this stage, others do not.

Stage two: Characteristics of the beginnings of this stage are that the bitch lies down on her side, often with her head up, looking at her hindquarters. Visible straining is evident and the foetal membranes appear at the vulva. The membrane (amnion) is rather like a bluish-white plastic bag lining the placenta and enveloping the foetus; when ruptured, it discharges a yellowish fluid. Not infrequently, the amnion ruptures before appearing at the vulva.

The normal presentation is head first but it is not uncommon for a pup to be presented tail first (breech birth). The pup may be delivered within the amnion. The bitch will lick vigorously at the sack, rupturing it with her teeth, and then continue to lick the puppy, cleaning it

thoroughly. While doing this she will chew through the umbilical cord.

If the foetal membranes or amnion appear at the vulva and no further progress is achieved after ten minutes then seek veterinary advice.

If the head of the pup appears and the bitch makes no attempt to remove the membranes, immediately remove any foetal membranes that may be obstructing the nostrils and mouth so that the pup can breathe freely.

The umbilical cord is usually broken when the pup is born. If cord is intact and the bitch does not break it by chewing through it, cut it using the following procedure:

Place a pair of scissors and thread in a dish of disinfectant. Tie the thread around the cord about 2 cm (¾ in) from the body, and knot it tightly. Cut the cord with the scissors ½ cm (¼ in) away from the knot, between the knot and placenta. If cord is broken at birth and bleeding, it should be tied off. Thoroughly swab the stump of the cord with disinfectant. The cord will dry out and drop off within a short period of time leaving a neat navel.

Stage three: The placenta or afterbirth is usually passed with the pup at the time of birth or shortly after. Make sure that a placenta is passed for each pup born. If the afterbirth is not passed within eight hours of the last pup, contact your veterinarian.

The bitch often chews through the umbilical cord and then eats the placenta. This is quite normal behaviour for the bitch in the birth process. If she eats a number of afterbirths it may cause vomiting and diarrhoea.

Once the first pup is born, the others usually follow fairly quickly so that all the pups are born over a period of approximately three to six hours. The puppies are usually born ten to 30 minutes.apart. Occasionally it happens that a bitch will give birth to a number of pups, then will relax and go into labour 24 hours later and produce another healthy pup.

ABNORMAL LABOUR

The bitch's labour usually proceeds without a hitch, but sometimes complications occur. If they do, it is important to recognise them as early as possible and to take quick knowledgeable action so that any danger to the life of the puppies and bitch is minimised.

In such situations, the wisest course to follow is to seek the help of a veterinarian immediately.

Puppy presented at the vulva: If the puppy presented at the vulva is in the normal head first position, but the bitch does not seem able to expel it, give assistance; but first, take certain precautions: Scrub your hands thoroughly and wear a surgical glove, if available, and wash the area around the bitch's anus and vulva with a non-irritant antiseptic, e.g. chlorhexidine.

THE BIRTH

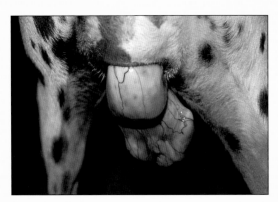

Birth: normal presentation, head first

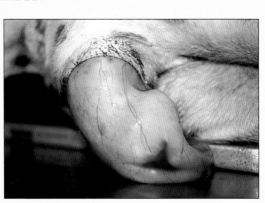

Breech birth: puppy presented tail first

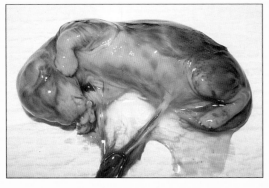

Puppy delivered within amnion

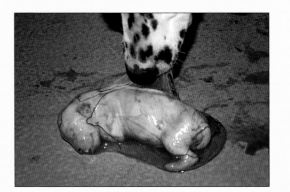

Bitch ruptures amnion sack

If the presentation is normal and the membranes are intact, break them to clear them away from the head, especially from the nose and mouth to help with the pup's breathing, and from that part of the body visible outside the vulva so that the person assisting at the delivery can get a better grip. Using a clean towel to get a better grip, take hold of the pup around the shoulder area and slowly pull downwards and outwards. If the pup will not budge, a twist to the left or right in conjunction with pulling will often bring about success. If there is no change, call your veterinarian.

One leg presented at the vulva: Before you put your finger into the vagina, make sure your hands have been scrubbed with a non-irritant disinfectant and lubricated, as it is necessary to prevent tissue damage and infection that may endanger the lives of the bitch and puppies. Feel for the other leg, pull it forward and then proceed to deliver the pup.

Hindquarters presented at the vulva: If the hindquarters are presented, take hold of the pup in the region of the hips and pull outwards and downwards. Avoid squeezing the abdomen as this may cause serious damage to the pup.

No puppy present at the vulva: Call your veterinarian if:
• the bitch has been straining for more than an hour and no pup appears;
• there are no obvious contractions and the bitch is distressed, continually getting up and down, looking at her flanks and crying;
• after 30 minutes of obvious straining and contractions, the bitch appears to give up, and her efforts are weak and less frequent.

CAESARIAN SECTION

This surgical procedure may be indicated for a bitch that cannot have puppies by normal delivery or that does not respond to labour-inducing drugs or obstetrical manipulation. Some of the reasons for a veterinarian performing a caesarian section are :
• pelvic deformity;
• puppies too big to pass through the pelvic canal;
• the bitch is more than three days overdue and does not go into labour;
• the life of the bitch or puppies are at risk.

POST-NATAL CARE

FIRST VISIT TO THE VETERINARIAN

It is a good idea to take the bitch and her puppies along to the veterinarian for a post-natal examination. The bitch will be checked to make sure no pups are left in the uterus and no afterbirths have been retained. The bitch may be given an injection of oxytocin to make the uterus contract, thereby expelling any debris and helping to control haemorrhage. The mammary glands will be checked to make sure the bitch has adequate milk for the pups. Tears or bruising of the vulva and vagina may necessitate an antibiotic injection.

The pups are checked for general health as well as for any defects, such as cleft palate and umbilical hernia.

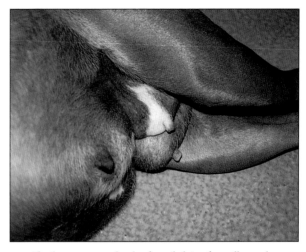

Check mammary glands after whelping for milk supply.

CARE OF THE BITCH

Once the pups have been born, there is sometimes a tendency to lavish attention and care on them, with a corresponding neglect of the bitch. In this situation, it is well to remember that the pups' viability depends on the health of the bitch. The care of the bitch after the birth should not be neglected and the following activities and observations should be established as routines.

• **Cleansing:** If the bitch's tail, vulva, and hindlegs are matted with blood and discharge, the area should be washed to make the bitch feel better and also to prevent the spread or growth of bacteria that may be harmful to the bitch and pups. Use an antiseptic, non-irritant wash, e.g. chlorhexidine. Do not use harsh disinfectants as they may scald the skin which may in turn cause the bitch to reject the pups. It is also important to wash off the remains of any soap, especially in the area of the mammary glands, because the taste may inhibit the pups from suckling.

When the bitch is being washed, place the pups in a basket or box with a blanket or towel where she can see them, thus allaying any anxiety she may feel.

• **Tears, bruising and swelling:** After the bitch has been cleaned, examine her for tears, bruising and swelling. Lift the bitch's tail out of the way so that the anus and vulva can be observed without hindrance.

Tears of any length or depth should be attended by your veterinarian who will stitch the wound and protect the bitch from infection with an antibiotic injection.

Swelling and/or bruising, if any, is normal and usually subsides over 48 hours. If the swelling is excessive and persists for longer, or is accompanied by severe bruising, the bitch is susceptible to infection, so consult your veterinarian.

Gentle, cold hosing of the swollen areas can have a three-fold action. First, it cleanses the area; secondly, the massaging effect of the water pressure will disperse and reduce the swelling; and thirdly, the coldness of the water will help to stop the bleeding that causes the bruising.

• **Vaginal discharge:** Small amounts of clear, serous discharge, sometimes blood-tinged, is normal up to a week after the birth. However, a constant drip of blood, a bloody brown discharge or pus coming from the vulva is abnormal. The bitch should be examined by a veterinarian if this is the case.

• **Mammary glands:** Examine the nipples to see that they are normal. Express milk from the nipples to make sure that there is a satisfactory flow and the status of the milk is normal.

If one mammary gland is larger than the others, it may be due to the fact that the pups have not suckled from it or there may be an infection of the gland, e.g. mastitis. If the mammary gland is infected, it is very painful to touch as well as being hot, swollen, hard and sometimes lumpy. It may be difficult to express the milk, which may be thick and discoloured. In acute cases, the bitch will have a high temperature. When treating the bitch for mastitis, remove the pups from her, apply hot foments, and consult with your veterinarian who will treat her with antibiotics.

• **The afterbirth (placental membranes):** The afterbirth may be expelled with the birth of each pup or immediately after. If the membranes have not come away from the bitch within eight hours, contact your veterinarian. If a placenta is visible, it may easily be removed by manually pulling on it with firm, even pressure. Using a piece of gauze or clean towelling will give you a better grip on the slippery membrane. If it is not removed in this way, an injection of oxytocin will be necessary to aid in separation and expulsion of the afterbirth from its attachment to the uterus.

• **Milk fever (Eclampsia):** Not uncommon in lactating bitches. It usually occurs in bitches that have a large litter and whose pups are older than two weeks.

The cause is due to the bitch's calcium levels being depleted; the calcium is lost in the milk.

The symptoms are mild muscular twitching and wobbliness, progressing to severe, uncontrolled muscular twitching and spasm. The pupils become dilated, and the respiration is rapid and shallow.

Immediately contact your veterinarian who will give the bitch injections of calcium and cortisone, which will reverse the symptoms rapidly. The pups may have to be removed temporarily from their mother. (See Orphan puppies, p. 193). The mother should be placed on a calcium–vitamin D supplement.

• **Hysteria:** Some mothers attack and kill their healthy puppies shortly after they are born. See your veterinarian regarding tranquillising the bitch. Closely observe the bitch and pups until they appear bonded to one another.

• **Poor milk production:** Some bitches, especially those having their first litter, have little or no milk. Your veterinarian can give the bitch hormone treatment to facilitate milk letdown. The suckling of the puppies aids in stimulating milk production.

THE PUPPIES

It is a thrilling experience to see your newborn puppies being licked and nuzzled by their mother as they suckle from her nipples. So far, the bitch has done most of the work. It is now up to those who assisted at the birth to do a little more.

A close watch should be kept on the puppies; what to do and when to do it will be determined primarily by the puppies' needs. The following guidelines are basic to the immediate care of the newborn puppies.

CARE OF NEWBORN PUPPIES

As soon as a puppy is born, check to see that it is breathing. If necessary, clear away any placental membranes or mucus that may be blocking the nostrils or mouth. If the puppy is not breathing, it should be given oxygen therapy by means of a resuscitator unit or by mouth to nose resuscitation (see p.109). The puppy has only a very small lung capacity, so use only short, shallow breaths, otherwise there is a risk of stretching or rupturing the lungs. Gently massage the chest with finger and thumb. Put the puppy in a head down position, with the head lower than the rest of the body, thus allowing the blood to flow more freely to the brain. Vigorous rubbing of the puppy's chest with a towel may stimulate breathing.

If the puppy is still not breathing, grasp it firmly in your hand with its head protruding between your index and middle finger, then raise the puppy above your head and proceed with an action as if you were going to throw it to the ground. Repeat the action four or five times. This action gets rid of the mucus from the nose and mouth, as well as stimulating respiration.

Allow the bitch to break the umbilical cord which is normally done at the time when she is licking, pulling and tearing at the foetal membranes around the pup to free it. Usually the stump of the umbilical cord is about two centimetres long. Swab the end with tincture of iodine. In three to four days the cord will wither and drop off.

If by chance the umbilical cord does not break, wait five to ten minutes before severing it. A ligature should be applied about 2 cm (¾ in) from the pup's body using thread soaked in disinfectant. The cord is then cut with scissors soaked in disinfectant 1 cm (⅓ in) from the ligature, between the ligature and the placenta. Swab the cut

A newborn puppy

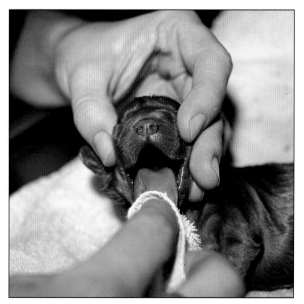
Clearing the mouth

THE UMBILICAL CORD

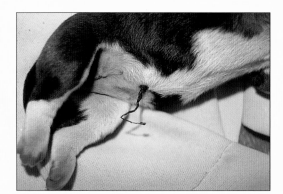

Umbilical cord ready to drop off

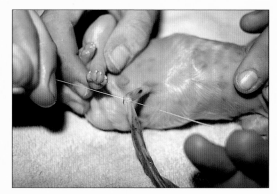

Tying the umbilical cord with thread

An alternative: breaking the cord with the fingers

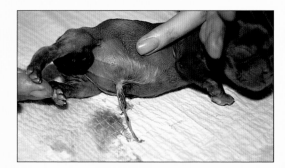

The broken umbilical cord

end with tincture of iodine. An alternative to cutting the cord is to break it using the fingers. Premature breaking of the umbilical cord may deprive the puppy of its maximum blood supply, thus starving the brain of oxygen with subsequent brain damage. If the end of the cord is bleeding, tie it off with a disinfected thread to control haemorrhage.

While the bitch is still in the process of having more puppies, if she is interested in the pups already born, licking and encouraging them to suckle, leave them with her. Otherwise, if she appears disinterested in the puppies, remove them to a box with a hot water bottle wrapped in a towel, and leave them there until all the puppies are born. Make sure the hot water bottle is not too hot and does not come in direct contact with the puppies.

If the puppies do not suckle the bitch (do not mistake mouthing of the teats for suckling), the failure to do so may be caused by weakness or deformity of the puppies, or by the bitch being cranky, or by some other factor.

Normally, the puppies will suckle within minutes after finding their way to the bitch's nipples. If a puppy does not suckle within a couple of hours, then, with one hand expressing milk from the bitch's nipple and the other hand holding the pup's head, place the puppy's

Newborn puppies should be kept warm.

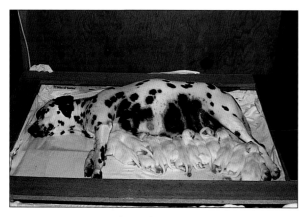

A contented bitch feeding her puppies.

partially opened mouth over the nipple. A good healthy puppy will start sucking immediately. Sucking can be stimulated by moving the puppy's mouth on and off the nipple.

Puppies suckle about every two hours in the first week. If they are getting adequate milk, they will be warm, relaxed and not crying. The puppy should almost double its weight in the first week.

Colostrum is the name given to the first milk that the bitch produces. It contains antibodies which give the puppies temporary immunity against infection for six to 16 weeks after birth. Colostrum is only produced by the bitch for about the first 24 hours after the puppies are born and they can only absorb the antibodies from it for about the first 36 hours of life. In addition, colostrum has a high vitamin content and food value, and guards against constipation.

The bitch licks the puppies around the anal and genital area stimulating them to urinate and defaecate.

ORPHAN PUPPIES

When puppies lose their mother at birth or shortly after, it strongly arouses our sympathy. Orphan puppies include not only the pups whose mother died during or shortly after birth, but also those puppies whose mother, for one reason or another, has no milk or cannot nurse her offspring.

• **Bottle feeding:** The puppies should be fed every two hours in the first week of life. Thereafter, the frequency of the feeds should be decreased and the amount increased, so that by the time it is two weeks old feeding every four hours is sufficient.

In the first week at each two-hourly feed, the puppies should receive about 5 ml (1 teaspoon) of milk substitute. (This can be varied according to individual demand.)

Two suggested formulas for substitute milk are:

• 1 cup of evaporated or powdered milk mixed with boiled water and made up to double the strength recom-

BOTTLE FEEDING

Bottle feed the puppy every two hours in its first week. By two weeks, every four hours is sufficient.

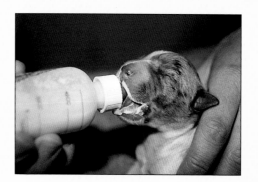

To bottle feed, hold the puppy firmly with its head elevated.

mended for babies on the container; 1 egg yolk; 1 teaspoon of glucodin.

• ½ cup of cow's milk; 1 egg yolk; 1 teaspoon of glucodin.

Note: If possible, express colostrum (first milk) from the bitch's nipples and give it to the orphan puppies either with the formula or separately.

Your veterinarian can supply you with a commercially prepared mother's milk substitute and an appropriate feeding bottle.

Warm the milk to body temperature before feeding. Hold the puppy firmly, with its head slightly elevated, and

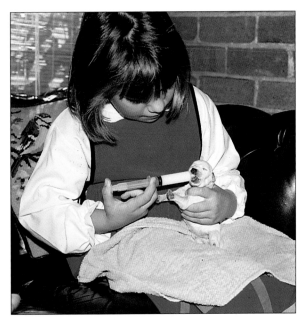

A syringe is an alternative to bottle feeding.

syringe and delivering the substitute milk into the stomach. The orphan puppy should be kept for about two weeks in a draught-free area at a temperature of 30°C or 85°F. Puppies do not have the ability to control or regulate their temperature. In the normal situation of being fed by the mother, they are kept warm by contact with the mother's mammary glands and the other puppies, and by moving about.

Rubbing the puppy around the anal and genital area with a small amount of vaseline will stimulate it to urinate and defaecate. The faeces will give you an indication as to whether the milk formula you are using is too rich or not. If the puppy has diarrhoea (fluid faeces), dilute the formula.

insert the teat into its mouth. Move the teat gently in and out of the mouth, expressing a small amount of milk to stimulate sucking.

The disadvantage of bottle feeding is that it is time-consuming, i.e. it involves cleaning the bottle and teat and holding the bottle while the puppy is feeding.

• **Foster mother:** In many cases, a foster mother is not readily available when urgently required. There is a greater possibility in a large breeding establishment of one being available. Some bitches are good foster mothers and readily accept an orphan puppy. If a bitch is available, place the orphan puppy with a litter of a similar size, otherwise, if the orphan is considerably smaller and weaker, it may not be able to compete for an adequate quantity of milk.

• **Stomach tube:** If the puppy will not take to bottle feeding or it is too time consuming, try feeding it by stomach tube, which is quicker and ensures that the puppy has received adequate nutrition. The equipment required is simply a piece of soft plastic tube 3 mm (¹⁄₁₀ in) diameter and 15 cm (6 in) long, attached to a syringe.

Before inserting the tube, measure the distance with the tube from the puppy's mouth to a point two-thirds along the rib cage and mark it. This will indicate how far the tube has to go in to reach the stomach.

Insert the tube through the mouth gently but firmly, pushing the tube over the back of the tongue, which should guide it into the oesophagus (food pipe) and eventually into the stomach. The mark on the tube when at the mouth indicates that the inserted end of the tube has reached the stomach. Make sure the tube is in the stomach and not in the lungs before pressing the plunger on the

FEEDING BY TUBE

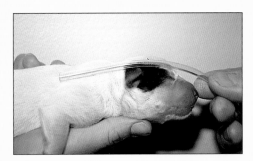

Measure the correct length of tube before inserting.

Gently but firmly insert the tube via the mouth.

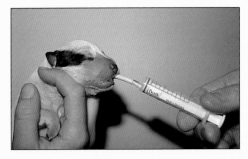

Make sure the tube is in the stomach before pressing the plunger.

A deformed puppy

DISEASES AND PROBLEMS OF THE NEWBORN OR YOUNG PUPPY

CLEFT PALATE

This is an opening in the roof of the mouth which can vary from a slit-like opening in the midline to virtually the entire roof of the mouth being absent.

Causes

• An iodine deficiency in the bitch during pregnancy.
• Administration of cortisone in the early stages of pregnancy.
• Other unknown causes.

Signs

• Milk coming out of the puppy's nostrils.
• Unable to suck properly.
• Weakness and poor development due to lack of nutrition.

Treatment

Take the puppy to your veterinarian to be humanely euthanased.

CONJUNCTIVITIS

The puppy's eyes open usually seven to ten days after birth. At that time, infection of the conjunctiva is usually noticed if present.

Cause

Usually staphylococcal or streptococcal infection.

Signs

• Eyelids stuck together.
• Pus oozing from the corner of the eyelids.
• Dry pus adhering to the edges of the eyelids.

Treatment

Warm bathing and gentle parting of the eyelids. Be careful not to pull the eyelids apart too abruptly because you may damage the rims. Once the eyelids are open, bathe them regularly to wipe away the pus and to prevent them sealing together again. If you are unable to part the eyelids or, once parted there is evidence of heavy pus discharge, see your veterinarian who will prescribe an antibiotic eye ointment.

DIARRHOEA

Diarrhoea can cause death in young puppies if it goes unchecked, particularly in the first few days of life.

Cause

Diarrhoea may be caused by infection or by the bitch's milk being toxic. In cases where the milk is toxic, usually the bitch has a discharge from the vagina indicating a uterine infection, the source of the toxins which enter the milk via the blood stream.

Signs

Greenish fluid faeces, inflamed raw anus, crying, bloated abdomen and rough harsh coat that tends to stand up.

Treatment

Treatment involves both the puppies and the bitch. The bitch should be treated by your veterinarian with antibiotics. The puppies may or may not require antibiotics, but ask your veterinarian to check them. Remove the pups from their mother until her infection is cleared. Keep the puppies warm and away from draughts. Hand feed them (see Orphan puppies, p.193).

FADING PUPPY SYNDROME

This term is used to describe a condition in puppies between one to seven days of age that show signs of weakness and lethargy, and die within 24 hours.

Causes

• Bacterial infections contracted from their mother via the placenta, vagina, mammary glands (milk) or from the broken end of the umbilical cord.
• Viral infections such as canine herpes virus, are implicated, but the significance of other viral infections is doubtful because of the protection received by the puppies from maternal antibodies in the colostrum (first milk).
• Toxoplasmosis may be a cause, and worms may play a role in the disease because of their debilitating effect.

Signs

Healthy, vigorous pups quickly become restless, cry as if distressed, refuse to suck, are cold to the touch, become weak, quiet, and die.

Treatment

Consult your veterinarian who will administer antibiotics and more intensive supportive treatment such as oxygen, fluids and electrolytes via a stomach tube.

Warm the puppy slowly and gently, to a temperature of 30°C or 85°F. If the puppy will still suck, provide nutrition and fluids by feeding a milk substitute, using a bottle and teat or eye dropper.

Prevention

Examination of the bitch and the stud dog and a post-mortem of the dead puppy will often explain the cause and assist in preventing repetition of the problem.

Assess your health care management practices, such as vaccination, worming and the hygiene of the breeding establishment, especially the whelping area.

HARE LIP

May be associated with cleft palate, but not necessarily.

Cause

A genetic inherited characteristic.

Sign

The upper lip does not join in the middle.

Treatment

Euthanasia.

HYPOTHERMIA

Newborn puppies are unable to regulate their body temperature. They rely on heat generated from the bitch's body (including her mammary glands), the close proximity of the other puppies, general activity, and on being in a draught-free, warm environment.

Cause

Mother rejects puppies; puppy removed from mother and placed in an unsuitable environment.

Signs

Initially, the puppy shows signs of increased activity, constant crying and is cold to the touch. Sucking is weak and little or no milk is ingested.

In a later stage, the puppy becomes weak, unco-ordinated, stops crying and cannot or will not suck. Often, the bitch rejects the puppy by pushing it away, further aggravating its hypothermia and causing it to go into a coma. Shake the thermometer down as far as the mercury will go and then check the puppy's temperature. If the temperature is below 35°C (90°F), hypothermia should be suspected.

Treatment

Slow, gentle heating can lead to complete recovery over 12 to 24 hours. Rapid warming can lead to shock and death.

NAVEL INFECTION

Cause

Infection which may progress up the cord and into the abdominal cavity causing peritonitis.

Signs

Indications of this problem are inflammation and redness of the stump of the umbilical cord with pus discharge and the skin of the abdomen around the base of the navel is often bluish in colour.

Treatment

Involves your veterinarian administering antibiotics, fluids, and keeping the pups warm.

Prevention

Is related to the general cleanliness of the environment, the correct handling of the umbilical cord and swabbing the end of it with iodine after it is severed.

UMBILICAL HERNIA

Fatty tissue or the intestine passes through a hole in the muscles of the abdominal wall and presses against the skin, forming a swelling.

Causes

• A congenital defect. If an umbilical hernia is a congenital defect, the bitch should not be used for breeding.

• The umbilical cord may be broken by the bitch or by a person assisting at the birth. An umbilical hernia can be caused by pulling on the cord too vigorously, damaging the abdominal muscles where the cord is attached.

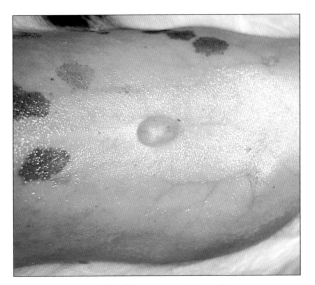

An umbilical hernia; note the swelling.

Puppies in the weaning stage

Sign

A swelling in the region of the navel which may be up to 2 cm (¾ in) or more in diameter.

Treatment

Many small umbilical hernias close up and disappear over a period of eight months. Nevertheless, it is wise to ask your veterinarian to evaluate the hernia and to recommend whether or not it should be corrected surgically.

If the hernia opening in the muscular wall of the abdomen is large enough, a loop of the intestine may become twisted in it and strangle itself, cutting off the blood supply to that portion of the intestine and necessitating emergency surgery to save the puppy's life.

WEANING

In general, start weaning when the puppies are about four weeks of age. The precise starting time will depend on the size of the litter, the bitch's milk supply and when you want the puppies to go to their new home.

As a starter for the weaned puppies, use some of the prepared baby foods or canned dog food mixed with water to form a sloppy paste. Smear some of the food around the mouth of the pup or entice it to suck the food from the end of your finger. Once the pup shows interest, introduce it to a flat dish or saucer containing the food.

Initially they walk in the food and make a mess, but soon get the idea of lapping it into the mouth. Once this is achieved, increase the consistency of the food to that of a more solid nature.

Provide the pups with water or milk in a dish but be careful as some pups may develop diarrhoea from cow's milk. If so, use a low lactose milk formula, such as Divetalac.

After a week the pups should be eating solid food readily from a bowl. It is a good idea to feed them four times a day. At this young age the pups should be exposed to a wide variety of foods in taste and texture, as some dogs become addicted to one type of food as they mature. In time, if it is discovered that the diet which the dog is accustomed to does not cover all its nutritional requirements, it may be difficult to get the dog to change and accept a better balanced diet.

If the bitch wants to feed them all the time during the weaning process, remove her from the pups while they are being fed solid food. They should be completely weaned over a four week period so that at eight weeks of age they are self-sufficient and ready to go to their new home.

197

By removing the pups from the bitch for periods during the weaning, the bitch's milk production will decrease so that at the time when the pups are fully weaned at eight weeks of age, the bitch will not have uncomfortable, swollen mammary glands full of milk.

WORMING

A worm paste or worm syrup may be easier to administer than worm tablets. The paste or syrup can be mixed with a small quantity of their favourite food or can be put directly into the mouth (see Worms, p. 95).

FLEA INFESTATION OF PUPPIES AND BITCH

Wash the bitch in an insecticidal shampoo, as the stronger insecticidal rinses may have an adverse effect on the puppies.

Make sure she is thoroughly rinsed and dried, especially in the area of her nipples so that the puppies do not ingest any of the insecticide, and its unpleasant taste or smell does not deter the pups from sucking.

Dip the pups for a couple of minutes in a bucket of warm water so that their heads are just above water level. While they are in the water, remove any fleas from their heads. Dry the pups thoroughly.

If the bedding is washable, give it a good scrub in the insecticidal shampoo and then rinse thoroughly. Otherwise, burn the bedding and replace.

COLLECTING YOUR PUPPY FROM THE KENNEL

Before you collect your puppy from the breeder, it is very important to be prepared for its arrival in its new home (see p. 47).

NECESSARY ITEMS FOR THE ARRIVAL OF THE NEW PUPPY

• Plastic food dish.

• Plastic water dish with a stable base (if the base is unstable, the pup may tilt the dish, spilling its contents).

• Basket or bed. Do not buy an expensive one as you may find the pup prefers to sleep in a discarded cardboard box. Buy a basket that can be readily cleaned.

• Collar. If a pup has a collar with an identity disc, you have a good chance of recovering your pup if it is lost or injured. The collar should be a very light one. Put it on so that two of your fingers can just fit underneath it. If it is too loose, it is liable to get caught on protruding objects or the pup is liable to flip it off with one of its paws and lose it.

When the pup arrives at your home, keep it inside. Help it feel secure, offer it affection, and provide it with a warm place to sleep. Put its basket in a small room such as the laundry where it can be confined at night. Feed it

When the new puppy feels secure, allow it to explore the garden.

at regular intervals (four times daily) with the food the breeder was using. If you want to change the diet, wait for a week and after that do it gradually.

Place the pup frequently onto newspaper. When it urinates and/or defaecates, reinforce its behaviour with praise. Remove any faeces, but leave the paper for a day or two because the odour in the paper will reinforce in the pup's mind that this is the place to urinate and defaecate (see Toilet training, p. 49).

After a number of days when the pup feels secure and happy with the environment inside the home, take it outside and let it explore the garden under close supervision. Over a period of a couple of weeks the pup will develop a sense of belonging and also a sense of where its boundaries are and will start to become protective about its territory.

Until the pup is big enough to defend itself, do not leave it outside alone during the day. Always keep your dog confined, as it will tend to wander, with the risk of being attacked by another dog or run over by a motor vehicle.

PUPPY CARE AND YOUR VETERINARIAN

When your puppy is six to eight weeks old, make an appointment to see your veterinarian for a thorough and detailed examination of your pet and to discuss all aspects of dog care, including:

• birth control (see p. 199).

• breeding (see p. 183).

• fleas, lice and ticks (see pp. 148,198;161;171).

• health problems (see pp. 38–42,172).

• training (see p. 47).

- nutrition and feeding (see p. 77).
- vaccination programmes (see p. 94).
- worms and worming (see p. 95).

BIRTH CONTROL

When your puppy is having its final vaccination at 16 to 18 weeks of age, it is an opportune time to discuss birth control with your veterinarian.

DESEXING

Females are usually desexed from five to six months of age, and males usually from seven to eight months of age.

If you do not want to breed, nor worry about such matters as isolating your bitch when she is on heat, giving her a contraceptive pill or injection at the correct time or what you should do with unwanted puppies, then it is advisable to have your bitch desexed. The male dog does not present the same worries, but if you are concerned about the fact that when it matures, it may become aggressive to humans or other dogs, wander in its search for a bitch on heat, cause you embarrassment by masturbating in public or mounting children and sometimes adults, then you should think seriously about desexing the dog.

Whether desexing be referred to as spaying, neutering, sterilising, or castrating, the same surgical procedure for removal of the reproductive organs is followed. In the female, the ovaries and uterus are removed, and in the male, the testicles are removed.

SURGICAL PROCEDURE FOR THE BITCH

- Make an appointment with your veterinarian.
- Do not give the bitch food or fluid for at least eight hours before going to the veterinary hospital in the morning.
- The bitch is given a general anaesthetic, the hair on the abdomen is shaved, and the skin is sterilised.
- The veterinary surgeon makes an incision about 3 cm (1 in) long in the skin and through the abdominal muscles to gain access to the abdominal cavity.
- The blood vessels supplying the ovaries and uterus are carefully tied off, and then the organs are removed.
- The incision in the abdominal muscles is closed by stitching with dissolvable suture material. The skin incision is closed using non-dissolvable suture material and the stitches are removed ten days after surgery.
- Usually the bitch is kept under observation overnight and goes home the next day.

On arriving home, there is very little need for post-operative care. There are no signs of pain or discomfort; the bitch eats normally and resumes normal activities. Leisurely activity is all right but do not allow the bitch to jump from a height or do anything strenuous which will put tension on the abdominal wound.

Most bitches do not worry about the wound, but a few do pull out the stitches soon after surgery, causing the skin wound to open up. If it does, it has to be restitched. However, if the skin wound does not open up and remains intact, keep your bitch quietly confined and the wound should heal as well as if the stitches were in place.

If you notice the bitch pulling at the stitches, there is only one way to stop her and that is to put an Elizabethan collar (see p. 163) around her neck. Leave the collar on 24 hours a day until the stitches are removed. Whilst wearing the collar, the bitch should be confined for her own safety. If she roams, she may be hit by a motor vehicle or have her head caught in the branches of a shrub. The bitch can sleep comfortably when wearing the collar, but you will either have to take the collar off to allow her to eat or leave the collar on and hold the food and fluids up to her mouth.

Sometimes owners ask the veterinarian about the feasibility of a tubal ligation. While this procedure is possible in bitches, keep in mind the difference in the purpose of the two types of surgery. Tubal ligation in humans is to prevent pregnancy but to allow a normal sex life. Removal of the uterus and ovaries in the bitch is not only to prevent pregnancy but also to prevent her from coming in season and being sexually interested in or attractive to male dogs. The problems of the bitch bleeding and male dogs hanging around fighting for her favours, urinating to mark their territory, howling and generally making a nuisance of themselves, will disappear.

SURGICAL PROCEDURE FOR THE MALE DOG

- Make an appointment with your veterinarian.
- Do not give the male dog food or fluid for at least eight hours before going to the veterinary hospital in the morning.
- The dog is given a general anaesthetic, the hair on and around the scrotum is shaved and the skin is sterilised.
- An incision is made in front of the scrotum to remove the testicles from which testosterone, the male sex hormone is produced. The blood vessels supplying the testicles are tied off before the testicles are removed. The incision is stitched and the stitches are removed ten day later.
- The dog recovers quickly and usually is allowed to go home the next day. Put the dog onto his normal diet and allow him free exercise.

Some owners are concerned that their dog might go into a psychological decline after being castrated. A male dog does not know that he has been castrated. Certainly his male characteristics will change but there is no reason to think that he will go into a 'psychological decline'.

Sometimes the veterinarian is asked about the feasibility of a vasectomy for the male dog. Keep in mind that the vasectomy would only stop the dog from helping to produce puppies. It would not put a stop to those unpleasant male characteristics such as fighting, wandering, chasing bitches on heat and sexual hyperactivity (masturbating).

POINTS OF VIEW FOR
CONSIDERATION BEFORE DESEXING

Some owners maintain that allowing their bitch to come in season and have a litter of pups before being desexed makes her a more contented dog. There is no known medical or psychological evidence to support this notion.

Other owners do not want their dog desexed because it will put on too much weight after desexing. Weight in the main is determined by genetic make up, the quantity and type of food eaten, and the amount of exercise taken. If the young pup is active, fed correctly, and the parents are slim, it should not get fat after being desexed.

When the bitch first comes in heat at ten to 12 months of age, she may be too immature physically to allow for normal pregnancy and birth; consequently, the puppies have to be delivered by caesarian section. The ideal age to start breeding with the bitch is at about 18 to 20 months, although she will come in season once or twice before reaching 20 months of age.

ALTERNATIVES TO DESEXING

Isolating your bitch

When the bitch comes in season (in heat), lock her up so that she does not have access to a male dog.

The success of this approach depends on being able to recognise when the bitch comes in season (in heat), and on keeping her confined in a dog-proof pen for approximately 18 to 21 days until she goes off heat. If she is confined to a normal fenced-off garden area, invariably a male dog will get in or she will get out, and more than likely pregnancy will result.

If you confine her inside the house, she will leave blood spots all over the place while she is in heat.

A reasonable percentage of bitches over six years of age that have not been desexed and have never had a litter of puppies develop a cystic infection of the uterus called Pyometra. This infection can be life threatening and is only cured by a hysterectomy if the infection is recognised early enough.

To sum up, isolating the bitch is not recommended as a long term method of birth control.

Contraceptive pill or injection

If you prefer to use the pill, consult your veterinarian for details of correct dosage and time to administer. If a bitch is on the contraceptive pill for a long time, a cystic infection of the uterus (Pyometra) may develop as a side effect.

The long-acting contraceptive injection is given every five months. This stops the bitch coming in season in that period. The injection has the same side effect as the pill. The contraceptive pill or injection is not recommended for a valuable breeding bitch.

The pill or injection method of birth control often fails because owners forget either to give the pill or to arrange the injection at the appropriate time.

INFERTILITY IN THE BITCH

A bitch in oestrus (in heat), if given the opportunity, will mate with a compatible male dog as often as two to three times a day for approximately a week. She invariably becomes pregnant, and given similar opportunities will continue to produce a healthy litter of puppies at regular intervals for many years.

The pedigreed (pure-bred) bitch in the controlled environment of a breeding establishment may not breed so well. The breeder may only allow the stud (male dog) to mate with the bitch once or twice. If the timing of the mating is not within 48 hours of the bitch ovulating, pregnancy is unlikely to follow. Many so-called cases of infertility are due to poor timing of the mating.

FACTORS AFFECTING
THE FERTILITY OF THE BITCH

NUTRITION

Obese bitches or bitches in very poor condition have a greater tendency to suffer infertility problems such as abnormal heat cycles or failure to conceive.

HORMONAL IMBALANCE

The bitch may be cycling irregularly or not at all. If a bitch's heat (oestrus) cycle lasts for more than 21 days, it is considered abnormal.

Cystic ovaries

This is one of the common causes of a prolonged heat cycle. Consult your veterinarian who can treat the condition using hormone therapy; if unsuccessful, the bitch may require surgery.

Silent heat cycles

Some bitches have 'silent' heat cycles, so called because the usual signs of swollen vulva and bleeding are not evident. The heat cycle goes unnoticed and the owner thinks that the bitch has not cycled.

If a bitch fails to cycle it could be due to immature ovaries or malfunction of the thyroid gland (hypothyroidism). Consult your veterinarian as to the cause and the appropriate treatments.

Immature ovaries

One of the treatments for immature ovaries is the use of a follicle stimulating hormone (FSH) which causes follicle development in the ovaries. If the treatment is successful, the follicles in the ovaries develop and the bitch comes on heat. 12 days after the first signs of oestrus (heat) the bitch is treated with a luteinising hormone (LH) injection to cause rupture of the mature follicle and release of the egg. The bitch should be mated shortly after the injection and as many times as is practical over the following 48 hours.

Hypothyroidism

Your veterinarian can diagnose hypothyroidism by a blood test and other signs, such as the hair becoming brittle and thinning and/or the skin becoming darker and thicker. Hypothyroidism can be treated successfully with thyroid hormone.

INFECTION

Any infection which has a debilitating effect on the bitch, especially for a period of time, can stop the bitch from cycling.

BACTERIA

Many bitches harbour bacteria in the reproductive tract; some are apparently harmless and others are known to be harmful or pathogenic. The latter are known to cause infection of the uterus.

A bitch may be suspected of having a uterine infection (metritis) if:

• there is pus discharge from the vagina;

• her heat (oestrus) cycles are irregular;

• she does not become pregnant after two or three matings;

• she gives birth to dead or weak, sickly puppies.

Bitches suspected of being infected should be swabbed by a veterinarian, preferably when they are in oestrus (on heat). The swab is cultured and if the result is positive, the bacteria are identified and an antibiotic sensitivity test is done to determine the best antibiotic to use against the infection.

Following the results of swabbing, your veterinarian will treat an infected bitch with the appropriate antibiotic.

BRUCELLOSIS

(See p. 132.) *Brucella canis*, a bacteria, is the major cause of infertility in the male and female dog in the US. The most common method of infection is by sexual intercourse. This particular bacteria has not been isolated as a cause of infertility in dogs in Australia.

Signs

An infected bitch may show signs of a temperature, swollen painful joints, enlarged lymph nodes, sterility, abortion during the sixth to eighth week of pregnancy, or the birth of stillborn or weak sickly puppies that die shortly after birth.

Some infected bitches do not exhibit any signs, harbouring the bacteria in the uterus and vagina. They transmit the bacteria during intercourse or via vaginal discharge.

Treatment

Dogs can be positively diagnosed by a blood test in your veterinarian's laboratory. The bitch and stud dog should be tested before mating and only mated if found to be free of the infection.

Long term treatment with antibiotics is often followed by a relapse, so that dogs which are positive to the blood test should not be used for breeding and should be removed from the breeding establishment.

Prevention

There is no effective vaccine currently available. Breeding dogs should be blood tested prior to mating and positive cases should be either desexed or removed from the breeding establishment.

PSYCHOLOGICAL PROBLEMS

A bitch isolated from other female dogs for prolonged periods may not cycle (come on heat). If this is the cause, placing the bitch with a group of bitches that cycle regularly may stimulate her to cycle. Also, the bitch may be stimulated to cycle if she is allowed to run with a male dog for a couple of months.

ABORTION (see p. 187)

INFERTILITY IN THE STUD
(MALE DOG)

It is a bitter disappointment to come face to face with the reality that your stud dog, which you had chosen so carefully, is infertile.

Infertility in the dog is a complex problem. In a broad sense, it may mean that the dog is unable to produce sperm, or that it can produce sperm which, for one reason or another, e.g. brucellosis, renders the bitch infertile.

FACTORS AFFECTING THE FERTILITY OF THE STUD

NUTRITION

Stud dogs that are obese or suffer from malnutrition and are in very poor condition have a greater tendency to suffer from infertility problems. Very little information is available on the relationship between nutrition and fertility in the dog.

INFECTION

A major cause of infertility in the male dog in the US. is the bacteria *Brucella canis*. It is a venereal disease, i.e. it is transmitted by sexual intercourse, although it can be spread by contact with infected secretions.

An infected dog may show signs of a temperature, swollen painful joints, enlarged lymph nodes, and swollen painful testicles. Over a period of time the testicles become hard and small. They are not painful to the touch. Sperm production is reduced or non-existent, rendering the dog infertile and a risk to any bitch with which he has intercourse.

Some infected dogs do not exhibit any signs of brucella infection. These dogs, called 'carriers', usually harbour the bacteria in the prostate gland. The bacteria are transmitted to the bitch at the time of sexual intercourse.

Treatment

Dogs can be positively identified by a blood test done in most veterinarian's laboratories. Working stud dogs should be tested every three months. The owner of the stud dog should require a veterinary certificate from the owner of the visiting bitch to prove that the bitch has been tested and found to be free of brucellosis (see p. 132).

Long-term treatment with antibiotics is often followed by a relapse, so that dogs which are positive to the blood test should not be used for breeding. They should be castrated and removed from the breeding establishment.

PSYCHOLOGICAL PROBLEMS

Some stud dogs are selective about the bitches they serve. They may reject a bitch because she is not at the correct stage of her oestrus cycle or for other reasons, such as her colour, size and age. In cases of rejection, the reason is not always obvious to the handler. Five minutes after having rejected a bitch, a stud dog may accept and serve another bitch vigorously.

When a mating is organised in a breeding establishment, the bitch should always be taken to the stud. In a strange environment, the stud is often unlikely to mate with the bitch because he feels insecure.

Some dogs that live in close contact with people and have little or no exposure to other dogs may be tentative and apprehensive in a mating situation.

Overuse of the stud dog may be the cause of lack of libido or sexual drive. Resting the stud from sexual activity and allowing it to mate at intervals of 48 hours or more should rectify the problem. In cases that have not responded to rest from sexual activity, testosterone (male sex hormone) has been used with varying degrees of success. Consult your veterinarian, as prolonged use of testosterone may eventually cause a reduction in the size of the testicles, depression of testosterone and sperm production, and result in permanent low libido with reduced fertility.

CONGENITAL PROBLEMS

Stud dogs that have small testicles, which are hard or soft on palpation, usually have poor quality semen and a lack of libido because their testicle activity is minimal. The testicles should feel firm and be of similar size.

Sometimes a dog may have testicles that have failed to descend (Cryptorchidism). This type of dog cannot be used at stud because he is infertile.

The Monorchid is a dog with only one testicle descended. He should not be used as a stud, even though he is fertile, because the condition is hereditary. This recommendation would still apply even if the other testicle, through hormone therapy or surgery could be made to descend and develop.

Normally, the testicles descend prior to birth. If both testicles are not present in the scrotum by six months of age, consult your veterinarian. Testicles that have not descended should be surgically removed because of their predisposition to cancer.

A Yorkshire Terrier

Opposite: A white Standard Poodle

BREED LISTS

KENNEL CLUB (ENGLAND)

HOUNDS

Afghan Hound
Basenji
Basset Fauve de Bretagne
Basset Hound
Bavarian Mountain Hound
Beagle
Bloodhound
Borzoi
Dachsbracke
Dachshund (Longhaired)
Dachshund (Miniature Longhaired)
Dachshund (Smooth-haired)
Dachshund (Miniature Smooth-haired)
Dachshund (Wire-haired)
Dachshund (Miniature Wirehaired)
Deerhound
Elkhound
Finnish Spitz
Fox Hound
Grand Bassett Griffon Vendeen
Grand Bleu de Gascoine
Greyhound
Hamiltonstovare
Ibizan Hound
Irish Wolfhound
Norwegian Lundehund
Otter Hound
Petit Basset Griffon Vendeen
Pharaoh Hound
Portuguese Warren Hound
Rhodesian Ridgeback
Saluki
Segugio Italiano
Sloughi
Swiss Laufhund (Jura)
Whippet

GUN DOGS

Bracco Italiano
Brittany
Drentse Partridge Dog
English Setter
German Longhaired Pointer
German Shorthaired Pointer
German Wirehaired Pointer
Gordon Setter
Hungarian Vizla
Hungarian Wirehaired Vizla
Irish Red & White Setter
Irish Setter
Italian Spinone
Kooikerhondie
Large Munsterlander
Pointer
Pointing Wirehaired Griffon
Retriever (Chesapeake Bay)
Retriever (Curly Coated)
Retriever (Flat Coated)
Retriever (Golden)
Retriever (Labrador)
Retriever (Nova Scotia)
Small Munsterlander
Spaniel (American Cocker)
Spaniel (American Water)
Spaniel (Clumber)
Spaniel (Cocker)
Spaniel (English Springer)
Spaniel (Field)
Spaniel (Irish Water)
Spaniel (Sussex)
Spaniel (Welsh Springer)
Weimaraner

TERRIERS

Airedale Terrier
Australian Terrier
Bedlington Terrier
Border Terrier
Bull Terrier
Bull Terrier (Miniature)
Cairn Terrier
Cesky Terrier
Dandie Dinmont Terrier
Fox Terrier (Smooth)
Fox Terrier (Wire)
Glen of Imaal Terrier
Irish Terrier
Kerry Blue Terrier
Lakeland Terrier
Manchester Terrier
Norfolk Terrier
Norwich Terrier
Parson Jack Russell Terrier
Scottish Terrier
Sealyham Terrier
Skye Terrier
Soft Coated Wheaten Terrier
Staffordshire Bull Terrier
Welsh Terrier
West Highland White Terrier

UTILITY GROUP

Boston Terrier
Bulldog
Canaan Dog
Chow Chow
Dalmatian
French Bulldog
German Spitz (Klein)
German Spitz (Mittel)
German Spitz (Klein) Development Register
German Spitz (Mittel) Development Register
Iceland Dog
Japanese Akita
Japanese Shiba Inu
Japanese Spitz
Keeshond
Leonberger
Lhaso Apso
Mexican Hairless
Miniature Schnauzer
Poodle (Standard)
Poodle (Miniature)
Poodle (Toy)
Schipperke
Schnauzer
Shar Pei
Shih Tzu
Tibetan Spaniel
Tibetan Terrier

WORKING GROUP

Alaskan Malamute
Anatolian Shepherd Dog
Australian Cattle Dog
Australian Kelpie
Bearded Collie
Beauceron
Belgian Shepherd (Groenendael)
Belgian Shepherd (Laekenois)
Belgian Shepherd (Malinois)
Belgian Shepherd (Tervueren)
Bergamasco
Bernese Mountain Dog
Border Collie
Bouviers des Flandres
Boxer
Briard
Bullmastiff
Collie (Rough)
Collie (Smooth)
Continental Landseer (Ect)
Dobermann
Eskimo Dog
Estrela Mountain Dog
Finnish Lapphund
German Shepherd (Alsatian)
Giant Schnauzer
Great Dane
Hovawart
Hungarian Kuvasz
Hungarian Puli
Komondor
Lancashire Heeler
Maremma Sheepdog
Mastiff
Neopolitan Mastiff
Newfoundland
Norwegian Buhund
Old English Sheepdog
Pinscher
Polish Lowland Sheepdog
Portuguese Water Dog
Pyrenean Mountain Dog
Pyrenean Sheepdog
Rottweiler
St Bernard
Samoyed
Shetland Sheepdog
Siberian Husky
Swedish Lapphund
Swedish Vallhund
Tibetan Mastiff
Welsh Corgi (Cardigan)
Welsh Corgi (Pembroke)

TOY GROUP

Affenpinscher
Australian Silky Terrier
Bichons Frise
Bolognese
Cavalier King Charles Spaniel
Chihuahua (Long Coat)
Chihuahua (Smooth Coat)
Chinese Crested
Coton Du Tulear
English Toy Terrier(Black & Tan)
Griffons Bruxellois
Italian Greyhound
Japanese Chin
King Charles Spaniel
Lowchen
Maltese
Miniature Pinscher
Papillon
Pekingese
Pomeranian
Pug
Yorkshire Terrier

AUSTRALIAN NATIONAL KENNEL COUNCIL

TOYS

Affenpinscher
Australian Silky Terrier
Bichon Frise
Cavalier King Charles Spaniel
Chihuahua (Long Coat)
Chihuahua (Smooth Coat)
Chinese Crested Dogs
English Toy Terrier (Black & Tan)
Griffon Bruxellois
Italian Greyhound
Japanese Chin
King Charles Spaniel
Lowchen
Maltese
Miniature Pinscher
Papillon
Pekingese
Pomeranian
Pug
Tibetan Spaniel
Yorkshire Terrier

TERRIERS

Airedale Terrier
American Staffordshire Terrier
Australian Terrier
Bedlington Terrier
Border Terrier
Bull Terrier
Bull Terrier (Miniature)
Cairn Terrier
Dandie Dinmont Terrier
Fox Terrier (Smooth)
Fox Terrier (Wire)
Glen of Imaal Terrier
Irish Terrier
Kerry Blue Terrier
Lakeland Terrier
Manchester Terrier
Norfolk Terrier
Norwich Terrier
Scottish Terrier
Sealyham Terrier
Skye Terrier
Soft Coated Wheaten Terrier
Staffordshire Bull Terrier
Welsh Terrier
West Highland White Terrier

GUN DOGS

Brittany

Chesapeake Bay Retriever
Clumber Spaniel
Cocker Spaniel
Cocker Spaniel (American)
Curly Coated Retriever
English Setter
English Springer Spaniel
Flat Coated Retriever
German Shorthaired Pointer
German Wirehaired Pointer
Golden Retriever
Gordon Setter
Hungarian Viszlas
Irish Red & White Setters
Irish Setter
Irish Water Spaniel
Italian Spinone
Labrador Retriever
Large Munsterlander
Pointer
Sussex Spaniel
Weimaraner
Welsh Springer Spaniel

HOUNDS

Afghan Hound
Basenji
Basset Griffon Vendeen Petit
Basset Hound
Beagle
Bloodhound
Borzoi
Dachshund (Longhaired)
Dachshund (Miniature Longhaired)
Dachshund (Shorthaired)
Dachshund (Miniature Shorthaired)
Dachshund (Wirehaired)
Dachshund (Miniature Wirehaired)
Deerhound
Elkhound
Finnish Spitz
Foxhound
Greyhound
Harrier
Ibizan Hound
Irish Wolfhound
Otterhound
Pharaoh Hound
Rhodesian Ridgeback
Saluki
Whippet

WORKING DOGS

Anatolian Shepherd Dog
Australian Cattle Dog
Australian Kelpie
Bearded Collie
Belgian Shepherd (Groenendael)
Belgian Shepherd (Malinois)
Belgian Shepherd (Tervueren)
Border Collie
Bouvier Des Flandres
Briard
Collie (Rough)
Collie (Smooth)
German Shepherd Dog
Hungarian Puli
Maremma Sheepdog

Old English Sheepdog
Polish Lowland Sheepdog
Shetland Sheepdog
Stumpy Tail Cattle Dog
Swedish Vallhund
Welsh Corgi (Cardigan)
Welsh Corgi (Pembroke)

UTILITY

Akita Inu
Alaskan Malamute
Bernese Mountain Dog
Boxer
Bullmastiff
Dobermann
German Pinscher
Komondor
Leonberger
Mastiff
Newfoundland
Pyrenean Mountain Dog
Rottweiler
Samoyed
Schnauzer
Schnauzer (Giant)
Schnauzer (Miniature)
Shiba Inu
Siberian Husky
St Bernard
Tibetan Mastiff

NON-SPORTING

Boston Terrier
British Bulldog
Chow Chow
Dalmatian
French Bulldog
German Spitz
Great Dane
Japanese Spitz
Keeshond
Lhasa Apsos
Poodle (Standard)
Poodle (Miniature)
Poodle (Toy)
Schipperke
Shar Pei
Shih Tzu
Tibetan Terrier

AMERICAN KENNEL CLUB (US)

SPORTING GROUP

Brittany
Pointer
Pointer (German Shorthaired)
Pointer (German Wirehaired)
Retriever (Chesapeake Bay)
Retriever (Curly-Coated)
Retriever (Flat-Coated)
Retriever (Golden)
Retriever (Labrador)
Setter (English)
Setter (Gordon)
Setter (Irish)
Spaniel (American Water)
Spaniel (Clumber)
Spaniel (Cocker)

Spaniel (English Cocker)
Spaniel (English Springer)
Spaniel (Field)
Spaniel (Irish Water)
Spaniel (Sussex)
Spaniel (Welsh Springer)
Weimaraner
Wirehaired Pointing Griffon

HOUND

Afghan Hound
Basenji
Basset Hound
Beagle (not exceeding 13 in)
Beagle (over 13 in, but not exceeding 15 in)
Black & Tan Coonhound
Bloodhound
Borzoi
Dachshund (Longhaired)
Dachshund (Smooth)
Dachshund (Wirehaired)
Foxhound (American)
Foxhound (English)
Greyhound
Harrier
Ibizan Hound
Irish Wolfhound
Norwegian Elkhound
Otterhound
Petit Basset Griffon Vendeen
Pharaoh Hound
Rhodesian Ridgeback
Saluki
Scottish Deerhound
Whippet

WORKING

Akita
Alaskan Malamute
Bernese Mountain Dog
Boxer
Bullmastiff
Doberman Pinscher
Giant Schnauzer
Great Dane
Great Pyrenees
Komondor
Kuvasz
Mastiff
Newfoundland
Portuguese Water Dog
Rottweiler
Saint Bernard
Samoyed
Siberian Husky
Standard Schnauzer

TERRIER

Airedale Terrier
American Staffordshire Terrier
Australian Terrier
Bedlington Terrier
Border Terrier
Bull Terrier (Colored)
Bull Terrier (White)
Cairn Terrier
Dandie Dinmont Terrier
Fox Terrier (Smooth)
Fox Terrier (Wire)
Irish Terrier

Kerry Blue Terrier
Lakeland Terrier
Manchester Terrier (Standard)
Miniature Bull Terrier
Miniature Schnauzer
Norfolk Terrier
Norwich Terrier
Scottish Terrier
Sealyham Terrier
Skye Terrier
Soft Coated Wheaten Terrier
Staffordshire Bull Terrier
Welsh Terrier
West Highland White Terrier

TOY

Affenpinscher
Brussels Griffon
Chihuahua (Long Coat)
Chihuahua (Smooth Coat)
Chinese Crested
English Toy Spaniel (Blenheim and Prince Charles)
English Toy Spaniel (King Charles and Ruby)
Italian Greyhound
Japanese Chin
Maltese
Manchester Terrier (Toy)
Miniature Pinscher
Papillon
Pekingese
Pomeranian
Poodle (Toy)
Pug
Shih Tzu
Silky Terrier
Yorkshire Terrier

NON-SPORTING

Bichon Frise
Boston Terrier
Bulldog
Chow Chow
Dalmatian
Finnish Spitz
French Bulldog
Keeshond
Lhasa Apso
Poodle (Miniature)
Poodle (Standard)
Schipperke
Tibetan Spaniel
Tibetan Terrier

HERDING

Australian Cattle Dog
Bearded Collie
Belgian Malinois
Belgian Sheepdog
Belgian Tervueren
Bouvier des Flandres
Briard
Collie (Rough)
Collie (Smooth)
German Shepherd Dog
Old English Sheepdog
Pulik
Shetland Sheepdog
Welsh Corgi (Cardigan)
Welsh Corgi (Pembroke)

INDEX

Italic page numbers refer to illustrations